Bloom's Major Literary Characters

King Arthur

George Babbitt

Elizabeth Bennet

Leopold Bloom

Sir John Falstaff

Jay Gatsby

Hamlet

Raskolnikov and Svidrigailov

Bloom's Major Literary Characters

Raskolnikov and Svidrigailov

Edited and with an introduction by
Harold Bloom
Sterling Professor of the Humanities
Yale University

CHELSEA HOUSE PUBLISHERS
A Haights Cross Communications Company
Philadelphia

A Haights Cross Communications Company

Printed and bound in the United States of America.

10 9 8 7 6 5 4 3 2 1

Library of Congress Cataloging-in-Publication Data

Raskolnikov and Svidrigailov / edited and with an introduction by Harold Bloom.
p. cm — (Bloom's Major literary characters)
Includes bibliographical references and index.
ISBN 0-7910-7671-7
1. Dostoyevsky, Fyodor, 1821–1881. Prestupenie i nakazanie. 2. Dostoyevsky, Fyodor, 1821–1881—Characters—Raskolnikov. 3. Dostoyevsky, Fyodor, 1821–1881—Characters—Svidrigailov. 4. Raskolnikov (Fictitious character) 5. Svidrigailov (Fictitious character) I. Bloom, Harold. II. Major literary characters. III. Title. IV. Series: Bloom's major literary characters.
PG3325.P73R37 2003
891.73'3—dc21

2003009315

Contributing editor: Amy Sickels

Cover design by Keith Trego

Cover: Courtesy Library of Congress

Layout by EJB Publishing Services

Chelsea House Publishers
1974 Sproul Road, Suite 400
Broomall, PA 19008-0914

www.chelseahouse.com

Contents

HAROLD BLOOM

The Analysis of Character

"Character," according to our dictionaries, still has as a primary meaning a graphic symbol, such as a letter of the alphabet. This meaning reflects the word's apparent origin in the ancient Greek character, a sharp stylus. *Charactēr* also meant the mark of the stylus' incisions. Recent fashions in literary criticism have reduced "character" in literature to a matter of marks upon a page. But our word "character" also has a very different meaning, matching that of the ancient Greek *ēthos*, "habitual way of life." Shall we say then that literary character is an imitation of human character, or is it just a grouping of marks? The issue is between a critic like Dr. Samuel Johnson, for whom words were as much like people as like things, and a critic like the late Roland Barthes, who told us that "the fact can only exist linguistically, as a term of discourse." Who is closer to our experience of reading literature, Johnson or Barthes? What difference does it make, if we side with one critic rather than the other?

Barthes is famous, like Foucault and other recent French theorists, for having added to Nietzsche's proclamation of the death of God a subsidiary demise, that of the literary author. If there are no authors, then there are no fictional personages, presumably because literature does not refer to a world outside language. Words indeed necessarily refer to other words in the first place, but the impact of words ultimately is drawn from a universe of fact. Stories, poems, and plays are recognizable as such because they are human utterances within traditions of utterances, and traditions, by achieving authority, become a kind of fact, or at least the sense of a fact. Our sense that literary characters, within the context of a fictive cosmos, indeed are fictional personages is also a kind of fact. The meaning and value of every character in a successful work of literary representation depend upon our ideas of persons in the factual reality of our lives.

Literary character is always an invention, and inventions generally are indebted to prior inventions. Shakespeare is the inventor of literary character as we know it; he reformed the universal human expectations for the verbal imitation of personality, and the reformation appears now to be permanent and uncannily inevitable. Remarkable as the Bible and Homer are at representing personages, their characters are relatively unchanging. They age within their stories, but their habitual modes of being do not develop. Jacob and Achilles unfold before us, but without metamorphoses. Lear and Macbeth, Hamlet and Othello severely modify themselves not only by their actions, but by their utterances, and most of all through *overhearing themselves*, whether they speak to themselves or to others. Pondering what they themselves have said, they will to change, and actually do change, sometimes extravagantly yet always persuasively. Or else they suffer change, without willing it, but in reaction not so much to their language as to their relation to that language.

I do not think it useful to say that Shakespeare successfully imitated elements in our characters. Rather, it could be argued that he compelled aspects of character to appear that previously were concealed, or not available to representation. This is not to say that Shakespeare is God, but to remind us that language is not God either. The mimesis of character in Shakespeare's dramas now seems to us normative, and indeed became the accepted mode almost immediately, as Ben Jonson shrewdly and somewhat grudgingly implied. And yet, Shakespearean representation has surprisingly little in common with the imitation of reality in Jonson or in Christopher Marlowe. The origins of Shakespeare's originality in the portrayal of men and women are to be found in the *Canterbury Tales* of Geoffrey Chaucer, insofar as they can be located anywhere before Shakespeare himself, Chaucer's savage and superb Pardoner overhears his own tale-telling, as well as his mocking rehearsal of his own spiel, and through this overhearing he is emboldened to forget himself, and enthusiastically urges all his fellow-pilgrims to come forward to be fleeced by him. His self-awareness, and apocalyptically rancid sense of spiritual fall, are preludes to the even grander abysses of the perverted will in Iago and in Edmund. What might be called the character trait of a negative charisma may be Chaucer's invention, but came to its perfection in Shakespearean mimesis.

The analysis of character is as much Shakespeare's invention as the representation of character is, since Iago and Edmund are adepts at analyzing both themselves and their victims. Hamlet, whose overwhelming charisma has many negative components, is certainly the most comprehensive of all literary characters, and so necessarily prophesies the labyrinthine complexities of the will in Iago and Edmund. Charisma, according to Max Weber, its first codifier, is primarily a natural endowment, and implies a primordial and idiosyncratic power over nature, and so finally over death. Hamlet's uncanniness is at its most suggestive in the scene of his long dying, where the audience, through the mediation of Horatio, itself is compelled to meditate upon suicide, if only because outliving the prince of Denmark scarcely seems an option.

Shakespearean representation has usurped not only our sense of literary character, but our sense of ourselves as characters, with Hamlet playing the part of the largest of these usurpations. Insofar as we have an idea of human disinterestedness, we tend to derive it from the Hamlet of Act V, whose quietism has about it a ghostly authority. Oscar Wilde, in his profound and profoundly witty dialogue, "The Decay of Lying," expressed a permanent insight when he insisted that art shaped every era, far more than any age formed art. Life imitates art, we imitate Shakespeare, because without Shakespeare we would perish for lack of images. Wilde's grandest audacity demystifies Shakespearean mimesis with a Shakespearean vivaciousness: "This unfortunate aphorism about art holding the mirror up to Nature is deliberately said by Hamlet in order to convince the bystanders of his absolute insanity in all art-matters." Of *Hamlet*'s influence upon the ages Wilde remarked that: "The world has grown sad because a puppet was once melancholy." "Puppet" is Wilde's own deconstruction, a brilliant reminder that Shakespeare's artistry of illusion has so mastered reality as to have changed reality, evidently forever.

The analysis of character, as a critical pursuit, seems to me as much a Shakespearean invention as literary character was, since much of what we know about how to analyze character necessarily follows Shakespearean procedures. His hero-villains, from Richard III through Iago, Edmund, and Macbeth, are shrewd and endless questers into their own self-motivations. If we could bear to see Hamlet, in his unwearied negations, as another hero-villain, then we would judge him the supreme analyst of the darker recalcitrances in the selfhood. Freud followed the pre-Socratic Empedocles, in arguing that character is fate, a frightening doctrine that maintains the fear that there are no accidents, that overdetermination rules us all of our lives. Hamlet assumes the same, yet adds to this argument the terrible passivity he manifests in Act V. Throughout Shakespeare's tragedies, the most interesting personages seem doom-eager, reminding us again that a Shakespearean reading of Freud would be more illuminating than a Freudian exegesis of Shakespeare. We learn more when we discover Hamlet in the Freudian Death Drive, than when we read *Beyond the Pleasure Principle* into *Hamlet.*

In Shakespearean comedy, character achieves its true literary apotheosis, which is the representation of the inner freedom that can be created by great wit alone. Rosalind and Falstaff, perhaps alone among Shakespeare's personages, match Hamlet in wit, though hardly in the metaphysics of consciousness. Whether in the comic or the modern mode, Shakespeare has set the standard of measurement in the balance between character and passion.

In Shakespeare the self is more dramatized than theatricalized, which is why a Shakespearean reading of Freud works out so well. Character-formation after the passing of the Oedipal stage takes the place of fetishistic fragmentings of the self. Critics who now call literary character into question, and who proclaim also the death of the author, invariably also regard all notions, literary and human, of a stable character as being mere reductions of deeper pre-Oedipal desires. It becomes clear that the fortunes of literary character rise and fall with the prestige of normative conceptions of the ego. Shakespeare's Iago, who wars against being, may be the first deconstructionist of the self, with his proclamation of "I am not what I am." This constitutes the necessary prologue to any view that would regard a fixed ego as a virtual abnormality. But deconstructions of the self are no more modern than Modernism is. Like literary modernism, the decentered ego came out of the Hellenistic culture of ancient Alexandria. The Gnostic heretics believed that the psyche, like the body, was a fallen entity, mechanically fashioned by the Demiurge or false creator. They held however that each of us possessed also a spark or pneuma, which was a fragment of the original Abyss or true, alien God. The soul or psyche within every one of us was thus at war with the self or pneuma, and only that sparklike self could be saved.

Shakespeare, following after Chaucer in this respect, was the first and remains still the greatest master of representing character both as a stable soul and a wavering self. There is a substance that endures in Shakespeare's figures, and there is also a quicksilver rendition of the unsettling sparks. Racine and Tolstoy, Balzac and Dickens, follow in Shakespeare's wake by giving us some sense of pre-Oedipal sparks or drives, and considerably more sense of post-Oedipal character and personality, stabilizations or sublimations of the fetish-seeking drives. Critics like Leo Bersani and René Girard argue eloquently against our taking this mimesis as the only proper work of literature. I would suggest that strong fictions of the self, from the Bible through Samuel Beckett, necessarily participate in both modes, the sublimation of desire, and the persistence of a primordial desire. The mystery of Hamlet or of Lear is intimately invested in the tangled mixture of the two modes of representation.

Psychic mobility is proposed by Bersani as the ideal to which deconstructions of the literary self may yet guide us. The ideal has its pathos, but the realities of literary representation seem to me very different, perhaps destructively so. When a novelist like D. H. Lawrence sought to reduce his characters to Eros and the Death Drive, he still had to persuade us of his authority at mimesis by lavishing upon the figures of *The Rainbow* and *Women in Love* all of the vivid stigmata of normative personality. Birkin and Ursula may represent antithetical and uncanny drives, but they develop and change as characters pondering their own pronouncements and reactions to self and others. The cost of a non-Shakespearean representation is enormous. Pynchon, in *The Crying of Lot 49* and *Gravity's Rainbow*, evades the burden of the normative by resorting to something like Christopher Marlowe's art of caricature in *The Jew of Malta*. Marlowe's Barabas is a marvelous rhetorician, yet he is a cartoon alongside the troublingly equivocal Shylock. Pynchon's personages are deliberate cartoons also, as flat as comic strips. Marlowe's achievement, and Pynchon's, are beyond dispute, yet they are like the prelude and the postlude to Shakespearean reality. They do not wish to engage with our hunger for the empirical world and so they enter the problematic cosmos of literary fantasy.

No writer, not even Shakespeare or Proust, alters the available stock that we agree to call reality, but Shakespeare, more than any other, does show us how much of reality we could encounter if only we retained adequate desire. The strong literary representation of character is already an analysis of character, and is part of the healing work of a literary culture, which implicitly seeks to cure violence through a normative mimesis of ego, *as if it were stable*, whether in actuality it is or is not. I do not believe that this is a social quest taken on by literary culture, but rather that we confront here the aesthetic essence of what makes a culture *literary*, rather than metaphysical or ethical or religious. A culture becomes literary when its conceptual modes have failed it, which means when religion, philosophy, and science have begun to lose their authority. If they cannot heal violence, then literature attempts to do so, which may be only a turning inside out of the critical arguments of Girard and Bersani.

I conclude by offering a particular instance or special case as a paradigm for the healing enterprise that is at once the representation and the analysis of literary character. Let us call it the aesthetics of being outraged, or rather of successfully representing the state of being outraged. W. C. Fields was one modern master of such representation, and Nathanael West was another, as was Faulkner before him. Here also the greatest master remains Shakespeare, whose Macbeth, himself a bloody outrage, yet retains our imaginative sympathy precisely because he grows increasingly outraged as he experiences the equivocation of the fiend that lies like truth. The double-natured promises and the prophecies of the weird sisters finally induce in Macbeth an apocalyptic version of the stage actor's anxiety at missing cues, the horror of a phantasmagoric stage fright of missing one's time, of always reacting too late. Macbeth, a veritable monster of solipsistic inwardness but no intellectual, counters his dilemma by fresh murders, that prolong him in time yet provoke him only to a perpetually freshened sense of being outraged, as all his expectations become still worse confounded. We are moved by Macbeth, however estrangedly, because his terrible inwardness is a paradigm for our own solipsism, but also because none of us can resist a strong and successful representation of the human in a state of being outraged.

The ultimate outrage is the necessity of dying, an outrage concealed in a multitude of masks, including the tyrannical ambitions of Macbeth. I suspect that our outrage at being outraged is the most difficult of all our affects for us to represent to ourselves, which is why we are so inclined to imaginative sympathy for a character who strongly conveys that affect to us. The Shrike of West's *Miss Lonelyhearts* or Faulkner's Joe Christmas of *Light in August* are crucial modern instances, but such figures can be located in many other works, since the ability to represent this extreme emotion is one of the tests that strong writers are driven to set for themselves.

However a reader seeks to reduce literary character to a question of marks on a page, she will come at last to the impasse constituted by the thought of death, her death, and before that to all the stations of being outraged that memorialize her own drive towards death. In reading, she quests for evidences that are strong representations, whether of her desire or her despair. Such questings constitute the necessary basis for the analysis of literary character, an enterprise that always will survive every vagary of critical fashion.

Editor's Note

My Introduction contrasts the radical nihilism and desperate solipsism of Svidrigailov with the hesitant "freedom" of Raskolnikov.

Edward Wasiolek observes that Raskolnikov's conversion is not wholly persuasive, while Robert Louis Jackson explores the ambiguities of consciousness in Dostoevsky's protagonist.

To Malcolm V. Jones Raskolnikov's humane qualities survive his crimes, a survival attributed by Roger B. Anderson to mythic thought.

Raymond J. Wilson III interprets Raskolnikov's dream as a clue to his subsequent development, after which Frank Friedeberg Seeley uncovers the positive aspects of Svidrigailov.

The confession of Raskolnikov is seen by Gerald Fiderer as a pattern of self-punishment, while R.E. Richardson emphasizes the theatricalism of Svidrigailov.

The violent narcissism of Svidrigailov is judged by Giles Mitchell to have created an authentic personal hell, after which Laura A. Curtis shrewdly surmises the excessive attachment of the sado-masochistic protagonist to his mother.

Richard Peace isolates symbolic elements in Raskolnikov while Alba Amoia perhaps optimistically credits love with resurrecting this ambiguous personage.

In a concluding essay, Nina Pelikan Straus deftly finds in both Svidrigailov and Raskolnikov a pathway to fulfilling feminist hopes for a better life.

HAROLD BLOOM

Introduction

Raskolnikov, a resentful student, plays with the terrible fantasy of murdering a greedy old woman, who as a pawnbroker exploits him. His phantasmagoria becomes reality when he kills not only her, but her half-witted stepsister as well. Once the crimes have been committed, the fate of Raskolnikov turns upon his encounters with the novel's three major characters. The first is Sonya, a pious and angelic young girl who has sacrificed herself as a prostitute, in order to care for her destitute siblings. Next is Porfiry Petrovich, a wise police investigator, who is Raskolnikov's patient nemesis. The most fascinating is Svidrigailov, a monument to nihilistic solipsism, and to cold lust.

In the intricate movements of the plot, Raskolnikov falls in love with Sonya, gradually realizes that Porfiry knows of his guilt, and increasingly sees his own potential for total degradation in the brilliant Svidrigailov. What the reader comes to understand is that there is deep division in Raskolnikov, between the urge to repent and the inner conviction that his Napoleonic self needs to be expressed in full. Dostoevsky himself is subtly divided, since Raskolnikov does not collapse into repentance until the novel's epilogue.

Crime and Punishment remains the best of all murder stories, a century and a third after its publication. We have to read it—though it is harrowing—because, like Shakespeare, it alters our consciousness. Though many among us deny the nihilism of Shakespeare's high tragedies of blood—*Hamlet*, *Othello*, *King Lear*, *Macbeth*—they are an inescapable origin for Dostoevsky's grand nihilists: Svidrigailov, Stavrogin in *The Possessed* (*The*

Devils), and old Karamazov, the father in *The Brothers Karamazov*. We never will know what Shakespeare's actual belief (or skepticism) was, while Dostoevsky became a clerical reactionary almost beyond our capacity to conceive. But for *Crime and Punishment* in particular, we ought to follow D. H. Lawrence's adage: Trust the tale, and not the teller.

Dostoevsky believed in a Christianity that is yet to come: when all of us would love selflessly, and so sacrifice ourselves to others, as Sonya does in *Crime and Punishment*. In that Christian phase, beyond civilization as we think we know it, could novels be written? Presumably, we would not need them. Tolstoy, who wanted Dostoevsky to be Russia's Harriet Beecher Stowe, insisted that he valued *Uncle Tom's Cabin* over *King Lear*.

Dostoevsky, essentially a tragedian, and not an epic moralist, did not agree with Tolstoy. I muse sometimes that Dostoevsky left the Russian army, at twenty-three, in order to pursue a literary career, and Rodion Raskolnikov is twenty-three in the dreadful summer when he gratuitously murders two women, so as to aggrandize his Napoleonic vision of his self. There is a submerged affinity between Raskolnikov's refusal to swerve from his self-estimate, and Dostoevsky's heroic quest to write eternal fictions, culminating in *The Brothers Karamazov*. Raskolnikov repents truly at last, in the novel's unconvincing epilogue, when he surrenders wholly to the Magdalene-like Sonya, as the hope for his Lazarus-ascension from death to salvation. But since Raskolnikov's tragic recalcitrance is inextricably bound up with Dostoevsky's heroic drive to compose great tragedy, the reader is unlikely to be persuaded by Raskolnikov's belated Christian humility. Dostoevsky is superb at beginnings, astonishing at middle developments, but oddly weak at endings, since his apocalyptic temperament (one might think) would render him adept in last things.

Readers who are open to the experiential darkness of *Crime and Punishment* may well ponder the split not only in Raskolnikov but the implied fissure in Dostoevsky himself, and may conclude that a recalcitrance in the novelist, dramatic rather than moral-religious, renders him reluctant utterly to transform Raskolnikov into a redeemed being. Happy endings are not consonant with works that feature the awesome nihilists Svidrigailov and Iago. When I think of *Crime and Punishment*, immediately Svidrigailov comes into my mind, and I shudder at his explanation as he pulls the trigger to commit suicide: "Going to America." This is the postnihilist (mere nihilist will not suffice) who tells Raskolnikov that Eternity exists; it is like a filthy bathhouse in the Russian countryside, crawling with spiders. Poor Raskolnikov, confronted with the real thing in Svidrigailov, the Way Down and Out incarnate, can be forgiven when he yearns for a vision more comforting, whether he believes in it or not.

There seems to me a real affinity between Raskolnikov and the murderer Macbeth, as there is between Svidrigailov and the Edmund of *King Lear*, another cold sensualist. Himself born in 1821, Dostoevsky more overtly associates the disturbing Svidrigailov with Lord Byron, made immensely popular in Russia by the national poet Pushkin, who also preceded Dostoevsky and Turgenev in their Shakespearean sympathies. Svidrigailov's criminal lusts, particularly excited by little girls, are a degradation of Edmund's and Byron's proclivities. But Raskolnikov, who is alarming enough, is several verges away from becoming a Svidrigailov, just as the murderous yet still sympathetic Macbeth is also a hero-villain, rather than a peer of Iago and Edmund.

Dostoevsky emulates Shakespeare by identifying the reader's imagination with Raskolnikov, even as Macbeth usurps our imaginations. Porfiry, the police inspector who brilliantly tortures Raskolnikov with uncertainty, presents himself as a Christian, but clearly causes distaste in Dostoevsky, who regards Raskolnikov's nemesis as a Western-influenced "mechanist," a manipulator of Raskolnikov's already tormented psychology. Sonya is as spiritually beyond the reader in the transcendental dimension as uncanny Svidrigailov exceeds us in the demonic mode. We have no place to go but Raskolnikov's consciousness, just as we have to journey with Macbeth into his heart of darkness. *We* might not murder old women or a fatherly monarch, but since in part we *are* Raskolnikov and Macbeth, perhaps in certain circumstances we might. Like Shakespeare, Dostoevsky makes us complicit in his hero-villain's murders. *Macbeth* and *Crime and Punishment* both are authentically frightening tragedies that do not purge us of pity, let alone of fear. Reversing Aristotle's socio-medical idea of catharsis, in which tragedy frees us of emotions not conducive to the public good, both Shakespeare and Dostoevsky have darker designs upon us.

It is this sharing in *Macbeth*'s terrible sublimity that allows *Crime and Punishment* to transcend depressing us, as we are led through a bad Petersburg summer in which a nightmare phantasmagoria becomes reality. Every wall we look at seems a hideous yellow, and the horror of a modern metropolis is portrayed with an intensity that rivals Baudelaire, or Dickens in his least affable moments. We begin to feel that in Raskolnikov's Petersburg, as in Macbeth's bewitched Scotland, we too might commit murders.

The question of how to read *Crime and Punishment* rapidly becomes, what causes Raskolnikov to become a murderer? He is replete with good qualities; his impulses are essentially decent, indeed humane. I marvel at the eminent modern Italian novelist Alberto Moravia, who found Raskolnikov a forerunner of Stalinist commissars, who were better known for oppressing others than for tormenting themselves. Raskolnikov, like his demonic parody Svidrigailov, is a self-punisher, whose masochism is absolutely incompatible with his professed desire to be a Napoleon. In one sense, Raskolnikov kills in order to discover whether he is a potential Napoleon, though he has every reason to believe that he is anything but that. Perhaps deeper is Raskolnikov's fierce guilt, which *precedes his crimes*. Whether he is a coarser version of Sonya's will-to-suffer, I rather doubt. Nor is he a passive double of Svidrigailov, all of whose malevolent sadism is a mask for "going to America" or suicide. It seems impossible to detach Raskolnikov from Dostoevsky, who at twenty-eight endured eight months in solitary confinement for being part of a radical group. Under sentence of death, he and his companions stood before a firing squad, and only then were reprieved. Four years of hard labor in Siberia followed, during which Dostoevsky became a thorough reactionary, a monarchist, and a devout follower of the Russian Orthodox Church.

Raskolnikov goes to Siberia for seven years, a light sentence for a double murder, but he has confessed his crimes, and the court has found him to have been at least in part insane, particularly when he killed. I don't see how an open, common reader could ascribe, with any certainty, any motive to Raskolnikov's transgressions in any ordinary meaning of "motive." Malignancy, deep rooted in Svidrigailov as in Iago and Edmund, has little place in the psyches of Raskolnikov and Macbeth, which makes their descents even more terrifying. Nor does one progress by looking for Original Sin in Raskolnikov and Macbeth. Both men suffer from powerfully proleptic or prophetic imaginations. Once either perceives a potential action to advance the self, he leaps the gap and experiences the crime as having been done, with all the attendant guilt. With so potent an imagination, and so guilty a consciousness, the actual murder is only a copy or a repetition, a self-wounding that lacerates reality, yet just to complete what in a way has already been done.

Absorbing as *Crime and Punishment* is, it cannot be absolved of tendentiousness, which is Dostoevsky's invariable flaw. He is a partisan, whose fierce perspective is always explicit in what he writes. His design upon us is to raise us, like Lazarus, from our own nihilism or skepticism, and then convert us to Orthodoxy. Writers as eminent as Chekhov and Nabokov have been unable to abide him; to them he was scarcely an artist, but a shrill would-be prophet. I myself, with each rereading, find *Crime and Punishment* an ordeal, dreadfully powerful but somewhat pernicious, almost as though it were a *Macbeth* composed by Macbeth himself.

Raskolnikov hurts us because we cannot cut loose from him. Sonya seems to me quite unendurable, but even Dostoevsky did not have the power to create a sane saint; I wince before her. Yet it is extraordinary that Dostoevsky could give us two supporting characters as vivid as Porfiry, the police inspector who is Raskolnikov's mighty opposite, and the amazingly plausible Svidrigailov, whose fascination is endless.

Porfiry, an accomplished investigator, is a kind of pragmatist, and a utilitarian, believing in the greatest good for the greatest number through the exercise of reason. Any reader (I assume), myself included, would rather dine with Porfiry than with the dangerous Svidrigailov, but I suspect Dostoevsky would have preferred Svidrigailov. Quite openly, Porfiry compares himself to a candle, and Raskolnikov to a circling butterfly, in a wonderfully composed waiting game:

> "What if I run away?" asked Raskolnikov, with a strange smile.
>
> "You won't run away. A peasant would run away, or a modern dissenter—the lackey of another's ideas, because you need only show him the end of your finger and, like Mr. Midshipman Easy, he will believe anything you like for the rest of his life. But you, after all, no longer believe even your own theory, why should you run away? What would you do in hiding? The fugitive's life is hard and hateful, and your first need is for a definite position and existence, and a suitable atmosphere, and what sort of atmosphere would you have? If you run away, you would come back of yourself. *You can't get on without us.*"
>
> (Translated by Jessie Coulson)

This is a deservedly classic moment in the history of "detective novels." What could be finer than Porfiry's "*You can't get on without us*," candle speaking to butterfly. One feels in this instance that even the superb Chekhov was wrong; underestimating Dostoevsky is hazardous, even if you don't esteem him.

More hazardous, and yet more memorable, is Svidrigailov, the authentic nihilist, and the end of what might be called the Shakespearean road in Dostoevsky (if one adds Stavrogin in *The Devils*). So strong and strange a character is Svidrigailov that I almost have to retract my assertion as to Dostoevsky's tendentiousness. Raskolnikov has confronted Svidrigailov, who has been pursuing Dunya Raskolnikov, the protagonist's sister. This is Svidrigailov on the woman who will reject him, then and always:

> In spite of Avdotya Romanovna's real aversion for me, and my persistently gloomy and forbidding aspect, she grew sorry for me at last, sorry for a lost soul. And when a girl's heart begins to feel *pity* for a man, then of course she is in the greatest danger. She begins to want to "save" him, and make him see reason, and raise him up, and put before him nobler aims, and awaken him to a new life and new activities—well, everybody knows what can be dreamt of in such circumstances. I realized at once that the bird had flown into the net of its own accord, and I began to make preparations in my turn. You seem to be frowning, Rodion Romanovich. There is no need; the affair, as you know, came to nothing. (Devil take it, what a lot of wine I'm drinking!) You know, from the very beginning I always thought it was a pity that your sister had not chanced to be born in the second or third century of our era, as the daughter of a ruling prince somewhere, or some governor or proconsul in Asia Minor. She would doubtless have been one of those who suffered martyrdom, and she would, of course, have smiled when they burnt her breast with red-hot pincers. She would have deliberately brought it on herself. And in the fourth or fifth century she would have gone into the Egyptian desert and lived for thirty years on roots, ecstasies, and visions. She is the kind of person who hungers and thirsts to be tortured for somebody, and if she does not achieve her martyrdom she is quite capable of jumping out of a window.

It is after Avdotya Romanovna's (Dunya Raskolnikov) failure to kill Svidrigailov (something he desires, rather more desperately even than he does her) that Svidrigailov "goes to America"—shoots himself. Svidrigailov's freedom, like Stavrogin's in *The Devils*, is absolute, and also is absolutely terrifying. Raskolnikov never repents, though in the epilogue he breaks down and yields to Sonya's saintliness. But it is Svidrigailov, not Raskolnikov, who runs away from Dostoevsky's ferocious ideology, and indeed runs out of the book. A reader may well want to murmur to herself. "Svidrigailov lives," though we probably won't scrawl that on subway walls.

EDWARD WASIOLEK

Crime and Punishment

From the first lines Raskolnikov is moving toward the crime. We meet him on the staircase: he slinks past the open kitchen where his landlady is with her humiliating demands for payment, goes out onto the hot, smelly summer streets, and then on to the rehearsal for the crime. For more than a month he has lain for whole days in his closet-like room, crushed by poverty, badgered by his landlady, eaten up by an idea that hovers like a tempting nightmare about the fringes of his belief. From the first lines we have a sense of "something having to give," and Dostoevsky plays upon this tension unabashedly. What has to be done has been incubating in his mind for more than a month, first only as a tempting flicker, then as a half possibility, and finally as a half-believed rehearsal. On the way to rehearse the crime, he has already measured off the steps to Alyona Ivanovna's house, studied the staircase, traced out the habits of the caretakers, and taken note of the layout. Dostoevsky uses the popular technique of giving the reader the criminal's intention and preparations so that he can, for suspense, play off what the criminal does against what he has prepared. He frankly exploits a "will-it-happen-and-will-he-get-away-with-it-if-it-happens" situation. Almost every detail contributes to the suspense: the lucky break of overhearing that Lizaveta will not be home at seven the next day, the unlucky break of

---

oversleeping and of finding Nastasya in the kitchen, the lucky break of the caretaker being absent and of the haywagon shielding his entrance into Alyona Ivanovna's building; after the murder the unlucky break of Koch's and Pestryakov's arrival when he is ready to leave, the unlucky break of their returning when he has started down the stairs, and the lucky break of the second-floor apartment being vacant. Throughout, Dostoevsky plays upon the most elemental springs of suspense: alarm and relief. The murder scene itself is a classic in technique from beginning to end. Raskolnikov has to ring three times, and for him and the reader there is acute tension between each ring. Before the third ring, Raskolnikov puts his ear to the door and has the sensation of Alyona putting her ear to the door also: murderer and victim sense each other's presence through the partition. When Alyona Ivanovna opens the door a crack, only her eyes are seen; and there is the suspense of not knowing whether she will let him in or not. Then there is the excruciating moment when she turns to the light to untie the string of the pledge, and Raskolnikov realizes—as he slips the hatchet out of its loop—that it would have to be then or never. Perhaps more than anything, the tension and drama of Raskolnikov's half-conscious rummagings during the murder come from Dostoevsky's use of sound, or rather from the lack of it. The windows are closed, and nothing is heard from the landing. There is only the dull sound of the axe falling on Alyona Ivanovna's head and her weak cry, the faint cry of Lizaveta, the sound of the keys, and the sound of Raskolnikov's heavy breathing. The murder takes place in a ghastly pantomime that throws into relief both the sound of the murder weapon and the sound of the keys. The scene ends with Saturday matinee thriller gestures: Koch and Pestryakov pull at the door; Raskolnikov, with two murdered women and a pool of blood behind him, watches the hook of the door bob up and down.

But no matter how skillfully done, such techniques touch only the superficial layers of our minds and feelings. If there were only this level, *Crime and Punishment* might be an interesting, surely an entertaining book, but it would not be a great book. However, *Crime and Punishment* is a great novel, and part of its greatness comes from a technique that assaults the reader's intellectual complacency and challenges him to continual refinement of understanding. Whenever the reader begins to relax into what he thinks he understands and can accept, Dostoevsky introduces some fact, some scene that contradicts what the reader expects and forces him to rethink the novel. The reader is constantly being challenged by Dostoevsky to reappraise what he has already concluded.

The reader quickly sees, for instance, that there is more to the crime than the murder, and thus more than the suspense of "Will he do it?" and "Will he get away with it?" He sees that the crime has a social significance.

Our sympathy is drawn toward Raskolnikov: he is poor and unable to continue his studies; his mother is ruining herself for him; his sister is being forced into voluntary prostitution by marrying Luzhin for his sake; he is young and talented, but for lack of money, his talent is wasted. And as he reminds us, there are thousands like him in St. Petersburg. On the other hand, the old hag Alyona Ivanovna, useless to everyone, lies in her lair like some spider, sucking out the blood of the best of Russian youth so as to erect some lasting monument to herself and to her soul after death. It is only a step from these considerations to the explicit justification of the crime as the "humanitarian" exchange of one worthless life for a thousand useful lives. The motive of economic necessity (no job, the economic plight of his family) suddenly becomes not *necessity* but a bold claim, *a right*. Crime is put forth as virtue, evil as good. What a moment before made a claim on our sympathy makes a claim on our judgment. It is an attack on our values, and for a moment the justification almost sounds believable; and although we are not taken in, the powerful argument provokes our attention. The other important motive Raskolnikov puts forth, the superman theory, makes the same kind of appeal-attack on us, but it is not radically different in kind. Mochul'sky and many before him have reasoned these into very different and even contradictory motives, but both justify crime for humanitarian reasons. The superman theory simply gives to exceptional people only the prescience to know what crimes are beneficial to humanity. After we have made our peace with both motives, we settle down to watch what is a misguided act run its course. According to our moral and aesthetic dispositions, the criminal must be pursued, caught, and punished in order to satisfy our legal sense, and he must be brought to see the error of his ways in order to satisfy our moral sense. And this seems to be precisely what happens: Raskolnikov runs, Porfiry pursues, Raskolnikov gradually sees that he was wrong, and he is caught, converted, and punished.

But Dostoevsky has a way of introducing a contradiction at a point where we feel we understand what is going on, and thus challenging us to think through our conclusions. As readers we are always sinking back into an aesthetic and moral sloth which Dostoevsky continually assaults. We classify certain situations and expect them to confirm our judgments and interpretations. His technique is to trap the reader into more and more refined explanations of Raskolnikov's motives, constantly to challenge our understanding, and to attack our moral predispositions. According to conventional moral explanations, Raskolnikov should be running from the crime, and he should begin with the wrong moral idea and be converted to the right one. But Raskolnikov, we shortly see, is not running away from the crime but *toward* it.

Raskolnikov wants to be caught. He commits two murders and leaves the door open; back in his room with his clothes stained with blood and his pockets bulging with stolen articles, he promptly falls asleep and sleeps until two o'clock the next day—with the door unlatched! When he is summoned to the police station the following day, he faints at precisely the moment when suspicion may fall on him. He had come fearing that the summons had to do with the crime and learns that it has to do with his failure to pay a promissory note. When he is relieved to learn that there is not the slightest suspicion of him, he faints so as to provoke suspicion. Later he again provokes suspicion upon himself by almost confessing to Zamyotov in a tavern, by returning to the scene of the crime and deliberately baiting the workman there (Porfiry later acknowledges that his return to the scene of the crime first aroused his suspicion), and by intentionally putting out clues to encourage Porfiry's suspicion and pursuit. In fact, the more we examine the elaborate pursuit of Porfiry, the more apparent it is that Raskolnikov has a stake in keeping the pursuit alive. It is almost comic, the way he breathes life into the pursuit, providing it with clues, offering himself as bait, and supporting it when it falters. When the scent fades into nothing but Porfiry's double-edged psychology, and when Porfiry himself admits in the last conversation he has with Raskolnikov that he has no clues, Dostoevsky tells us that "Raskolnikov felt a rush of a new kind of terror. The thought that Porfiry thought him innocent began to frighten him suddenly." After this, only Svidrigaylov is left to incriminate him, and yet when he learns that Svidrigaylov is dead, "Raskolnikov felt as if something had fallen on him and was suffocating him." Why? Raskolnikov is terrified and crushed by the thought of not being pursued; and when the last person who can incriminate him dies (Svidrigaylov), he incriminates himself by confessing his crime.

But need this trouble us? Dostoevsky had told us in his famous letter to Katkov, in which he outlined the plot of *Crime and Punishment*, that the criminal would want to be punished, presumably from guilt. Can we not see Raskolnikov's punishment as a sign of his guilt and his desire to atone for his crime? He has killed, recognizes his error, and seeks his punishment. It is not our moral anticipations that are violated by Raskolnikov's elaborate pursuit of punishment, but only our dramatic anticipations. Raskolnikov does not believe he is wrong. He believes he has a right to kill when he lies in his attic room, when he kills the moneylender, when he "seeks his punishment," and indeed when he gives himself up. Raskolnikov seeks punishment, but acts as if he feels no repentance. It is here that the dialectic can help us, for the desire for punishment in Dostoevsky's metaphysic need not be redemptive. The meetings between Raskolnikov and Sonia in the second half of the novel illustrate brilliantly the dialectical nature of Dostoevsky's world.

Raskolnikov visits Sonia twice, first to rehearse his "confession" and then to confess. The first visit is weirdly beautiful: the harlot and the murderer gathered over the reading of the Holy Book; the pale flickering of candlelight over the feverish gaze of Raskolnikov and the terrified look of Sonia. Sonia is wretched and shamed and pleased (*ey bylo i toshno i stydno i sladko*) by his visit. She feels herself defenseless before him. She is shamed at having him where she receives her guests, and timid in the defense of her beliefs and hopes. After Sonia has finished reading the Lazarus passage, Raskolnikov gets up, and with trembling lips and flashing eyes he falls down before her and says, "I did not bow down to you, I bowed down to all suffering humanity." This phrase has been underlined by critics since de Vogüé as a key to the novel because, presumably, it shows a repentant Raskolnikov, one who after killing a human being now recognizes his debt to human beings. *In fact, it is but another expression of the self-willed and rationalizing Raskolnikov*. It is a bookish reassertion of his first self-flattering and self-deceptive humanitarian motive. He bows down to those who have suffered out of pride and not out of humility. We are quick to accept Raskolnikov's bowing to suffering humanity as a sign of repentance because we expect the criminal to have a change of heart, and especially because we expect such a change of heart to take place under the influence of the Bible. But if we read carefully, we see how the dramatic situation contradicts our conventional expectations.

Raskolnikov does his best in this visit to provoke in Sonia the kind of revolt against society that he himself has carried on. He starts out—before the reading of the Lazarus passage—by cruelly insisting on the desperate and hopeless fate that awaits Katerina, Sonia, and especially the children. Katerina will die, and the children will have to share Sonia's terrible life, or at best Sonia will get sick, and Katerina will have to go begging in the street, bang her head against stone and die. The children will have nowhere to go, and Polya will end up a prostitute like Sonia. Without mercy he tears one illusion after another from Sonia, attacking even her most precious protection, her belief in God. He does this by suggesting with malicious joy that God does not exist. It is at this point that he inconsequently asks her to read Lazarus. He listens to the reading of Lazarus, not because he has changed or is changing, but because he is fascinated that someone in such a hopeless position should be buoyed up by something so odd. After the reading, he calls upon her to follow him, because both of them are "damned." But the road he calls her to follow is his, and not hers. He repeats what he said at the beginning: it is folly to cry like children that God will not permit terrible things to happen. In answer to Sonia's agonized cry as to what is to be done, he answers: "What's to be done? We have to break what must be broken once and for all—that's what must be done; and we must take the suffering upon ourselves. What? You don't understand? You'll understand later. Freedom and power—power above all. Power over all trembling creatures and over the anthill. That's our goal." It is his suffering, and not hers, he offers. And his suffering is a suffering of pride and will; it is a suffering of "power over all trembling creatures and over the anthill."

In his second visit to her, he confesses; but before he confesses he makes explicit what he had done in the first visit. In his first visit he had asked her to follow his path by proving to her how hopeless her own path (faith in God) was. In his second visit he puts the choice of his way of life to her only. He asks her, hypothetically, to "kill" to do "good." Both have come from the funeral dinner, where Luzhin had, from petty revenge, tried to ruin Sonia and the Marmeladov family. Raskolnikov asks Sonia: "Suppose this were suddenly left up to you—I mean, whether he or they should go on living, whether, that is, Luzhin should live and go on doing wicked things or Mrs. Marmeladov should die. How would you decide which of the two should die? I ask you." Sonia answers as only she can—that it is not up to her to decide who is to live. Once again, as in the first visit, he changes suddenly from torturer to supplicant. He asks her to forgive him and then confesses. But the confession is no more than the "bowing down to suffering humanity" a sign of repentance. After he has finished, Sonia cries out in terrified compassion that they will go to prison together, and he replies, a hateful and arrogant smile playing on his lips, "I, Sonia, may not want to go to prison." And after Sonia calls upon him to "take suffering upon him and by suffering redeem himself," he answers: "How am I guilty before them? Why should I go? What will I say to them? Why, the whole thing's an illusion. They themselves are destroying people by the million and look on it as a virtue. They're knaves and scoundrels, Sonia. I won't go." Later, he will say the same thing on the eve of confessing to the authorities when he comes to take leave of Dunia and when she reminds him that he has shed blood. He answers with impatience: "Which all men shed ... which flows and has always flowed in cataracts, which men pour out like champagne, and for which men are crowned in the Capital and afterwards called the benefactors of mankind." And he adds a few minutes later, "Never, never have I understood why what I did was a crime. Never, never have I been stronger and more convinced than now."

To be sure, he had committed a crime; he had stepped over the line of the permitted, but that line had been traced arbitrarily by those who had power. The criminal breaks only arbitrary laws, and with daring and strength enough he can make his own laws. He is consequently violating nothing but the wills of others, doing only what society itself has always done. His crime was, therefore, according to the rules of society; liberated from fear and habit, he had a perfect right to commit a crime. With clear logic, he acknowledges that those in power have a perfect right, even an obligation, to assert their restraint of his freedom. He had a right to commit his crime, and they had a right to pursue and punish him for it, and victory lay waiting for the stronger and cleverer. What is clear, then, is that Raskolnikov needs the duel with Porfiry, needs the pursuit, and when this flags, he needs the punishment that society inflicts on him. And he needs all this without having changed his mind about the "rightness" of his crime. Why should he pursue punishment when he is convinced that he has a right to kill? *So that he can prove his strength by bearing the punishment.* If he hasn't been strong enough to carry off the idea of his superman indifference to moral feelings, then he will be strong enough to bear society's punishment. It is not guilt or atonement that drives him to pursue his pursuers, but pride and self-will. He had committed the crime to prove his superiority; he pursues punishment and suffering to protect this superiority. Even more, he committed the crime in order to fail. At the end of Part Three, he summarizes all the reasons why he has failed, and concludes: "And, finally, I am utterly a louse ... because I am perhaps viler and more loathsome than the louse I killed, and I felt *beforehand* that I would say that to myself *after* killing her!"

His strength in failure is not an alternative to strength in success, because he expected from the beginning to fail. He had not committed the crime to be reborn, but to fail. We have something of the same kind of process already at work in *The Double*. Golyadkin creates his "enemies" as Raskolnikov provokes his pursuers; Golyadkin knows beforehand (the same word *predchustvovat'*, literally "to prefeel," is used by Golyadkin and Raskolnikov) that he will be thrown out of Klara's party, that the "Double" will appear, and that he will be taken away to a madhouse; he knows he will fail, but he pursues failure anyway. Raskolnikov does the same thing for an analogous purpose. Golyadkin can keep alive the image of himself as "good," as long as he can keep alive the image of those who are preventing him from being good. Raskolnikov can keep alive the conception of himself as "superior," as long as he can keep alive an image of society that prevents him from being superior. He provokes pursuit so as to show his strength in bearing the punishment, but he also provokes it—and this is perhaps more important—so that they victimizers be the pursuers and he, the pursued; they, the victimizers and he, the victimized; they, the oppressors, and he, the oppressed. By its pursuit of him society confirms what Raskolnikov has made of it. If he can sustain the image of society against which he has revolted, he can sustain his belief in the rightness of his crime. By failing, he makes the kind of world and the kind of Raskolnikov he wants.

We are here at the core of Raskolnikov's motives. In his confession to Sonia, he is explicit about false motives. He is not a victim of economic conditions, nor of hunger, nor of lack of money. He admits to Sonia that he stayed in his room on purpose and went hungry out of spite. He knows that he might have supported himself as had Razumikhin, if he had wanted to. "Ah, how I hated that garret! And yet I wouldn't go out of it. I wouldn't on purpose! I didn't go out for days together, and I wouldn't work, I wouldn't even eat, I just lay there doing nothing. If Nastasya brought me anything, I ate it, if she didn't, I went all day without; I wouldn't ask, on purpose, out of spite." And he is explicit about his real motives:

> I wanted to murder, Sonia, without casuistry, to murder for my own sake, for myself alone! I didn't want to lie about it even to myself. It wasn't to help my mother I did the murder—that's nonsense—I didn't do the murder to gain wealth and power and to become a benefactor of mankind. Nonsense! I simply did it. I did the murder for myself, for myself alone, and whether I became a benefactor to others, or spent my life like a spider catching men in my web and sucking the life out of men, I couldn't have cared at that moment. And it was not the money I wanted, Sonia, when I did it. It was not so much the money I wanted, but something else. I know it all now. Understand me! Perhaps I should never have committed a murder again, if I followed the same road. It was something else I wanted to find out, it was something else that led me on: I had to find out then, and as quickly as possible, whether I was a louse like the rest or a man. Whether I can step over or not.... Whether I am some trembling creature or whether I have the *right*....

To kill, of course, as Sonia cries out. Raskolnikov killed the moneylender for himself, and for himself alone. This has apparently been too bare and simple a motive for critics who have busied themselves looking for Raskolnikov's motives in incest, homosexuality, and earth mothers. In the context of Dostoevsky's metaphysic "for himself alone" is a profound statement, pointing to the self's capacity to exercise its freedom and power without limit. He killed to see whether or not he had the right to step across: step across what? Obviously, the conventional (and to him arbitrary) line of right and wrong, where he can make his own right and wrong. Raskolnikov kills to prove that he is free, and if anything—including the taking of another's life—is interdicted, then he is not free. Raskolnikov fails because he did not have the courage to kill, with indifference, because he chose the most "useless" member of society when he should need no reasons to kill; and because he suspected beforehand that he would not be able to kill indifferently. He does the act anyway so as to confirm his weakness and turn it into strength by giving the reason for his failure to society and thus keeping inviolate his superiority.

But it is all a mad drama of the self making its own reality to fit its dream of itself, and in the face of failure, remaking reality with the failure. In Dostoevsky's metaphysic this remaking of reality illustrates the self's capacity for endless self-justification, its ability to seize with endless refinement upon anything to impose its own image on the world and to support its own belief of itself. Raskolnikov kills the old pawnbroker, visits pain and punishment upon himself, and finally confesses so that he can justify his own rightness and destroy any suggestion of his wrongness. This explains his vicious reaction, even in prison, to any suggestion of another kind of Raskolnikov. According to his theory he should be insensitive to what he does, indifferent to the fate of others, and sublimely content to be proud and independent. But he is not: he takes the drunken Marmeladov home, leaves money out of pity for Mrs. Marmeladov, feels compassion for the young girl on the boulevard who had just been raped and anger at the rake who follows her. He asks Polya to love him, listens sentimentally to the organ grinder, and talks nostalgically about the beauty of falling snow. He desires unaccountably to be with other people, feels disgust for the very act of murder that is supposed to prove that there is no reason to be disgusted with anything, and falls unaccountably in love with Sonia.

But he hates this "other" Raskolnikov that erupts from some suppressed layer of his consciousness to contradict the image of himself as sublimely independent of life he does not control. When these feelings of love, compassion, and beauty erupt, he dismisses them contemptuously, as in the boulevard scene concerning the raped girl: "Anyway to hell with it! Let them! That's how it should be, they say. It's essential, they say, that such a percentage should go every year—that way—to the devil." Frequently he misinterprets these eruptions of another Raskolnikov. After caring for Marmeladov and giving sympathy and love to the dying man and his family, he feels a great sense of rebirth and exhilaration: "The sensation might be compared to that of a man condemned to death who has quite unexpectedly been pardoned." Clearly, the upsurge of life within him—a short time before he had looked upon a dead universe—is caused by the sympathy and love that had welled up within him for another person. But he misinterprets it as a pledge of the rebirth into will and power:

> "Enough!" he said solemnly and resolutely. "I'm through with delusions, imaginary terrors, and phantom visions! Life is real! Haven't I lived just now? My life hasn't come to an end with the death of the old woman! May she rest in peace—enough, time you leave me in peace, madam. Now begins the reign of reason and light and—and of will and strength—and we'll see now! We'll try our strength now," he added arrogantly, as though challenging some dark power.

Again and again he is moved to actions he does not understand but cannot help. His visits to Sonia, both in rehearsal and in confession, show this double character. He has, as has been shown, challenged Sonia to join him in revolt, blasphemed against her faith, confirmed himself in his rightness, and yet, though his "suffering" is a suffering of pride, he is still drawn mysteriously to her. He invites her to join him, but he is happy she doesn't; and if she had, he would have hated her.

It may appear that the compassion, love, and suffering Raskolnikov feels contradicts the elaborate explanation by which these positive motivations are corrupted by his will. Not at all. The fact that both poles exist in him at once dramatizes the most refined point of Dostoevsky's moral dialectic. Raskolnikov shows how the will attempts—and in part succeeds—in corrupting every virtue to its own uses. He feels compassion for the raped girl on the boulevard, and yet leaves her indifferently to her fate; he loves Sonia, but tries to corrupt that love by inviting her to share his self-willed revolt; he pursues punishment from some deep-seated unconscious urge to "reunite" himself with his fellow men, but he attempts and succeeds in corrupting it—at least on a conscious level—into a weapon of self-justification. But even while he is attempting and succeeding in part to corrupt every sign of another nature, these other impulses move him relentlessly—by a logic beyond his intentions and his will—toward another kind of issue. The battle is intense, and he tries with fury to kill every sign of weakness within him, or to use the weakness as a weapon of self-justification. It is not a simple matter of attempting to corrupt his good impulses and failing. In part, he attempts and succeeds. When he bows down to "suffering humanity," he is not repentant; and when he confesses to Sonia and indeed later to the authorities, he is not confessing from a chastened heart or from changed convictions. Dostoevsky knows that the will has almost infinite resources in justifying itself, but the will is not his entire nature. The will, for Raskolnikov, apparently cannot prevail against what is the most deep-seated and essential part of his character.

The pledge of another kind of logic, and of the existence of God, is made to lie upon the evidence of these impulses of compassion, love, and communion with one's fellow men. They properly prepare for the redemptive scene in the epilogue. Dostoevsky sees the opposed impulses in Raskolnikov's nature as the signs of two kinds of "logic" that are basic to the human condition. They correspond to the two poles of his moral dialectic. There is God, and there is the self. Each has roots in the real impulses of men. There is no bridge between these two natures, and man is poised in fearful anxiety with every choice between them. Raskolnikov carries these twin impulses throughout the novel; and in the second half of the novel, he confronts them objectified in the persons of Sonia and Svidrigaylov. His choice between these impulses is dramatized as a choice between Sonia and Svidrigaylov. The skill with which Dostoevsky expresses this choice in structure, incident, and detail is commensurate with the refinement of his dialectic.

Sonia and Svidrigaylov are doubles of Raskolnikov in that they embody in a fully developed manner the two impulses he carries within him. The first half of the novel is structured by Raskolnikov's visits to Alyona Ivanovna; the second half of the novel by his visits to Sonia and Svidrigaylov. Sonia, the symbol of true rebirth in faith, balances antithetically the image of the murdered Alyona Ivanovna, the symbol of false rebirth. Raskolnikov now visits Sonia instead of Alyona, and instead of death, there is birth in the reading of the story of Lazarus. If the murder is the central point of the testing of the rational principle, the confession becomes the central point of the testing of Raskolnikov's rebirth. Appropriately, since these two scenes balance each other, there is a rehearsal for the confession as there was for the murder scene. To be sure, Raskolnikov attempts to corrupt Sonia, and his listening to her reading of Lazarus and his confession do not come from compassion and repentance. But Sonia remains uncorrupted, and the mysterious attraction Raskolnikov feels for her is already a sign of Raskolnikov's acceptance of what she represents.

In going to see Svidrigaylov, Raskolnikov goes toward the destructive idea that had ruled his life in the first half; he goes to meet the ultimate consequences of the idea. Everything about this line of action is characterized by limitation and futile circularity. Raskolnikov and Svidrigaylov hunt each other out to learn from the other "something new," but when they meet—significantly near Haymarket Square, where Raskolnikov's idea grew into decision to act—they are like mirrors reflecting each other's dead idea. Sonia had offered Raskolnikov a new word; Svidrigaylov, the old word, only in grimmer, more naked terms than he had known it. Between the two Raskolnikov wavers, coming to a decision only with the death of one part of himself, only after Svidrigaylov—the objective correlative of the part—has acted out his play of self-destruction.

All of Svidrigaylov's actions, after Raskolnikov visits him in the inn near Haymarket Square, are a preparation for death, culminating in the grim ritual in the small hotel on the eve of his suicide. The hotel and its small empty room, cold veal, mice, and the Charon-like lackey are like a foretaste of the dismal hell that Svidrigaylov's fancy had accurately divined for itself. It is at this point, while Svidrigaylov prepares for death and Raskolnikov struggles with his dilemma, that Dostoevsky shows most vividly the ties and differences between the two men. Svidrigaylov's room looked like an attic: it was so small and low "that Svidrigaylov could scarcely stand up in it"; and the wallpaper was torn and yellowish. In a room that is, in fact, a replica of the small attic room where Raskolnikov's monstrous idea had come to birth, Svidrigaylov prepares to bring it to an end. End touches beginning, and, in his attempt to show the relationship between Svidrigaylov and Raskolnikov, Dostoevsky seems to bring the dreams Svidrigaylov has on his last night into correspondence—not wholly exact—with those Raskolnikov had earlier. Svidrigaylov's first dream is of a spring day on which he looks at the dead body of a girl who had apparently killed herself because of the atrocity he had committed on her body. Raskolnikov's first dream is of the mare beating, which, in the final furious shout of a frenzied peasant—"Why don't you strike her with an axe?"—is linked with his killing of the moneylender. Svidrigaylov looks with apathetic curiosity at the body of his victim; Raskolnikov reacts with furious aversion to the image of the victim-to-be. Svidrigaylov's second dream is of a little girl in whose eyes, even as he tries to protect her, he sees a reflection of his rapacious lust; Raskolnikov's, of his futile attempt to kill again Alyona Ivanovna. Raskolnikov is unable to act in his dream as he had in his conscious state; Svidrigaylov is able to act in no other way. At the point at which the ties between the two are about to be severed, the dreams, pointing perhaps to the essential nature of both men, show the unbridgeable gulf between them.

Now as Svidrigaylov prepares to meet the end to which the self-willed principle had brought him, the circumstances of the beginning of the crime are recreated. As on the night when he committed the atrocity which had led to the girl's death, the wind howls, it rains, and he goes, as before, to find a bush under which he can crawl and douse himself with the water he hates so much. At the precise moment, at dawn, when Svidrigaylov kills himself Raskolnikov—who had been wandering around St. Petersburg all night—is peering into the muddy waters of the Neva contemplating suicide. With Svidrigaylov's death, Raskolnikov turns to confess. One part of himself, the self-willed principle, dies; the life-giving principle, objectified in Sonia, remains.

Raskolnikov carries within him the antithetic poles of Dostoevsky's dialectic: human logic and divine logic. There can be no compromise between them. The English word "crime" is exclusively legalistic in connotation and corresponds to the "human logic"; but the Russian word for crime, *prestuplenie*, carries meanings which point both to human and divine logic. *Prestuplenie* means literally "overstepping," and is in form parallel to the English word "transgression," although this word no more than "crime" is adequate to translate *prestuplenie* because of its Biblical connotations. But *prestuplenie* contains both poles of Dostoevsky's dialectic, for the line of the permitted which one "oversteps" may be drawn both by human or by divine logic.

Because the two impulses of self and God battle within him to the very end, Raskolnikov's confession is at once a sign of his self-will and his acceptance of God. He confesses because he will no longer be pursued, and it is only by his confession that he can provoke the punishment and hence the image of society he wants; yet he is simultaneously being moved toward the kind of punishment that Sonia wants him to accept. The battle between the two principles continues to the very end. Dostoevsky resolves the conflict by legislating Raskolnikov's conversion. The conversion is motivated, as indeed suicide or a new crime is motivated, in Raskolnikov's character. Dostoevsky does not really have grounds for ending the conflict, and it would have been much better, I believe, to have ended the novel with Raskolnikov's confession. The confession itself is at once, as I have explained, a self-interested and a selfless act. This is to say that the confession would have dramatized at the very end of the novel the fury of the conflict, and the effort of the will to penetrate and corrupt even the holiest of gestures.

But Dostoevsky was not yet ready to grant so much to his antagonists. He had dramatized masterfully the strength and power of the self, and his very skill had increased the probability of the self's domination of Raskolnikov. But he had also discerned the springs of another "nature" in Raskolnikov's compassion, and he had set this against the powerful and cunning self-interest of Raskolnikov's nature. For the moment Dostoevsky settles the issue by nudging Raskolnikov into God's camp. But Dostoevsky will not be satisfied with his own solution, and again and again he will grant more and more to his antagonists, so as to test his belief that man can be reborn into selflessness.

ROBERT LOUIS JACKSON

Philosophical Pro and Contra in Part One of Crime and Punishment

I suffered these deeds more than I acted them.

—Oedipus

The burden of Part One is the dialectic of consciousness in Raskolnikov. This dialectic propels him to crime and, in so doing, uncovers for the reader the "motives" leading him to crime: motives deeply rooted in his character and in his efforts to come to terms with the necessities of his existence. Leo Tolstoy grasped the essence of the matter when he wrote that Raskolnikov lived his "true life" when he was

> lying on the sofa in his room, deliberating not at all about the old woman, nor even as to whether it is or is not permissible at the will of one man to wipe from the face of the earth another, unnecessary and harmful person, but whether he ought to live in St. Petersburg or not, whether he ought to accept money from his mother or not, and on other questions not at all relating to the old woman. And then at that time—in that region—quite independent of animal activities—the question of whether he would or not kill the old woman was decided. ("Why Men Stupefy Themselves," 1890)

But if the fundamental matters or issues over which Raskolnikov deliberates are very immediate and practical ones, his responses to these matters have broad implications that have direct bearing on the crime. Here we may rightly speak of a moral-philosophical pro and contra.

Part One begins with a "test" visit (*proba*) to the old pawnbroker and ends with a visit-for-real in which Raskolnikov murders the old lady and, incidentally, her sister Lizaveta. The murder itself is also, in a deeper sense, a "test" or experiment to determine whether he has the "right" to transgress. Raskolnikov starts out in a state of indecision or irresolution (I, 1) and ends with a decisive action-murder (I, 7): an apparent resolution of his initial indecision. But does the murder really constitute a resolution of Raskolnikov's dialectic? Does he really "decide" to murder the pawnbroker? Or does not "chance," rather, serve to mask his failure to decide with his whole being? Is he master or slave here? The final line alone of Part One suggests the answer: "Fragments and shreds of thoughts swarmed in his head; but he could not get hold of a single one, he could not dwell on a single one, in spite of all his trying" (I, 7). Raskolnikov's dialectic of consciousness continues to be dramatized in his thoughts, actions and relationships after the murder (Parts II–VI). It is only in the epilogue (chap. 2) that this dialectic is dissolved—not resolved—on a new, developing plane of consciousness.[1]

The movement from test to test, from rehearsal to experimental crime, from theory to practice, is marked by a constant struggle and debate on all levels of Raskolnikov's consciousness. Each episode—the meeting with Marmeladov and his family (chap. 2), Raskolnikov's reading of his mother's letter with its account of family affairs (chap. 3), his encounter with the violated girl and the policeman (chap. 4) and his dream of the beating of the mare (chap. 5)—is marked by a double movement: a motion of sympathy and a motion of disgust, of attraction and recoil; each episode attests to what one critic has called Raskolnikov's "moral maximalism";[2] yet each attests to a deepening scepticism and despair on the part of Raskolnikov, a tragic tension toward crime in both a psychological and philosophical sense.[3]

The immediate issues of this pro and contra are nothing more or less than injustice and human suffering and the question of how one shall respond to them. But the deeper evolving question—on which turns Raskolnikov's ultimate response to injustice and suffering—is a judgment of man and his world: is he a morally viable creature or simply and irredeemably bad? Do man and the world make sense?[4] Raskolnikov's murder of the old pawnbroker is the final expression of the movement of his dialectic toward a tragic judgment of man and society. The ideological concomitant of his paralysis of moral will (the scenes following his chance encounter on the street with Lizaveta) is a rationalistic humanism that is unable to come to terms with evil in human existence; lacking larger spiritual dimensions, this ideology ends by postulating incoherence and chaos in man and his environment and, in turn, a universe in which man is a victim of "fate."

The stark realism and pathos of Marmeladov's person and family at first cools the hot and agitated Raskolnikov. The novel rises to its first epiphany in the tavern: out of the troubled posturing and grotesquerie of Marmeladov comes a mighty prose poem of love, compassion, and forgiveness (echoing Luke 7, 36–50); it constitutes an antithesis to Raskolnikov's proud and rebellious anger. Raskolnikov visits the Marmeladovs, responds warmly to them, and leaves some money behind. But the same scene, focusing on the hopelessness and tragedy of Raskolnikov's environment, evokes finally incredulity and despair in him. If Marmeladov's "confession," which opens chapter 2, accents the central redemptive notes in *Crime and Punishment*, the final lines of the chapter stress antithetical notes of despair and damnation. The sight of human degradation is so overwhelming as to evoke in Raskolnikov fundamental doubts about man and human nature. Stunned that people can live in this way, that indignity, vulgarity and discord can become an accepted part of one's life, Raskolnikov explodes: "Man can get used to anything—the scoundrel [*podlets*]!" These strange ruminations follow: "But what if man really isn't a *scoundrel*, man in general, I mean, the whole human race; if he is not, that means that all the rest is prejudice, just imaginary fears, and there are no barriers, and that is as it should be!" (I, 2). These lines are crucial in posing the underlying moral and philosophical issues of *Crime and Punishment*.

The motif of "adaptation" is heard throughout Dostoevsky's works—from *Poor Folk* (1846) through *Notes from the House of the Dead* (1860–61) to *The Brothers Karamazov* (1881). It attests, from one point of view, to human endurance, the will to survive; yet from another view, it is a deeply tragic idea, implying that man will yield feebly to suffering, oppression, injustice, unfreedom, in short, to triumphant evil. Man in this conception is man as the Grand Inquisitor finds him: weak and vile. Such adaptation arouses only contempt in the rebellious Raskolnikov. His rebellion, of course, implies a positive standard or norm of human behavior, morality, life. Merely to speak of man as a "scoundrel" for adapting to evil is to posit another ideal, to affirm, by implication, that man ought not to yield weakly to degradation and evil. But the thought that occurs to Raskolnikov at this point is one which links him directly with the Grand Inquisitor. We may paraphrase his thought as follows: what if all this vile adaptation to evil is *not* a deviation from a norm; that is, what if villainy pure and simple is, *ab ovo*, the human condition? What if—as Raskolnikov later puts it—every one of the people scurrying about on the streets "is a scoundrel and predator by his very nature" (VI, 7)?

If such be the case, if man is truly defective by nature, then all our moral systems, standards, injunctions, pejorative epithets (the very word "scoundrel") are senseless "prejudices," "imaginary fears"; it follows that if human nature is, morally speaking, an empty plain, then "there can be no barriers," all is permissible, "and that is as it should be!"[5]

Svidrigailov, the character who comes closest to a complete embodiment of the principle that "all is permissible," also poses the question that Raskolnikov is deliberating, though more dispassionately and cynically. Defending himself against the charges that he persecuted Dunia in his home, he observes:

> Just suppose, however, that I, too, am a man, *et nihil humanum* ... In a word, that I can be attracted and fall in love (and of course that doesn't happen to us according to our own will), then everything's accounted for in the most natural manner. The whole question boils down to this: am I a monster or am I a victim? Well, and what if I am a victim? (IV, 1)

Barely concealed in Svidrigailov's jocular question, of course, is the issue of human nature, the character of man. The underlying ethical and finally philosophical import of his question—"Am I a monster or am I myself a victim?"—is clear: does a consideration of my acts—man's acts ("Just suppose ... that I, too, am a man") fall under the rubric of ethics or the laws of nature? Are we really responsible for our behavior? Is the morally pejorative epithet "monster" (or "scoundrel") really in order? Are we not simply creatures of "nature"? Svidrigailov, one notes, likes to appeal to "natural" tendencies; very much like the Marquis de Sade's alter ego Clément (*Justine*, 1791) or Dolmancé (*La philosophie dans le boudoir*, 1795), he appeals to "nature" as a reason for disposing entirely of moral categories or judgment. "In this debauchery, at least, there is something constant, based even on nature, and not subject to fantasy," Svidrigailov remarks in his last conversation with Raskolnikov[6] (VI, 3). Indeed, Svidrigailov's conception of man would appear to be wholly biological—"Now I pin all my hope on anatomy alone, by God!" (IV, 1)—a point of view that certainly undercuts any concept of personal responsibility or free will. The concept "*homo sum, et nihil humanum a me alienum puto*" ("I am a man and nothing human is alien to me") was for Dostoevsky a profoundly moral concept, implying the obligation squarely to confront human reality. "Man on the surface of the earth does not have the right to turn away and ignore what is taking place on earth," he wrote in a letter in 1871, "and there are lofty *moral* reasons for this: *homo sum et nihil humanum*, etc." Svidrigailov, of course, takes the concept as an apologia for doing whatever one pleases. To be a man, in his view, is to be open to all that is in nature, that is, to nature in himself; it is to be in the power of nature (if not to *be* nature) and, therefore, not to be responsible. We have noted that he pins his hopes on "anatomy." But his hopes for salvation through Dunia, and his final suicide, are evidence that his confidence in anatomy has its cracks and fissures. In the final analysis, then, even for Svidrigailov (though infinitely more so for Raskolnikov), the concept "monster or victim?"—morally responsible or free to commit all vilenesses?—is a fateful *question*; precisely this fact, in Dostoevsky's view, distinguishes man, even the Svidrigailovs, from de Sade's tigers and leopards.

The problem raised by Raskolnikov and Svidrigailov, and lived out in their life dramas, is posed directly by Ivan Karamazov. Apropos of his belief that man is incapable of Christian love, Ivan observes: "The real issue is whether all this comes from people's bad qualities or simply because it is their nature." Raskolnikov's pessimistic conjecture at the conclusion of chapter 2 (and, even more, the evidence of his dream in chapter 5) can be compared with Ivan's bitter judgment of man in his famous "rebellion." It can be described as the opening, and dominant motif, in a prelude to murder. The whole of *Crime and Punishment* is an effort to refute this judgment of man, to provide an answer, through Raskolnikov himself, to his own tragic conjecture. The action in Part One, however, is "moved" by the almost syllogistic logic of Raskolnikov's pessimistic conjecture.

Chapter 2, then, contains the extreme moral and philosophical polarities of the novel: affirmation of the principle of love, compassion and freedom (which will ultimately embrace Raskolnikov through Sonia) and the principle of hate, a pessimistic view of man as a "scoundrel" by nature, and a projection of the idea that "all is permissible." The events of chapter 2 bring Raskolnikov full circle from compassion to nihilistic rage. Exposed is that realm of "underground," ambivalent consciousness where love is compounded of pain, and hate—of frustrated love; where extreme compassion for suffering and for the good are transmuted into a contempt for man; where that contempt, finally, signals despair with love and with the good and nourishes that urge for violence and sick craving for power that is born not only from an acute sense of injustice but from a tragic feeling of one's own real helplessness and irreversible humiliation. Here is our first contact with the matrix of Raskolnikov's "theoretical" crime, with the responses that will find explicit formulation in Raskolnikov's article and arguments. Here is the protean core of those shifting, seemingly contradictory "motives" (what Mochulsky has termed the "idea of Rastignac"—altruistic, utilitarian crime, and the "idea of Napoleon"—triumph over the "anthill," etc.[7]). Here we see how the raw material of social and psychological experience begins to generalize into social and philosophical "point of view"—ultimately, into those "ideas" of Raskolnikov that will tragically act back again upon life and experience.

The same cyclical pattern we have noted in chapter 2 dominates chapter 3. The chapter opens on a subtle note that disputes the depressing and abstract conjectures of Raskolnikov. Nastasia, the servant girl, brings him soup, chatters about food, about Raskolnikov's affairs. She is the epitome of a simplicity, warmth, and goodness that cannot be gainsaid. She is a kind of spiritual harbinger of Raskolnikov's mother, whose letter he receives. This letter, like the encounter with Marmeladov and his family, evokes a similar picture of self-sacrificing people who are helpless before the evil in the world, before the Luzhins and Svidrigailovs. Raskolnikov begins reading the letter with a kiss ("he quickly lifted it to his lips and kissed it") but ends it with "a heavy, bilious, angry smile" playing around his lips. The letter produces, finally, the same ugly sensations as the scene in the Marmeladov household, the same sympathy and compassion turning into rage and rebellion. Raskolnikov goes out for a walk as though "drunk": his shapeless body reflects his inner rage and distress. His initial defense of the violated girl (chap. 4) is followed almost immediately by a sense of "revulsion," a raging amoral anger. Starting out, then, with a gesture of goodness, Raskolnikov characteristically ends by abandoning the girl to evil in a classical gesture of "underground" malice.

During Raskolnikov's walk (the early part of chapter 4), the central philosophical motif on the nature of man—the area of his vacillations—emerges in his reflections on his mother, Dunia and their situation. He comprehends their sacrifice for him as an ascent to Golgotha, but in bitterness casts his mother and sister among the innocents, those "Schilleresque 'beautiful souls'" who wave the truth away, would rather not admit the vile truth about man. Dunia, like Sonia, Raskolnikov realizes, is prepared to suppress her moral feelings for the one she loves, for him. Raskolnikov almost venomously rejects the idea of such sacrifice, sale of one's freedom, peace of mind and conscience. It is a rejection, of course, of the Christian spirit of sacrifice. "Dear little Sonia, Sonia Marmeladov, Sonia eternal, while the world lasts! But this sacrifice, this sacrifice, have you taken the measure of your sacrifice, both of you? Have you really? Do you have the strength? Will it be of any use? Is it wise and reasonable?" Raskolnikov's choice of words is symptomatic of his ideological illness. To the impulses of the heart he opposes, in his bitterness and despair, utility, scales, self-interest. And, of course, here is rich soil for the cultivation of ideas of utilitarian crime (I, 6). The appeal of utilitarian ethics emerges from a despairing sense of the *uselessness* of all human striving for justice and truth, from a sense of the vileness of human nature, and a conviction that "people won't change, and nobody can reform them, and it's not worth the effort!" (V, 4).

Raskolnikov rightly understands that what he opposes and rejects (that is, the principle of love and self-sacrifice) is "eternal"; he rejects it in part out of despair with evil, but in part in the name of a false principle of self-affirmation and "triumph over the whole anthill," a false principle of "freedom." "And I know now, Sonia, that whoever is strong and self-confident in mind and spirit is their master!" (V, 4) "Understand me well," Dostoevsky wrote in *Winter Notes on Summer Impressions* (1863), "voluntary, fully conscious self-sacrifice, utterly free of outside constraint, sacrifice of one's whole self for the benefit of all, is in my opinion the sign of the highest development of individuality, of its supreme power, its absolute self-mastery and its most complete freedom of its own will." Raskolnikov's rejection of his family's spirit of self-sacrifice, at least in part, reflects his own distance from Dostoevsky's concept of self-sacrifice and, chiefly, from the ideal of authentic freedom that such a spirit of self-sacrifice implies.

But Raskolnikov's powerful impulses to good and his high potential for self-sacrifice are short-circuited by a sense of overwhelming injustice and evil, of absurd imbalance in the "scales" of good and evil. In the face of the world's misery, the rapacious Svidrigailovs and Luzhins, the pitiful and loathesome spectacle of *man-adapting*, Raskolnikov rebels: "I don't want your sacrifice, Dunia; I don't want it, mother dear! As long as I live it shall not come to that! It shall not, shall not come to that! I refuse to accept it!" (I, 4)

Dostoevsky uses the word "anguish" to express Raskolnikov's state of mind. His rebellion, indeed, looks back on the revolt of the man from the "underground" and forward to Ivan Karamazov's rebellion against divine harmony (if it be based on the innocent suffering of children). Deeply responsive to human suffering, Ivan, in his indignation, returns to God his "ticket" to future harmony; yet this same humanitarian revolt, with its despair in a meaningful universe, leads him unconsciously to sanction the murder of his father. This same ethical paradox lies at the root of Raskolnikov's crime. Starting out with love and compassion for the "eternal" Sonias, for Dunia and his mother, Raskolnikov ends up with a rejection of love and sacrifice and with a rage at evil: a rage which itself becomes disfigured, evil. This rage, in its origins ethically motivated, deforms Raskolnikov and accentuates in him the elements of sick pride and self-will.

It is no accident that in this state of mind Raskolnikov's thought is led back to his projected crime. "It shall not come to that": he is "robbing" his family, he feels; but what can he do? The letter from his mother exposes his helplessness in a realm that is dear to him, drives him onto the path of action. Either action or renunciation of life: "humbly accept my fate as it is, once and for all, strangle everything I have within me, and give up every right I have to act, to live and to love!" Suddenly a thought flashes through his mind. This is the "'monstrous' dream" (*bezobraznaja mechta*, l, 1) of his crime, but now no longer a dream or vision, but taking on "some new and terrifying form that he had not known before." This new and threatening form is revealed to him in his "terrible dream" (*strashnyj son*) in chapter 5: the beating and killing of the mare.

Raskolnikov's dream, echoing earlier incidents, situations, and emotional experience, is a psychological metaphor in which we may distinguish the various responses of Raskolnikov to his projected crime: his deep psychological complicity in, and yet moral recoil before, the crime. What has received less attention, however, is the way in which the underlying philosophical pro and contra is revealed in the separate elements of the dream (pastoral church and cemetery episode, tumultuous tavern and mare-beating scene); how the scene of the beating itself, this picture of Russian man and reality, raises the central and grave question of Part One: what is the nature of man? In its oppressive realism, and in the pessimism of its "commentary" on man, this dream yields only to the tale "Akulka's husband" in *Notes from the House of the Dead*: at the center of that episode is the stupefied life of the Russian village, the persecution and murder of a peasant girl. The story is the nethermost level of Dostoevsky's "hell": here there is no light, only brutality, ignorance, absolute loss of control, and the violation of all that is sacred: beauty, human dignity, life.

The opening recollection in Raskolnikov's dream, though dominated by an atmosphere of impending evil, embodies Dostoevsky's pure aesthetic-religious ideal. Everything is sacred form, harmony, and reverence in the boy's first memory of the tranquil open landscape, the stone church with its green cupola, the icons, the simple rituals, the cemetery and, finally, the tombs of his grandmother and younger brother with their clear promise of resurrection. "He loved this church" and its atmosphere. In this, Raskolnikov's purified and almost completely submerged memory of sacred form, spirituality and beauty, there lies, without question, the seed of Raskolnikov's own moral and spiritual renewal. But the path to the church and cemetery—to resurrection—goes by the tavern on the edge of town, with its crowd of drunken, brawling peasants with their "drunken, fearsome distorted faces," their "shapeless and hoarse singing." Here, everything is desecration and deformation. The faces of the people in Raskolnikov's nightmare tell the tale: this is a demonized universe.[8] It all created an "unpleasant impression" on the boy. On the deepest level of the dream, then, we may speak of the coexistence—passive, we shall see—of two barely contiguous worlds: the ideal world of Christianity, with its aesthetic-religious ideals, and the real world claimed by the devil.

But now again, as Raskolnikov dreams, it is a holiday, a day of religious observance; the peasants, however, are drunk and in riotous spirits. There is an overloaded cart drawn by a poor mare. Then, suddenly, a drunken crowd of peasants, shouting and singing, emerge from the tavern, "blind drunk, in red and blue shirts." At the invitation of the driver, Mikolka, they pile onto the cart, followed by a "fat, red-faced peasant woman" in a "red calico dress ... plumed and beaded ... she was cracking nuts and laughing. In the crowd all around they're laughing, too." Then, the effort to start the cart and the brutal process of beating, and finally killing, the mare commences. This terrible and terrifying scene is simultaneously a rehearsal for murder and a statement on man. "Don't look," the father tells the boy. But Dostoevsky forces the reader to look at the beating, at the crowd, at himself. ("Man on the surface of the earth does not have the right to turn away.") "My property!" screams the peasant Mikolka in his drunken rage on three separate occasions, as he violently smashes away at the mare. This is a scene of absolute evil: here surface in a strange symbiosis what for Dostoevsky are the most predatory instincts in man: violence, sensuality and property-mindedness. The message of "my property" (*moyo dobro*) is clear: what is mine, what I covet and own, releases me from all moral obligations, because it is my good that is involved; the use of the word "*dobro*" here—property, goods, but also ethical "good"—subtly suggests the smashing of all moral norms or "barriers," the triumph of raw egoism over any moral imperative in human relations. "My property! What I want—I go ahead and do!" (*Chto khochu, to i delaju!*) "Now I shall do just as I want with all of you because I have lost control of myself," cries the murderer of Akulka in *Notes from the House of the Dead.* The motif "all is permissible" permeates Raskolnikov's nightmare, as it does "Akulka's Husband" and Ivan's stories of the cruelties inflicted on children. This is a grim statement on man.

Others, too, participate in the orgy of violence, or watch passively from the sidelines, laugh, enjoy the spectacle, or just go on "cracking nuts." There are some voices of condemnation. But they are drowned out. Even the old man who shouts indignantly—"What are you about, are you a Christian or a devil?"—becomes demonized, is unable, finally, to restrain his laughter as he watches the mare, "a bag of bones," kicking about.

"'Thank God, this is only a dream!'" exclaims Raskolnikov. But the dream was out of Russian life; reality, Dostoevsky liked to emphasize, was more fantastic than fiction. The mare-beating scene is the center of world evil, and it is not surprising that at this moment, on the threshold of crime, Raskolnikov's soul was "in confusion and darkness."

Are the people who inhabit Raskolnikov's nightmare "monsters" or "victims"? Ivan's question—and it is really Raskolnikov's as well—is very much to the point here: "the real issue is whether all this comes from people's bad qualities or simply because it is their nature." Raskolnikov's nightmare—the terrible event at its center—provides a tragic answer to this question; and if human nature is a moral wasteland, then "there are no barriers, and that is as it should be!" Raskolnikov's social—philosophical *conclusions* here embodied in the action of his own psychodrama—represent a precipitous movement toward murder.

Certainly, the fractured character of Raskolnikov's moral consciousness is revealed in this dream. The boy identifies with the suffering mare, with the victim, as Raskolnikov does, initially, in his various encounters in Part One. Here there is anguish to the point of hysteria. The boy cries and screams and at the end puts his arm around the mare's "dead, bloodstained muzzle, and kissed her, kissed her on the eyes, on the mouth." But, as in Raskolnikov's waking hours, anguish turns into rage, and the boy "suddenly leaps up and flings himself on Mikolka, striking out in a frenzy with his fists." Mikolka is clearly the oppressor, the embodiment of the principle of self-will. He may easily stand in for types like the pawnbroker, Luzhin, or Svidrigailov, vicious people exploiting and degrading innocent people like Dunia, Lizaveta, or Sonia, quiet timid creatures with gentle eyes like those of the mare. It is against these vicious people that Raskolnikov revolts. But in his revolt he is himself transformed into a monstrous, shapeless Mikolka, and himself becomes the alien oppressor, exalted by a new morality that crushes the "guilty" and innocent alike. In the image of the child, then, Raskolnikov recoils from the horror that Raskolnikov, the man, contemplates; but in the image of Mikolka, Raskolnikov prefigures his own role as murderer. Raskolnikov's dream has often been described as revealing the last efforts of his moral conscience to resist the crime. This is true: the dream is a battle; but it is a battle that is *lost*. On the philosophical plane, as a statement on man, the dream is the tragic finale to the pro and contra of Part One, the final smashing of "barriers."

The dream gives expression, finally, to a central paradox. Here is hell, or, in any case, the postfall world plunged in terrible evil. Yet the evil is witnessed and judged essentially from the point of view of the innocent, prefall mentality of the child. The world of the "fathers"—the adaptors, objectively indifferent to good and evil—is discredited ("Come along and don't look ... it's not our business"); their Christianity at best (witness the "old man") is shameful and frightening: Christian ethics dissolve into the aesthetics of laughter, the enjoyment of suffering, a Sadean realm that Dostoevsky explored in *Notes from the House of the Dead.* The Christian ethos is not in men's hearts. The church is out of town, literally, but also in a metaphorical sense: it is *hors de combat*, passive. The real, active tension in the nightmare—dramatic and ideological—is in the almost Quixote-like opposition of absolute evil with absolute innocence: the inflamed demonic violence and sensuality of Mikolka, and the pure, idyllic sensibility, goodness, and anguish of the child. But the child, though rightfully protesting cruelty and evil, is unable conceptually to integrate evil in his prefall universe. This is essentially the problem, as Dostoevsky conceives it, of such types as Raskolnikov and Ivan: idealists, humanists, they are unable, at root, to disencumber themselves of their utopian dreams, their insistence on the moral absolute. Raskolnikov, very much like his sister, is a chaste soul.

In the final analysis, what Dostoevsky finds missing in Raskolnikov (and, perhaps, in himself as well) is precisely a calm, reconciling Christian perspective, precisely an attitude that, while never yielding to evil, nonetheless, in ultimate terms, accepts it as part of God's universe, as cloaked in the mystery of God's truth. Such a perspective, indeed, we find in Zosima in *The Brothers Karamazov*. Dostoevsky strained in this direction, made his final conscious choice in this direction, indeed gives clear evidence of this choice (Raskolnikov's ultimate choice, we must believe) in the prelude to the nightmare. Yet at the same time he invested the child's suffering and rage with deep pathos and anguish. The child's pure nature is ill-equipped to cope with reality or even grasp the deeper coherence of life's processes. Yet it seems a cardinal feature of Dostoevsky's own outlook that all genuine moral feeling must arise from an open confrontation of the pure ideal with reality. Such a confrontation, on the plane of everyday life, may be unpleasant, disruptive, unrealistic, even absurd; but as Ivan Karamazov observes to Alyosha, "absurdities are frightfully necessary on earth. The world rests on absurdities, and without them, perhaps, nothing would ever have taken place in it." In Raskolnikov's nightmare only the pure vision of the child, only the sacred indignation of an unsullied soul, holds out any hope to a world that is all but damned.

"Freedom! freedom!" is Raskolnikov's predominant sensation after his nightmare. "He was free now from that witchcraft, that sorcery, those spells, that obsession" (I, 5). The nightmare is catharsis, purgation, momentary relief; it is only a "dream"; yet this "dream" brings him face-to-face with himself. "God! ... will I really? Will I really take the ax, will I really hit her on the head, split open her skull, will I really slip in the sticky warm blood," he reflects on awakening. "Good Lord, will I really?" The day before, he recalls, he had recoiled from the idea of crime in sick horror. And now he remarks inwardly, and significantly: "Granted ... that everything [his plans for the murder] ... is clear as arithmetic" but "really I know that I shall never decide on it in spite of everything!" Indeed, Raskolnikov will never *decide* to commit the crime, never consciously, actively and with his whole moral being, choose to kill or—the reverse—choose not to kill. His "moral resolution of the question" will never go deeper than "casuistry" (I, 6). And yet he will kill! He will lose his "freedom" (which in any case, after his nightmare, is deceptive) and be *pulled* into crime and murder (so it will seem to him) by some "unnatural power." Like Ivan Karamazov—but unlike Ivan's brother Dmitry—Raskolnikov will allow circumstances to shape his destiny. Here a contrast with Dmitry is instructive. Dmitry spent the two days before the murder of his father (which he did not, in the end, commit) "literally casting himself in all directions, 'struggling with his fate and saving himself,' as he himself put it later." Dmitry's open, if naive, recognition of his opposite impulses and freedom to kill or not to kill, as well as his awareness of competing "philosophies" within him, are the crucial internal factors that help to "save" him in the end from the crime of murder. Raskolnikov's dialectic of consciousness also constitutes a struggle, but his dialectic moves him toward, not away, from the crime; in the end, one "philosophy" triumphs: he loses his freedom (he blames the crime, significantly, on the "devil") and yields to his obsession; Dmitry, on the other hand, triumphs over his obsession (and, equally significantly, attributes his victory to "God").

Raskolnikov's deeply passive relationship to his crime often has been noted.[9] Yet this passivity is not a purely psychological phenomenon; it is, Dostoevsky clearly indicates, closely linked with Raskolnikov's world outlook, an area of very intense activity for Raskolnikov. As Raskolnikov realizes later on—and as his own thinking and language suggest—he is dominated at the time of the crime by a belief in "fate," a general superstitious concern for all sorts of chthonic forces, perhaps even a taste for the occult (elements that, in Svidrigailov, have already surfaced in the form of "ghosts"). Raskolnikov's problem is directly alluded to in Dostoevsky's notes to the novel. "That was an evil spirit: how otherwise could I have overcome all those difficulties?" Raskolnikov observes at one point. And a few lines later these significant lines: "I should have done that. (*There is no free will. Fatalism*)." And, finally, these crucial thoughts: "Now why has my life ended? Grumble: But God does not exist and so forth." Dostoevsky's own thought emerges even in these few notes: a loss of faith in God—or in the meaningfulness of God's universe—must end with the individual abandoning himself to a notion of "fate."

Raskolnikov shares his proclivity toward fatalism with a number of Dostoevsky's heroes, for example, the man from the "underground," the hero of "A Gentle Creature," and Aleksey Petrovich (*The Gambler*, 1866).[10] The similarity between Raskolnikov's and the gambler's problems is striking. Both are dominated by a sterile, rationalistic outlook; both place themselves in a position of challenging "fate"; both lose their moral awareness in the essential act of challenge (murder, gambling); both seek through their acts to attain to an absolute freedom from the so-called laws of nature that are binding on ordinary men; both, in the end, conceive of themselves as victims of "fate." Such types continually are seeking their cues or directives outside of themselves. Quite symptomatic, in this connection, is Raskolnikov's prayerful remark after his dream: "O God! show me the way, that I may renounce this cursed dream of mine!"

The fateful "circumstance" that struck Raskolnikov "almost to the point of superstition" and that seemed a "predestination of his fate" (I, 5) was his chance meeting with Lizaveta, a meeting that, in Raskolnikov's view, sets into motion the machinery of fate. Raskolnikov returned home after that meeting "like a man condemned to death. He had not reasoned anything out, he was quite incapable of reasoning; but suddenly with all his being he felt that his mind and will were no longer free, and that everything had suddenly been finally decided" (I, 5). Similarly, Raskolnikov responds to the conversation he overhears in a restaurant—by "coincidence" two men give expression to "precisely the same thoughts" that had been cropping up in his own mind—as "something preordained, some guiding hint":

> This last day ... which had so unexpectedly decided everything at once, had caught him up almost automatically, as if by the hand, and pulled him along with unnatural power, blindly, irresistibly, and with no objections on his part; and he was caught, as if by the hem of his coat in the cog of a wheel, and being drawn in. (I, 6)

Dostoevsky is not projecting an "accident" theory of personal history; but neither does he deny the role of chance. Chance is the eternal "given"; without it there would be no freedom. Raskolnikov's encounter with Lizaveta was accidental (though not pure accident); it was by chance that he overheard the conversation in which he recognized his own thoughts (although, as Dostoevsky wrote in his letter to M. N. Katkov on the novel, the ideas that infect Raskolnikov "are floating about in the air"). But these chance elements only set into motion a course of action that was seeking to be born, albeit without the full sanction of moral self.

What is crucial in Raskolnikov's situation is not so much the factor of chance as *his disposition to be guided by chance*, his readiness, as it were, to gamble, to seek out and acknowledge in chance his so-called "fate."[11] What is crucial to his action is the general state of consciousness that he brings to the moment of critical accident: and consciousness here is not only his nervous, overwrought state, but the way he conceives of his relationship to the world. Such is the background of Tolstoy's perception that Raskolnikov's true moment of decision and his "true life" occurred not when he met the sister of the old lady, not at the time of the murder when he was "mechanically" discharging the energy accumulated in him, "not when he was acting, but when he was thinking, when his consciousness alone was working"—and in realms affecting the total scope of his existence.

Raskolnikov seized upon the various chance incidents that preceded the murder as the action of "fate," but did not recognize that fate here had all the iron logic of his own, inner fatality. His passivity—that state of drift in which he evades the necessity of choice and abandons all moral responsibility—is motivated, then, not only by his deep and unresolved moral conflicts but by a muddled rationalistic, *fatalistic* outlook that itself denies freedom of choice or moral responsibility, an outlook that in the end posits an incoherent universe. This outlook is not something that Raskolnikov merely picked up in reading or table talk. The sense of a blind, meaningless universe, of a loveless world dominated by an "evil spirit"[12]—and this is conveyed by Part One—emerges from Raskolnikov's confrontation with the concrete social reality of Russian life, with the tragedy of the "lower depths": its hopeless poverty, its degradation, its desolation. It is this confrontation with the human condition that violates the purity of Raskolnikov's ideal, that ruptures his faith in moral law and human nature, that bends him toward a tragic view of man and toward a universe ruled by "blind fate."[13] It is this confrontation—in which compassion and contempt for man form an intimate dialectic—that nourishes the related structures of his "ideas" or ideology: his altruistic utilitarian ethics and his Napoleonic self-exaltation and contempt for the "herd." It is this confrontation that underlies his murder of the old pawnbroker.

Consciousness, of course, is not passive here. Raskolnikov, half-deranged in the isolation and darkness of his incomprehensible universe (the model of which is his little coffinlike room), actively reaches out into "history," into his loveless universe to rationalize his own responses to reality and his own psychological needs. He is an intellectual. His "ideas," moreover, acquire a dynamic of their own, raise him to new levels of abstraction and fantasy, and provide him, finally, with a "theoretical" framework and justification for crime. Yet, whatever the independence of these "ideas" (as we find them in his article or circulating freely in taverns and restaurants), they acquire their vitality, their force only insofar as they mediate the confrontation between individual consciousness and social reality; only insofar as they give expression to Raskolnikov's intimate social and psychological experience, to his deepest, organic responses to the world about him.

In one of his notebooks, Dostoevsky refers to himself with pride as the first to focus on

> the tragedy of the underground: it consists of suffering, self-punishment, the consciousness of something better and the impossibility of achieving that "something"; and, chiefly, it consists in the clear conviction of these unhappy people that all are alike and hence it is not even worth trying to improve. Consolation? Faith? There is consolation from no one, faith in no one. But another step from here and one finds depravity, crime (murder). Mystery.

The profoundly responsive Raskolnikov, one might say, voluntarily takes on himself that "tragedy of the underground," experiences it internally, morally, in all its aspects and agonizing contradictions. His final "step" should have been love—a step *toward* humanity; instead, experiencing the tragedy of life too deeply, and drawing from that tragedy the most extreme social and philosophical conclusions, Raskolnikov (a victim of his own solitude, ratiocination, and casuistry), took a step away from humanity into crime, murder, mystery.

Such is the practical denouement of the philosophical pro and contra—the dialectic of consciousness of Raskolnikov—in Part One.

Notes

1. Raskolnikov's inability to focus his thoughts on anything, his inability consciously to "resolve" anything after his reconciliation with Sonia in the epilogue ("he was simply feeling") constitutes, of course, a qualitatively different state of consciousness from the chaos of mind experienced right after the murder. The almost symmetrical opposition of these two "moments" of consciousness is not accidental; the movement or shift from one to the other constitutes the movement in Raskolnikov's consciousness from hate (unfreedom) to love (freedom).

2. See N. M. Chirkov's essay in this collection, p. 53.

3. In turn, Raskolnikov's internal conflict in Parts II–VI may be regarded as a reverse movement, a tension toward redemption.

4. These questions, of course, are explicit in *The Brothers Karamazov*.

5. Raskolnikov's intense moral concerns provide evidence, of course, that man is not "a scoundrel and predator" by nature. And it is, finally, the idea of adaptation as testimony to man's endurance and will to live that is ultimately accepted by Raskolnikov. Thus, Raskolnikov, after an encounter with prostitutes on the streets, declares that it would be better to live an eternity on a "square yard of space" than to die. "To live and to live and to live and to live! How true that is! God, how true! What a scoundrel man is! *And he's a scoundrel who calls him a scoundrel for that*," he added a minute later. (II, 6) My italics.

6. His cruel tastes, Clément argues in *Justine*, are given to him by "Nature." "Oh, Thérèse, is there any crime here? Is this the name to designate what serves Nature? Is it in man's power to commit crimes?" Nature's "primary and most imperious inspirations" enjoin man "to pursue his happiness at no matter whose expense. The doctrine of brotherly love is a fiction we owe to Christianity and not to Nature." "But the man you describe is a monster," Thérèse protests, while Clément rejoins: "The man I describe is in tune with Nature." "He is a savage beast," insists Thérèse. And Clément retorts: "Why, is

not the tiger or the leopard, of whom this man is, if you wish, a replica, like man created by Nature and created to prosecute Nature's intentions?" (Cf. The Marquis de Sade, *Justine* [New York: Grove Press, 1965], pp. 607–8.) From the sensualist-philosopher de Sade to the philosopher-sensualist Svidrigailov is no step at all. In his novels, particularly in *The Brothers Karamazov*, Dostoevsky comes to grips with the thoughts expressed here (the question of whether Dostoevsky actually read de Sade is beside the point, though references to de Sade in his works, especially in *Notes from the House of the Dead* suggest familiarity with his work). Dostoevsky's own point of view, though antithetical to de Sade's in the final analysis, is complex and, like everything else in his thought, antinomian. What is certain, however, is that for him the Christian doctrine of brotherly love is not a "fiction"; or, put in another way, this doctrine—in the face of what Dostoevsky fearfully detects in man's earthly sensual nature—is the most important "fiction" in human existence, without which, he insisted once in his notebooks, life on earth would be "senseless."

7. See Konstantin Mochulsky's discussion of Dostoevsky's search for "motives" in his essay in this collection.

8. The contrasts here reflect, of course, the fundamental creative tension Dostoevsky posits in human existence between man's quest for the moral and aesthetic ideal, on the one hand, and his earthly nature with its potential for violence and deformation, on the other. See my discussion of this problem in *Dostoevsky's Quest for Form: A Study of His Philosophy of Art* (New Haven: Yale University Press, 1966), in particular pp. 40–70.

9. See, for example, W. D. Snodgrass, "*Crime and Punishment*: The Tenor of Part One," *The Hudson Review*, 13 (1960): 241.

10. *The Gambler*, of course, was written at the time Dostoevsky was finishing *Crime and Punishment*, and it reflects Dostoevsky's preoccupation with Raskolnikov's state of mind. For a perceptive study of *The Gambler*, see D. S. Savage, "The Idea of *The Gambler*," *Sewanee Review*, 58 (April, 1950): 281–98. For a consideration of the problem of chance and fate in "A Gentle Creature," see my essay "On the Uses of the Motif of the Duel in Dostoevsky's 'A Gentle Creature,'" in *Canadian-American Slavic Studies*, 6, no. 2 (Summer, 1972): 296–64.

11. The same conception is at the basis of Tolstoy's psychologically profound presentation of Anna Karenina's first meeting with Vronsky at the railroad station. See my essay, "Chance and Design in *Anna Karenina*," in *The Disciplines of Criticism*, edited by Peter Demetz et al. (New Haven: Yale University Press, 1968), pp. 315–329.

12. The idea of an "evil spirit" as the embodiment of oppressive fate crops up in *Winter Notes on Summer Impressions* (1863) where Dostoevsky speaks in the chapter "Baal" of a "proud spirit" dominating all the misery and squalor of London.

13. See, in this connection, Raskolnikov's bitter complaint about "blind fate," in the epilogue (chap. 2).

MALCOLM V. JONES

Raskol'nikov's Humanitarianism

I

Many attempts have been made to trace Raskol'nikov's ideological antecedents and to show their roots in European and particularly Russian, polemics of the time. In an article published in *Encounter* in 1966[1], Joseph Frank describes how Raskol'nikov's preoccupations reflect Russian culture in the early and the mid-1860's. He draws attention to the way in which Raskol'nikov's crime is planned on the basis of a utilitarian calculus and on an assumption about the primacy of reason over the non-rational, typical of the Russian intelligentsia of the period. He further points to the recent shift among the intelligentsia from utopian socialism to an "embittered elitism," which stressed the right of a superior individual to act independently for the welfare of humanity. He sees reflected in *Prestuplenie i nakazanie* the transition from utopian socialism to nihilism and the "schism among the nihilists" about which Dostoevskii himself wrote.[2] Professor Frank also draws parallels between the views of Pisarev and his group—their use of the utilitarian calculus and social Darwinism—and Raskol'nikov's ideological position. He traces the "Nietzschean" elements in Raskol'nikov to Zaitsev. This analysis is presented to support Frank's thesis that "His [Dostoevskii's] aim was to portray the inescapable contradictions in this radical ideology of Russian Nihilism. To do so, he adopted his usual procedure (in his mature

From *Canadian-American Slavic Studies* 8, no. 3 (Fall 1974).

work) of imagining its 'strange, incomplete ideas' put into practice by an idealistic young man whose character traits embody its various conflicting aspects."[3] He continues:

> Now Dostoevsky knew very well that the emotional impulses inspiring the average Russian radical were generous and self-sacrificing. They were moved by love, sympathy, altruism, the desire to aid, heal and comfort suffering—whatever they might believe about the hard-headedness of their "rational egoism." The underlying foundation of their moral nature was Christian and Russian (for Dostoevsky the two were the same), and in total disharmony with the superimposed Western ideas they had assimilated, and on whose basis they believed they were acting.[4]

Other scholars have, of course, filled in other details about the origins of Raskol'nikov's ideas. References are made to the influence of Stirner, Napoleon III and others.[5] B. G. Reizov, in a recent article in *Izvestiia AN SSSR*[6] traces the literary and ideological antecedents of Raskol'nikov back more than half a century. He finds analogues of Raskol'nikov's belief that crime may be justified in the interests of the welfare of mankind as a whole, or of a needy and suffering member of it, in Schiller's Karl Moor, Balzac's Rastignac, Bulwer-Lytton's Eugene Aram, Victor Hugo's Claude Gueux and Jean Valjean, and many others.[7] In a similar way he traces the cult of the great man, the hero-figure, in the decades preceding Raskol'nikov.

But to judge from recent work in the Soviet Union, the most contentious aspect of Frank's argument is his view that the underlying foundation of the moral nature of Raskol'nikov's generation was Russian and Christian. Interest in this and related problems has been greatly stimulated of late among Soviet scholars by V. Ia. Kirpotin's provocative and scholarly study, *Razocharovanie i krushenie Rodiona Raskol'nikova*.[8] Although he does not wish to deny Christian elements in Raskol'nikov's attitudes, his emphasis is quite different. He finds the origins of Raskol'nikov's sensitivity to the injustice of life in utopian socialism rather than in Russia's Christian traditions. Indeed, he lays some emphasis on the fact that Dostoevskii's ideas—and hence, with some modifications, Raskol'nikov's—about a future Golden Age and universal harmony, derive not from Orthodoxy, but from Christian utopian socialism, from George Sand, Considérant, Hugo, Belinskii and the Petrashevtsy.[9] He would presumably want to say about Frank's article that he overlooks an important aspect of the psychology and ideological history of Raskol'nikov and the real-life nihilists: that their generosity, their self-sacrificing nature, love, sympathy, altruism, the desire to aid, heal and comfort suffering derive at least in part from the tradition of utopian socialism which, like the nihilism which succeeded it, had its roots in the culture of Western Europe rather than in that of Holy Russia.

Raskol'nikov, according to this argument, is a disillusioned utopian socialist. Kirpotin contends that there are clear indications in the novel of a residual utopian socialism which has still not taken leave of Raskol'nikov. Raskol'nikov "is unable to root out completely from his soul the convictions of former years; his scepticism is superimposed on a love and pity for others, which has been pushed aside from his consciousness, but not completely excluded ... disillusionment could not force out of the conscious and subconscious regions of Raskol'nikov's mind the feelings, associations, thoughts, sympathies and antipathies which had their origins in the ideology of the democratic and revolutionary utopian socialist movement."[10]

Of course, this view has not been unanimously accepted by Soviet critics, but what evidence is there that Raskol'nikov had passed through such a phase in the last three years, as Kirpotin avers? Apart from analogies with real-life nihilists, Kirpotin finds evidence in the text: in the parallels, for instance, between Raskol'nikov's dream of the old horse beaten to death by a drunken peasant and a poem by Nekrasov containing a similar incident;[11] in Raskol'nikov's reference to the new Jerusalem, which, Kirpotin argues, is to a socialist New Jerusalem;[12] in the similarities between the scene where Raskol'nikov pauses on the Nikolaevskii Bridge and looks across the Neva to the Winter Palace, with passages in *Slaboe serdtse* and *Peterburgskie snovideniia v stikhakh i proze*, interpreted by Kirpotin as yearnings for the New Jerusalem, a utopian-socialist Golden Age of the Future.[13]

It is perfectly plausible to suggest that a real-life Raskol'nikov might have been a disillusioned utopian socialist; it is true that Raskol'nikov's development is consistent with such a hypothesis; it is undeniable that in other works Dostoevskii exhibited a preoccupation with such themes. Yet, in the text of the novel, there are insufficient grounds for making this assumption. The evidence adduced by Kirpotin can be explained perfectly satisfactorily without importing this hypothesis at all. It might be argued, on Kirpotin's side, that it was unnecessary for Dostoevskii to make Raskol'nikov's socialist past explicit, because his readers would naturally have made this assumption. This is very much what Kirpotin does argue. It might also be stressed that too much explicitness might have run into trouble with the censor or with the editor of *Russkii vestnik*, Katkov. Dostoevskii could be sure that his novel would, on publication in 1866, be read by people who were themselves set in the socio-cultural situation depicted and evoked in his novel. Nevertheless, it remains true that he found it unnecessary to include references to Stirner, Napoleon III or Zaitsev, or to others whose names have been associated with Raskol'nikov's views and whose identity his readers would certainly have been unlikely to guess. Raskol'nikov, like other of Dostoevskii's heroes, transcends the immediate ideological context of his time. He dreams in solitude; he is alienated not only from the social structure of his day, but also from other people as individuals. He is not a run-of-the-mill nihilist of the sixties; he may be in some sense a true product of his time, but he is also a distinct and exceptional individual, even if not in the way he would like to think. E. Knipovich has indeed replied to Kirpotin's argument in roughly these terms in an article in *Znamia* in 1971,[14] arguing that Raskol'nikov had never been a socialist and that he follows in the Romantic tradition of Napoleon-worship. The reader does not need to be aware of the ideological problems of Russia in the 1860's—interesting though they may be—to appreciate the dynamic of Raskol'nikov's personality, his aspirations, his crime and the unfolding drama; hence the wide appeal of the novel among readers quite ignorant of this context. Similarly, Dostoevskii is not greatly concerned to inform the reader of the precise, concrete details and origins of Raskol'nikov's humanitarian feelings and aspirations, either in his recent past, or as embodied in his Napoleon theory. What matters is the general ethos which permits their development.

In one sense, it does not matter to the dynamic of the novel whether the emotional and intellectual origins of Raskol'nikov's humanitarian feelings are of Orthodox Christian or utopian socialist origin: what matters is that they are consistent with Raskol'nikov's acts of compassion, with his response to Sonia, with his sympathy for the ideals and values of his sister Dunia, with his eventual confession and projected "resurrection." But whether or not one feels able to accept Kirpotin's argument, he has rendered the student of Dostoevskii a signal service in drawing his attention to a neglected fact about Raskol'nikov. There is a clear disjunction between those of his humanitarian views and feelings which are associated with his Napoleon theory and those which are associated with his intuitive sympathy for his suffering neighbor. The essence of the disjunction may be expressed in Dostoevskii's own formula: it is the difference between the ideals of the man-god and the God-man[15] (between humanism and hominism as a recent Marxist writer has put it in a wider context)[16] between a proud, general sympathy for an abstract humanity, in whose interests many lives may be taken, and a humble compassion for one's neighbor, however lowly and insignificant. Yet to appeal here to the concept of the man-god in analysing Raskol'nikov's humanitarianism is insufficiently precise. It would be useful to have a clearer idea of the nature of those humanitarian values displayed by Raskol'nikov which do not correspond to those of primitive Christianity.[17] The interesting question arises: are there grounds within the novel for a more precise definition of the complex of ideas, images and feelings which constitute this aspect of Raskol'nikov's humanitarianism, and do they have a clear socio-cultural origin?

II

If Kirpotin's thesis that Raskol'nikov is a disillusioned socialist is contentious, the thesis that he is a disillusioned idealist is less so. Dostoevskii himself later wrote—in the notebooks which were to form the drafts for *Podrostok*—"nihilism is ... the last stage of idealism."[18] Moreover, if there is a part of him which responds to Sonia's primitive Christianity, there is a part which responds to the high moral principles and virtue of Dunia.

Svidrigailov perceives Raskol'nikov's idealism very clearly and taunts him with Schillerism (which seems to be a rough equivalent in his mind.) He also perceives the link between Raskol'nikov the idealist and Raskol'nikov the nihilist:

> "So you lay claim to strength? Ha, ha, ha! You quite surprised me, Rodion Romanich, although I knew in advance that it would turn out like that. You talk to me about vice and aesthetics! You are a *Schiller*! You are an *idealist*! That is just as it should be of course, and it would have been surprising if it were otherwise, but it's somehow strange when you come across it in real life. What a pity that I have so little time, for you're a most interesting individual! By the way, do you like Schiller? I like him tremendously."[19]

A little later, Raskol'nikov objects:

> "I've had quite enough of your horrible and disgusting anecdotes, you low, depraved sensualist!"
>
> "Listen to the Schiller! A real Schiller! just listen to him! *Où va-t-elle la vertu se nicher*? Do you know, I think I shall go on telling you these stories just for the pleasure of hearing your frantic protests."[20]

Svidrigailov does, of course, touch Raskol'nikov on a raw nerve. His solicitude for Dunia is not completely explicable in terms of family relations, though this element in the situation no doubt intensifies his feeling. But Raskol'nikov is genuinely disgusted. It is not his compassion which is aroused; his reaction brings together moral and aesthetic outrage. It is his sense of what is honorable and what is dishonorable, what is virtuous and what is vile in Svidrigailov's behavior which is stirred. There are numerous other incidents which confirm the importance of these idealistic "Schillerian" values for Raskol'nikov, his sense of honor, dignity, not to say pride. For instance, Raskol'nikov feels not only intellectually, but also morally superior to both Luzhin and Svidrigailov. One may note, too, his angry refusal to accept money from Svidrigailov on his sister's behalf, whereas Sonia, by contrast, is quite ready to do so on behalf of both herself (and, indirectly, Raskol'nikov) and her family.

When Svidrigailov uses the term "Schiller" to taunt Raskol'nikov, he is not, of course, using it in a socio-cultural sense. It is true that only a particular socio-cultural background makes the term available to him, but that is a different matter. He does not imply that Raskol'nikov is personally acquainted with Schiller's works. He uses the expression primarily as a *psychological* term, to denote the fact that Raskol'nikov is influenced in his behavior by a complex of ideas, emotions and values, which are like those commonly associated with the name of Schiller.

A number of Dostoevskii scholars have made allusions to the use of Schiller's name in the novel. The Soviet scholar Terekhov has written: "The name of Schiller serves in Dostoevskii's philosophical novels simply as a symbol of moral purity and sublime humanitarian aspirations, synonymous with the ideal of 'the man and the citizen', from which his rebel heroes will not be parted, even though their very protest, according to Dostoevskii, contains the basis for amoral behavior. Such are Raskol'nikov and Ivan Karamazov."[21] But this is as far as he goes.

N. Vil'mont, in his 300-page essay on Dostoevskii and Schiller,[22] devotes more than 100 pages (including digressions) to problems associated with *Prestuplenie i nakazanie*, and he advances arguments highly relevant to this question, but the question of Raskol'nikov's psychological Schillerism remains unresolved, indeed barely posed. Yet there can be no doubt that such a complex of ideas and emotions plays an important role in Raskol'nikov's psychological economy.

If Raskol'nikov has a sense of moral superiority in his relations with Luzhin and Svidrigailov which sits oddly with his claim to be above morality, he also has a marked aesthetic sense. His disgust with himself for committing the murders has little or nothing to do with Christian compassion for the victims, or with repentance. It is aesthetic disgust with himself for stooping to murder such an "old louse" as the woman moneylender, when his hero-figure, Napoleon, grandly left whole armies to perish. He has to try to persuade himself that Napoleon would have done the same in his position: "Would he have felt disgusted to do it because it was far from monumental and—and wicked too? ... he wouldn't have felt disgusted at all and ... indeed it would never have occurred to him that it was not monumental."[23]

But the argument is not convincing; Raskol'nikov has already consoled himself with the thought that Porfirii will never imagine that a person who considers himself a Napoleon would commit the murders of an old woman and her sister, "His aesthetic sense won't allow him. 'A Napoleon crawl under an old woman's bed?' Oh, rubbish!"[24] And, shortly afterwards, Raskol'nikov turns on himself with the words, "Oh, I'm an aesthetic louse, and nothing more."[25] Such aesthetic and moral Schillerism plays an important part in Raskol'nikov's attitudes and behavior, although his nihilistic attitudes prompt him to despise it.

When he is about to give himself up and he has his last interview with Dunia, he is racked by this very problem. He exclaims that he is going to give himself up out of cowardice, and the following dialogue ensues:

> "Brother, brother, what are you saying! You shed blood, didn't you?" cried Dunia in despair.
>
> "Which all men shed," he answered almost in a frenzy, "which is being shed and has always been shed on earth, in torrents, which pours out like champagne, and for which people are crowned with laurels in the Capitol and called benefactors of mankind. If you look more closely, you'll see. I too wanted to do good to people, and I should have done hundreds and thousands of good deeds, to make up for one piece of stupidity. Actually, it wasn't stupid, but just clumsy; the idea itself wasn't nearly as stupid as it seems now that it has failed ... (Failure makes everything look stupid). By this piece of stupidity I simply wanted to put myself in a position of independence, to take the first step, to get hold of the necessary funds, and then everything would have been put right by the immeasurable good, relatively speaking.... But I couldn't keep it up, because I'm rotten! That's all there is to it. All the same, I'm not going to adopt your attitude: if I'd succeeded, I should have been hailed as a benefactor to mankind, but now it's off to gaol with me!"
>
> "But that's all wrong, Rodion, you've got it all wrong. You don't know what you're saying!"
>
> "Ah! the wrong *form*, not the right aesthetic form! Well, I simply don't understand why blowing people up with bombs or slaughtering them in a siege according to all the rules is a more acceptable form. The fear of aesthetics is the first sign of impotence! I have never, never, understood that more clearly than

> I do now, and I understand my 'crime' less than ever. I have never felt stronger and more convinced than at this moment! ..."[26]

In this dialogue, we not only see Raskol'nikov wrestling with the hold which aesthetic form has over him, but we see another aspect of his Schillerism as well: the humanitarian motives which underlie his crime. It is true that they are not the dominant motives, but there is no doubt that they are real. It is also of some significance that they attain an unwonted degree of prominence in conversation with Dunia. For Raskol'nikov's Schillerism turns out to be in some measure a family characteristic. Because of her role in Raskol'nikov's confession (foreseen by Raskol'nikov before he commits the murder) Sonia has naturally attracted more attention from the critics than Dunia has. But Dunia is by no means an inconsiderable figure in the plot. Though she comes into her own only in the Svidrigailov plot, she plays an important role in the Raskol'nikov plot as well. Nor are the two roles wholly distinct. It is both symbolically and psychologically significant that Svidrigailov is effectively removed from the scene and ceases to haunt Raskol'nikov as the result of his defeat in his duel with Dunia. Dunia and Svidrigailov here fight out that very issue between virtue and demonic passion which is reflected in Raskol'nikov's attitude to Svidrigailov illustrated above. Raskol'nikov's battle against Svidrigailov is won not by himself, but by Dunia, as, conversely, it had been Raskol'nikov's protests which had rid his sister of Luzhin. As Versilov, in *Podrostok*, is said to have on either side of him "a heavenly angel" and "an earthly queen,"[27] so, in the same metaphorical sense, has Raskol'nikov.

The reader is left in no doubt that Dunia and her brother have much in common, in temperament as well as in external features. Their mother attests this, in affirming in her son the presence of those qualities of impulsiveness in defense of virtue, and indignation in the face of vice, which Svidrigailov notices.[28] The point is made obliquely in other ways. Porfirii, for example, remarks that Raskol'nikov is, in his opinion, one of those men who, even if he were disembowelled, would stand and look at his torturers with a smile, provided he had found God or something to believe in.[29] Similarly, Svidrigailov says of Dunia that, had she lived in bygone days, she would undoubtedly have suffered martyrdom, and she would most certainly have smiled when her breast was burnt with red-hot pincers.[30] Dunia brings to the mind of the infatuated Razumikhin the queen who darned her stockings in prison, retaining even there her regal dignity.[31] She shares characteristics of several of Schiller's heroines, not to mention analogous characters in George Sand and Dickens. She is proud, fiery, capable of self-sacrifice for a loved-one, courageous, self-confident, generous, strong-minded, sometimes patient and sensible, sometimes over-impetuous, on the look-out (as with Svidrigailov before the novel opens) for someone to save. What is more, she is dazzlingly beautiful.[32]

Raskol'nikov is related by family ties to Dunia and their mother (both of whom he himself accuses of Schillerism).[33] But although it is Dunia who brings about Svidrigailov's defeat, it is not Dunia who brings about Raskol'nikov's renewal. This is effected by contact not with Schillerian virtues (which Dostoevskii saw as the first stage of nihilism—and these virtues after all bring Dunia to the point of attempted murder) but with the virtues of humility, compassion and insight, and the voluntary acceptance of purification through suffering, which Dostoevskii associates with Christianity. It is the 'pure prostitute',[34] not the girl who is 'almost morbidly chaste',[35] who saves Raskol'nikov; the heavenly angel, not the earthly queen. This fact reflects Dostoevskii's own turning to the ideals of primitive Christianity rather than to those of Christian socialism—irrespective of what he may have had to omit from the novel—*pace* Kirpotin—at the behest of Katkov.[36]

If the break between Schillerism and nihilism appears to be a drastic one, the gap between altruistic humanitarianism and a Nietzschean will to power is bridged in the Napoleon legend. It is also plainly exhibited in the work of Schiller himself. N. Vil'mont points out that in *Die Räuber* (which intermittently haunted Dostoevskii from the age of ten to his last years) ethical and religious problems very similar to those of *Prestuplenie i nakazanie* are posed.[37] Franz Moor believes that right is on the side of the victor and that the force of law is relative to the strength of the individual. Karl Moor tries to overcome the injustice and cruelty of the world by taking to arms—to put the world to rights by force. Both are eventually routed. The Marquis Posa in Schiller's *Don Carlos* is obliged to have recourse to duplicity in order to advance his humanitarian ideals, and the Queen rightly discerns in him an element of personal pride.[38] Needless to say, both these plays were not only a part of what Schiller meant to Dostoevskii personally, but part of what the word Schillerism meant to cultivated Russians of his—and Svidrigailov's—generation as a whole. Nor should we overlook the fact that the idea of a man who makes his way to power, if necessary by crime, but who becomes a true father of his people is embodied by Schiller in his sketch for *Demetrius*.[39] It is inconceivable that Dostoevskii did not have this sketch in mind in his early, abortive, plan to write his own *Boris Godunov*. It is known that he planned to write another play called *Mariia Stiuart*.[40] Thus the idea of creating a hero who achieves what Raskol'nikov sets out to achieve, but who is overcome by retribution, had been in Dostoevskii's mind for many years. It was only in the 1860's that he was able to realize it in contemporary terms. It is not in the least surprising, therefore, within the context of the literary and historical traditions of the time, to find Raskol'nikov speaking as he does to Dunia. If Schillerism and nihilism seem logically distinct at first, they often merge in Raskol'nikov's mind, as when he muses to himself: "Now begins the reign of reason and light—and of will and strength!"[41] Hegel would have had no difficulty in showing the "logical" connection between them.

If the demonic and the humanitarian are often blurred in Raskol'nikov, it is not surprising if the primitive Christian response and the Schillerian response are often indistinguishable. Are his acts of charity, described at his trial,[42] primarily beautiful Schillerian deeds, or acts of spontaneous self-sacrifice and compassion? What about the episode when he defends Sonia against the false charges laid against her by Luzhin?[43]—an episode, incidentally, bringing together and giving scope to several aspects of Raskol'nikov's personality. What about the future which Dostoevskii projects for him?[44] It surely cannot be imagined that Raskol'nikov will become a sort of male Sonia. It is perhaps easier to imagine, as Mochulsky does, that Raskol'nikov is not really resurrected spiritually at all, and that the last lines of the novel are a "pious lie," a sop to the readers of Katkov's journal.[45] But it is not impossible to imagine a Raskol'nikov resurrected through a synthesis of his latent idealism, his intelligence and vigor, and the experience of suffering seen through the eyes of Sonia. It is noteworthy that, from their various standpoints, Porfirii, Dunia and Sonia foresee Raskol'nikov's renewal by means of suffering.[46]

So it is appropriate that towards the end of the novel Sonia and Dunia become good friends in what might be seen as a spiritual marriage and mutual recognition of the Schillerian idealist and the primitive Christian. Dunia venerates Sonia and Sonia does not consider herself worthy even to look at Dunia.[47]

III

The argument of Section II, in a nutshell, is that, in taunting Raskol'nikov with the name of Schiller, Svidrigailov puts his finger on an important aspect of Raskol'nikov's ideological and psychological make-up, which often merges with other aspects of his personality in his actual behavior. Indeed, the step from Schillerian idealism to nihilism is, however wide the gulf may appear, in practice but a short one, experienced by some of Schiller's own heroes. Svidrigailov, after a moment's reflection, finds the link quite natural and calls to mind Schiller's works. In applying the term "Schillerism" to Raskol'nikov seriously and systematically, no attempt has been made (or implied) to suggest that it derives from a reading of Schiller, or that Dostoevskii intended this. Although the currency of the term—Porfirii uses it as well as Svidrigailov and Raskol'nikov himself—derives from a concrete socio-cultural environment, the word is used here in a psychological sense. Whether the possession of such a complex of ideas, feelings and values might have inclined Raskol'nikov towards utopian socialism—for the ideas of a lost Arcadia and of a future universal harmony appear also in Schiller[48]—can be left to those who care to argue about such things. It does not preclude the possibility, but simply points to the emotional roots which Raskol'nikov seems to share with his sister.

Only at one point in the foregoing section have I suggested that Dostoevskii's own youthful Schillerism and familiarity with Schiller's works might have had some bearing on the development of this side of his much younger, fictional character. For the purposes of the main argument, the 'influence of Schiller on Dostoevskii' is, in all but minimal terms, irrelevant. Yet, of course, Dostoevskii was greatly influenced by Schiller, especially in the early and mid-1840's,[49] and provided this issue is kept logically distinct, there can be no harm in concluding with some pertinent remarks in this connection.

By the early sixties, it is clear that Schiller's name signified at least two different things for Dostoevskii. On the one hand, it could mean indulging in idealistic fantasy, pathetically divorced from real life.[50] On the other, it could mean the very best in the tradition of humanism, something to be taken very seriously, whatever guise it might assume in an age when Schiller himself was out of fashion.[51] Dostoevskii set to work on *Prestuplenie i nakazanie* in the autumn of 1865. As recently as the winter of 1864–65, he had included in *Epokha* (nominally the issue for November, 1864, though by this time the periodical was about two months late appearing), Strakhov's translation of Kuno Fischer's *Die Selbstbekenntnisse Schillers* ("*Samopriznaniia Shillera*")[52], which would have reminded him of just those aspects of Schiller's work which point forward to Raskol'nikov. His work on Schiller during the forties with his brother Mikhail would also have been brought to mind by a letter (dated December 14, 1864) from the Kursk Province, expressing sympathy on Mikhail's death. It came from someone Dostoevskii had not seen for many years and whose name he associated with the ethos of Schiller's work. The writer recalled their shared Romantic past and concluded his letter with a couplet celebrating the friendship of youth. It was from I. N. Shidlovskii[53]. If Russia had passed on to more violent and desperate ideas by the 1860's, the character of Raskol'nikov testifies—albeit obliquely—to Dostoevskii's notion that "Schiller" had entered the flesh and blood of Russian society[54]. By Raskol'nikov's time, Schiller's name and heritage had been clouded over and blended with other names and influences. Svidrigailov belongs to Dostoevskii's generation, and consider what has happened to his "Schillerism." But Raskol'nikov is still only twenty-three. What survives in him is the ethos, the psychological disposition, the ideals and the values. And this will also be true of some of Dostoevskii's later heroes, as Terekhov suggests.[55]

NOTES

1. Joseph Frank, "The World of Raskolnikov," *Encounter*, XXVI (June 1966), 30–35.

2. F. M. Dostoevskii, "Gospodin Shchedrin ili raskol v nigilistakh," *Epokha* (May 1861).

3. Frank, p. 33.

4. Ibid.

5. See, for example, F. I. Evnin, "Roman *Prestuplenie i nakazanie*," *Tvorchestvo F. M. Dostoevskogo* (Moscow, 1959), p. 153; L. P. Grossman, *Dostoevskii* (Moscow, 1962), pp. 347–348; Y. Ia. Kirpotin, *Razocharovanie i krushenie Rodiona Raskol'nikova* (Moscow, 1970), for varying views.

6. B. G. Reizov, "*Prestuplenie i nakazanie* i problemy evropeiskoi deistvitet'nosti," *Izvestiia Akademii Nauk SSSR, seriia literatury i iazyka*, XXX, 5 (1971), 388–399.

7. *Ibid.*, p. 389.

8. Kirpotin, note 5.

9. *Ibid.*, pp. 119-120.

10. Ibid., p. 48.

11. *Ibid.*, pp. 48–51.

12. *Ibid.*, pp. 56–57.

13. *Ibid.*, pp. 42–46.

14. E. Knipovich, "Legendy i pravda," *Znamia*, XI (1971), 216–223. There are other grounds for objecting to Kirpotin too, some of them methodological, but it has to be said that Kirpotin's is in many respects an interesting and stimulating book.

15. F. M. Dostoevskii, "Dve polovinki," *Dnevnik pisatelia* (August 1880), ch. iii.

16. V. Gardavskii, *God is not yet dead* (Harmondsworth, England, 1973), p. 52.

17. I use the term 'primitive Christianity' to denote the ideals and values of the New Testament, in particular of the Sermon on the Mount, by way of contrast to the distinctive rituals and traditions of the Russian Orthodox Church in Dostoevskii's day. Kirpotin rightly points out that Sonia is not a churchgoer and that there is nothing particularly Orthodox about her faith; Kirpotin, pp. 169 ff.

18. *F. M. Dostoevskii v rabote nad romanom 'Podrostok'*, eds. I. S. Zil'bershtein and L. M. Rozenblium, *Literaturnoe nasledstvo*, 77 (Moscow, 1965), p. 128.

19. F. M. Dostoevskii, *Prestuplenie i nakazanie*, Pt. vi, ch. iii.

20. *Ibid.*, Pt. vi, ch. iv.

21. S. F. Terekhov, "Shiller v russkoi kritike 50–70 godov xix v.," *Fridrikh Shiller, stat'i i materialy*, eds. R. M. Samarin and S. V. Turaev (Moscow, 1966), p. 144. However, G. M. Fridlender, whom Terekhov quotes, holds a view which approximates to mine. See G. M. Fridlender, *Realizm Dostoevskogo* (Moscow-Leningrad, 1964), p. 283.

22. N. Vil'mont, *Velikie sputniki* (Moscow, 1966), ch. i: "Dostoevskii i Shiller," pp. 7–316.

23. Dostoevskii, *Prestuplenie i nakazanie*, Pt. v, ch. iv.

24. *Ibid.*, Pt iii, iii, ch. vi.

25. *Ibid.*

26. *Ibid.*, Pt. vi, ch. vii.

27. F. M. Dostoevskii, *Podrostok*, Pt. iii, ch. xii, sect. 1.

28. Dostoevskii, *Prestuplenie i nakazanie*, Pt. i, ch. iii.
29. *Ibid.*, Pt. vi, ch. ii.
30. *Ibid.*, Pt. vi, ch. iv.
31. *Ibid.*, Pt. iii, ch. ii.
32. *Ibid.*, Pt. iii, ch. i.
33. *Ibid.*, Pt. i, ch. iv.
34. *Ibid.*, Pt. iii, ch. iv (a description of Sonia. The term 'pure prostitute' is, of course, a conventional one, not Dostoevskii's).
35. *Ibid.*, Pt. vi, ch. iv. This is Svidrigailov's expression.
36. Kirpotin (pp. 138–177) argues that the passages Dostoevskii had to omit from the novel would have established the utopian socialist credentials of both Raskol'nikov and Sonia. This thesis is, of course, not proven, though it is difficult to conceive of a better-argued case. Kirpotin himself argues for the roots of Sonia's Christianity in the New Testament rather than in Orthodoxy (see note 17).
37. Vil'mont, pp. 191–192.
38. F. Schiller, *Don Carlos*, act IV, sc. xxi.
39. F. Schiller, *Demetrius*, in that part of the drafts which was never rewritten in dramatic form.
40. Cf. the excerpt from the memoirs of A. E. Rizenkampf published in A. S. Dolinin, ed., *Dostoevskii v vospominaniiakh sovremennikov*, 2 vols., (Moscow, 1964), I, 112. See also Grossman, note 5, p. 36 and M. P. Alekseev, "O dramaticheskikh opytakh Dostoevskogo," *Tvorchestvo Dostoevskogo, 1821–1881–1921. Sbornik statei i materialy*, ed. L. P. Grossman (Odessa, 1921), pp, 41–62.
41. Dostoevskii, *Prestuplenie i nakazanie*, Pt. ii, ch. vii.
42. *Ibid.*, Epilogue, ch. 1.
43. *Ibid.*, Pt. v, ch. iii.
44. *Ibid.*, Epilogue, ch. ii.
45. K. Mochulsky, *Dostoevsky, His Life and Work*, trans. M. A. Minihan (Princeton, 1967), p. 312.
46. Dostoevskii, *Prestuplenie i nakazanie*, Pt. vi, ch. ii; Pt. vi, ch. vii; Pt. v, ch. iv.
47. Ibid., Pt. vi, ch. viii.
48. Cf. "Die Götter Griechenlands" and the *Briefe über die ästhetische Erziehung des Menschen*.
49. There are numerous accounts of Schiller's influence on Dostoevskii and on interesting parallels, far too many to list here, and some on special aspects of their relationship. Apart from N. Vil'mont (note 22), a useful general survey may be found in E. K. Kostka, *Schiller in Russian Literature* (Philadelphia, 1965), pp. 214–250, which contains a bibliography.
50. Cf. the excerpt from the memoirs of O. Pochinkovskaia published in Dolinin (note 40), II, 161.
51. See F. M. Dostoevskii, "Knizhnost' i gramotnost', stat'ia pervaia," *Vremia* (July 1861), "Smert' Zhorzh Zanda," *Dnevnik pisatelia* (June 1876), ch. i, sect. i; "Nechto o Shillere," *Vremia* (February 1861).
52. K. Fischer, *Die Selbstbekenntnisse Schillers* (Frankfurt a. Main, 1858); N. N. Strakhov's translation was published in *Epokha* (November 1864), under the title "Samopriznaiia Shillers."
53. Letter from I. N. Shidlovskii to F. M. Dostoevskii (14 December 1864), in the possession of the State Lenin Library, Moscow, GBL, *f* 93, ii, *op*. 9, *ed. khr*. 143a.
54. F. M. Dostoevskii, "Knizhnost' i gramotnost', note 51.
55. Terekhov, note 21.

ROGER B. ANDERSON

Raskol'nikov and the Myth Experience

Raskol'nikov is a modern attestation to man's age-old desire for a special meaning in his life above and beyond the ordinary routine of day-to-day activity. His deepest need is to "step over" some barrier, to perceive and touch something of transcendent significance that lies on the other side. Such a need immediately puts him at odds with a modern urban society where the individual is called upon to choose his identity and behavior patterns from among the established categories offered him. Hence Raskol'nikov's difficulties with his studies, potential career, family relations, friendships, and available social philosophies. Raskol'nikov's dilemma involves two related compulsions: first, rebellion against a normative reality that would have him be a passive spectator to things as they are; second, active struggle to find some structure of higher meaning within which he can place himself and thereby define himself as meaningful. In this latter respect he is a refinement of the Underground Man's rebellious principle of "freedom at any price," the desire to alter mathematical or social equations to accommodate subjective, "unrealistic" demands.

When Raskol'nikov "steps over" the limits of his society's laws he enters another dimension of being which bears many names. Depending on the variable philosophical preferences of the reader, this dimension can be called Christian, mystical, existential, or orthodox Marxist. These labels are

---

From *Slavic and East European Journal* 20, no. 1 (Spring 1976).

all valid in that each can properly adapt Raskol'nikov's experience to a system of philosophical values. But Raskol'nikov's journey into himself is such a basic fact of human experience that it underpins each of these systems and does not depend on any one of them for its meaning. It is therefore appropriate to discuss the hero in terms that are not governed or limited by any single philosophy to which his condition might have reference.

Raskol'nikov seeks to achieve a radical alternative to ordinary reality, not merely to add to that reality or adjust it in some way. His search for an alternative has its own coherence and rhythm of development; its tap root goes deep into the human personality. This radical alternative is not operative on the conscious level in Raskol'nikov, but rather, wells up on its own. From the first hint to the reader that he is preparing to commit murder, and thereby defy a basic limit of his society, he is subject to a state of mind which is dream-like, out of touch with the palpable world, distinctively "other." His higher logical faculties prove inadequate before the press of unconscious preoccupations, and he falls back on a more basic mode of thought and behavior that can appropriately be called primitive. The breakdown of his rational control is present virtually from the beginning of the novel, as evidenced by his disturbed sense of time, feverish hallucinations, lethargy, neurotic fixation on small details, dreams, inability to concentrate. Reality is distorted into an alogical mass having its own symbolic composition. Raskol'nikov comes into a unique state of being in which inchoate demands for the radical alternative consistently displace ordinary social standards in order to find expression. We perceive in Raskol'nikov a demand for psychological truth rather than objective facts.

The purpose of this article is to assess Raskol'nikov's developing pattern of thought and behavior, his "stepping over," by examining certain common denominators of myth theory. The intent is to suggest that, as in myth, Dostoevskij's alienated hero spontaneously reaches back into the human inventory of unconscious thought, images, and actions to create his own special meaning and sense of purpose. Myth is conceived here as more than the resuscitation of single mythological motifs—the "Earth Mother" that Vjaceslav Ivanov invokes in his treatment of the novel,[1] Edward Wasiolek's references to the minotaur quality of the old pawnbroker woman and her maze-like apartment building,[2] or L. J. Kent's remarks on the mythic quality of Raskol'nikov's final dream in Siberia.[3] Such motifs are present and can surely be catalogued with illuminating results, as Ivanov does so evocatively, for example. The present study leaves such particularized motifs in favor of analyzing certain basic characteristics of mythic thinking and action as human activity. These characteristics will then be applied to Raskol'nikov's development in order to illustrate Dostoevskij's use of them.

Allen Watts's definition of myth is particularly apt for the present discussion: "Myth is to be defined as a complex of stories ... which, for various reasons, human beings regard as demonstrations of the inner meaning of the universe and of human life."[4] Watts's definition emphasizes the central issue of a significant continuity which the individual seeks to establish between his conception of self and some qualitatively higher sphere of sacral importance in life. When this perceived continuity is absent or disrupted to a sufficiently serious degree, due to adverse external (physical or social) factors, then man, through myth, falls back on extremely basic images of himself, the nature of his crisis, and how to live through it. He unconsciously assigns these elements a place within a transcendent system of values that restores his primal demand for extra-ordinary order and meaning. Herein lie the tools of rebellion and redefinition as a response to the intolerable psychological sensation of estrangement from one's temporal world. The specifics of this upward reach will vary (e.g., Christian or existential understanding of *Crime and Punishment*, totemic or animistic ramifications for myth). But the impulse in man to manufacture meaning from within when it is seriously threatened from without remains structurally the same.[5] The contemporary mythopoetic theorist Philip Wheelwright puts the question succinctly when he states: "Now a world bereft of radical significance is not long tolerated; it leaves man radically unstable."[6] The function of myth is to provide that "radical significance" for man, whatever its name might be at any given time.

Society does not fill Raskol'nikov's basic need for continuity of meaning between himself and a higher order of significance. He is pronouncedly out of joint with his world, a *raznočinec* in psychological and spiritual, as well as social terms. As Renato Poggioli phrases it, Raskol'nikov is subject to the "disorder of vital consciousness" but is surrounded by the "order of a devitalized society."[7] None of society's institutions such as religion, education, or social philosophy provide him with clear guidance in defining what his life is for and what his cosmic role might be.[8] The bureaucratic and arbitrary power typical of a city like Petersburg accelerates the process of alienation. Raskol'nikov's needs are sacral, while the models of behavior held out to him by his environment are secular and unresponsive to his mythic urge. Without recourse to the mediating forces of his culture, he embarks on his quest in painful isolation. His need to matter is forced back upon itself, and he grapples alone to express it amidst urban stresses that would diminish him.[9] S. R. Hopper perhaps voiced Raskol'nikov's dilemma when he summed up the dilemma of modern man in the words "myth today has gone underground."[10]

Raskol'nikov's state of mind is properly called mythopoeic because of its drive to find and experientially touch sacral meaning in life. The neo-Kantian philosopher Ernst Cassirer has written extensively about mythopoeic cognition, terming it a structural faculty of the mind found in all mankind, whatever the historical time or place. Mythic thinking is a special mode of mental activity which is alogical and essentially imagistic. It is the dark side of logic (what Cassirer terms "discursive thought")[11] and has enormous appeal to man when he is under severe psychological stress. Logic is predicated on man's acceptance of the palpable limits of his world (physical and social); he orients his wants and concept of self within these limits. There is an unquestioned line dividing his inner self, his fantasy or imagination, from the "reality" of his surrounding environment. In mythopoeic (mythic) thinking man profoundly alters this relationship. Through intensive preoccupation with fantasy and imagination the Cartesian line between inner needs and outer "reality" dissolves. The individual is then subjectively free to change his world and make it responsive to him in a personally satisfying manner (Cassirer, 19). Man's needs become the very center of his relation to life, and logic pales before its symbol-making powers.[12] Following the same line as Cassirer, the French philosopher of myth Mircea Eliade maintains that man has an inborn intolerance for an absurd world (i.e., one in which he is a mere observer). Man has always been ready to expend any amount of energy to project a structure for the universe which will accommodate his direct participation in its secrets.[13] Hence the idea of man's search to participate in transcendent meaning, the cornerstone of myth.

The mythic mind, then, discriminates on the basis of unconscious needs, rather than logical categories. It seeks to discover some higher meaning which stands behind the simple facts and rational probabilities of immanent existence. Symbols become real in such thinking; they embody needs rather than simply represent them in an abstract scheme of the intellect (Cassirer, 56–57). What is extraneous to needs is brushed aside in myth: "Focusing of all forces on a single point is the prerequisite of all mythic thinking and mythical formulation" (Cassirer, 33). Raskol'nikov's intensive concentration on a limited number of objects, people, and events which assume symbolic value for him (or, more accurately, for the coherent system of unconscious needs that are furiously at work in him) is mythic in this sense.

One has only to think of the atmospheric detail that fills *Crime and Punishment* to encounter such intensive, as opposed to extensive thinking. The world Raskol'nikov lives in resonates to the cluttered and tense workings of his unconscious. Objective facts are transmuted until they fit his own preoccupations. His cramped room reflects his inner sense of oppression; his abhorrence of and attraction to water are spontaneous outward projections of his own ambivalent attitude toward confession. His dreams and conversations with others constantly make free use of actual people and physical facts to focus his own confused hopes and fears. When he looks around him he sees parts of himself, all of which are stamped with his own past and options for the future. Anyone or anything that cannot be so invested is simply ignored. As in mythic thinking, his world springs to symbolic life when he projects his inner needs, fears, and hopes into it. He "steps over" in his thinking into a personalized world where "objective reality" no longer competes with his subjective demand for continuity and significance. Herein lies the basis of Raskol'nikov as a mythic figure who pursues his own definition "in a higher sense," who seeks to utter "a new word."

Dostoevskij consistently pursued the massive shift in man's mind out of the ordinary workaday world into the extraordinary realm of higher meaning, of myth. In a letter of February–March 1869 he stated, "What most people call almost fantastic and exceptional is for me sometimes the very essence of the real."[14] He was passionate in fighting against the materialistic philosophy that would carve up man's psychic relation with himself and his world into neat rational categories. Dmitrij Merežkovskij spoke directly to this issue of mythic reality when he said: "Dostoeievski feels how visionary reality is; to him life is only a phenomenon, only the external covering beneath which is concealed that which is incomprehensible and forever hidden from the [rational] mind of man. He seems almost intentionally to eliminate the boundary between dreamland and reality."[15] Such remarks, with their emphasis on a subjectively ordered world for the individual, are a virtual recapitulation of the mythopoeic state of mind as described by Cassirer.

M. M. Baxtin approached this topic—cognition colored by personal need—from a formal vantage point when he elaborated his idea of Dostoevskij's polyphonic technique of narration. Each character has his own unique complex of inner compulsions which profoundly determines how he views and evaluates the meaning of his world. Each character interprets his surroundings and other characters in terms of these personal compulsions: "A multiplicity of independent and differentiated voices and consciousness, genuine polyphony of fully valued (*polnocennyx*) voices, really emerges as the distinguishing mark of Dostoevsky's novels."[16] Baxtin is interested in the variety of subjective narrative sources that populate Dostoevskij's novels, including *Crime and Punishment*. But implicit in his principle is the mythic notion of symbol making, i.e., that the individual views his world through a unique aura of internally ordered and unconscious preoccupations. For Baxtin, as for modern students of mythic thinking, "reality" is rendered plastic under such conditions. Its shape is malleable under psychological pressure within the individual.

Dostoevskij shares with myth a man-centered vision of the physical world. In both cases descriptions of events and objects bear the stamp of some human issue. Northrop Frye conceives of the natural world in myth as a storehouse of potential symbols which man uses to play out his quest for integration with cosmic forces.[17] Dostoevskij's world is the city, rather than nature, but the principle still holds. Raskol'nikov's special need for a vital essence that will include him personally dominates all physical aspects of the city for him, and in the process gives it a distorted and fantastic appearance. His inner drives for significance order and subordinate his environment just as much as the human pursuit of some higher meaning or achievement in Prometheus, Theseus, Icarus, or Gilgamesh organizes nature for them. The Soviet critic V. F. Pereverzev made a telling observation when he remarked: "Behind nature he [Dostoevskij] sees man."[18]

A concentration on human issues implies vigorous action. With both Dostoevskij and myth, symbol-making leads to *dromenon*, i.e., to a personalized acting out of symbols and their meanings.[19] This is one of the chief values of ritual in savage societies. Here man experientially unites with his projections and integrates their special value back into his own being. Without his active participation in these projections, the mythic process is aborted and the participant remains alienated from the higher meaning he seeks. Kierkegaard's aphorism that "man lives forward and understands backward" speaks to this point. Of course, this pattern of activity is not altogether comprehensible to the logical observer because of intellectual distance. Mythic action bypasses the intellect, as does mythic cognition, and allows traditional man to focus the competing hopes, fears, and urges of his own unconscious, and to live them out. He can assign them identity within the process of ritual and interact with them directly. As he comes to believe in the reality of his own projections he can more easily accept the validity of his inner contradictions and the unspoken needs that give rise to his projections. Without really understanding it, man comes profoundly into touch with his inner self through mythic action and ritual.

It is helpful to view Raskol'nikov's psychic adventures from the perspective of *dromenon*. Many critics have emphasized the dramatic quality of *Crime and Punishment* along with its irregular narrative line and unclear motivations. Raskol'nikov also lives forward and learns backward. As outsiders we are often adrift in his shifting impulses (his love for and rejection of his family, his conflicting urges to be a superman and to confess his crime). His assignation of extreme value to certain details (water, closed spaces, money) and people (especially Svidrigajlov and Sonja) are parts of a symbolic system which defies external logic, yielding meaning for the hero slowly, only as he experientially lives through it. As in myth ritual, Raskol'nikov engages in an extrarational pattern of activity which brings to the surface unconscious urges in him. Without knowing why, he attaches these urges to things and people around him. As will be shown, he interacts vigorously with them and works out their special symbolic meaning for himself. Not unlike a performer of ritual, Raskol'nikov lives through his inner unconscious demands for special meaning in the external world, with the result that he comes into more profound contact with himself.

Raskol'nikov's ritualistic activity is grounded in his act of murder and in the way he redefines himself as a result of the act. On the one hand he kills the old pawnbroker woman as a dramatization of his right to the higher status of a superman, a "new law maker." He strives in the process towards ego-expansion, strength of will, and the "go-it-alone" mentality of one who can endure the isolation that results from power. The enigmatic drive in him towards confession implies its opposite—abnegation of an isolating will and submission before authority. The inner split in Raskol'nikov is typically treated as an either/or moral proposition with strong Christian overtones (i.e., the mutually exclusive choices of Satanic pride vs. humility and love). If we back up one step into the mythic view, however, we see that both choices perform a common function for him. Both release him from an essentially passive role in the world of externally defined "reasonableness," well-ordered time schedules, crystal palaces, good sense, family expectations, and orderly social behavior. Both allow him personally to "negate the negation" imposed on him by his social environment. To put it in structuralist terms, both choices are stressed elements for him.[20] That is, the axis of Raskol'nikov's relation to higher meaning runs through self-assertion and submission alike; they function toward the same goal. The axis is the stable mythic element which resolves the paradox of his seemingly opposed alternatives—ego-expansion and ego-dissolution. Either activity satisfies his need to project a sense of cosmic value, to name it, and finally to incorporate its vitality back into himself. Each option is a convenient form, a vessel into which he pours the energy of his mythic reach toward sacral significance.

The similarity in function of ego-expansion and ego-dissolution unites their opposed moral appearance for Raskol'nikov. But for Dostoevskij, as for the mythic mind generally, higher significance is not a matter of single or discrete categories which can be directly pursued along some linear path. Paradox is unavoidable in both. The questions of light or dark, up or down, good or bad, life or death are not appropriate in mythic thought. The question of an "either/or" proposition (e.g., the superman theory vs. confession) is similarly out of place for Raskol'nikov. Basic elements of thought and action in the mythic realm rest upon mutual implication light and darkness infer one another, to speak of life necessarily entails the question of death as an unspoken alternative. Dostoevskij criticism has persistently approached this central issue of paradox and built-in dialectic both on the ideological level[21] and on the formal level. Baxtin's insights into the identity of Dostoevskij's characters as inseparable from their duality and inner tension are most appropriate here. His point is that two contrary voices, engaged in active dialogue, are the minimum of being in Dostoevskij's characters. Each "voice" implies the other.[22] The tension Baxtin sees in a character like Raskol'nikov has a dynamic force, the function of which is to mediate the character's movement into special knowledge about his inner self.

Although Baxtin limits his principle to Dostoevskij's novels, terming them original in world literature because of a dialectical nature of the inner character, he has actually stated the age-old essence of mythic thought. C. G. Jung speaks often of the necessary role of paradox and dialectic in myth and in man's unconscious (myth being one of the chief enterprises of the unconscious in Jung's view). Unlike rational logic (based on discrete categories of thought and linear causality) the common denominator of the unconscious is a Janus-like duality and tension. Here no important issue has a single value but, rather, each implies its opposite with which it actively interacts.[23] The dialectic is dynamic and constructive in mythic action as in Dostoevskij's hero. As Baxtin says of Dostoevskij's characters (including Raskol'nikov) and as Jung says of mythic regions of the unconscious, man is a function of his inborn system of contrary but interdependent forces.

The collateral functions of superiority and confession explain their proximity in many of Raskol'nikov's peak experiences. In the Crystal Palace restaurant he engages in both activities at once. He liberally drops clues about the murder that lead Zametov to suspect him. But he also "tweaks Zametov's nose" with his audacity. Similarly ambivalent behavior typifies Raskol'nikov's conversations with Porfirij. Moving between self-incriminating clues (which propel him toward confession) and adroit forensics designed to exhibit his cool intellectual superiority (a natural feature of his self-image as a superman), Raskol'nikov uses both to heighten his sense of what Poggioli has called "vital consciousness" (29). In his own mind, both serve to free him momentarily from ordinary reality imposed from without (i.e., the good sense of not drawing attention to himself). His postures as superman and confessor are virtually independent of his conscious will, and he is constantly amazed as he watches the drama of his own destiny unfold in their interaction.

One of the most poignant examples of Raskol'nikov's excursion from objective reality into mythic action occurs in his dream-like conversation with the painters when he returns to the murder scene. His behavior is again compulsive in its duality. He asks to be led to the police with the intent of confessing (ego-dissolution), but the bystanders refuse to become involved. In a twinkling he turns the moment into an audacious exhibition of his power to act by flaunting his willingness to confess (ego-expansion). Both motives are crystallized in the hero's gesture when, like a somnambulant, he pulls the door bell:

> The same bell, the same tinny sound! He pulled it a second, a third time; he listened and remembered. The old tormenting terrible sensation began to bring back to him ever clearer and more vivid memories; he shuddered at every tinkle, but he felt more and more pleasure.[24]

The bell is a concrete image which Raskol'nikov uses to invoke in himself a sense of something supremely important. It is not merely a psychological return to the macabre sensations of the murder that he accomplishes in his unconscious compulsion. He exists for the moment in a qualitatively different dimension of being in which he is not talking with people of this world. He uses the situation, the bell, the bystanders as raw material to position himself in a choice-making situation, either one of which brings him into experiential contact with something he sees as having cosmic value. He cares little how the situation might turn out, for he has succeeded in "stepping over." He is in a suspended state while his innermost drives for meaning well up in him, seize him, force him to act and speak, and directly affect his destiny.[25]

The alternate paths of superman and confession are thus parts of a paradoxical situation in which Raskol'nikov's options are so basic in their mutual opposition that they imply one another. The dramatic and dynamic quality of the inner dialectic is clear, but there is an implicit danger in seeing it as moved along primarily by other characters, i.e., Svidrigajlov and Sonja. It is all too convenient to suggest a God-centered interpretation of Raskol'nikov in his choice between incarnate goodness (Sonja) and evil (Svidrigajlov).[26] The question of the hero's reach for something higher is very much man-centered when viewed from the mythic perspective, and it goes beyond any single set of religious beliefs. The mythic view suggests that Raskol'nikov selectively maneuvers other characters into roles that meet competing needs which are already formed and at work in him; he has forms that demand content to fill them. He "creates" Svidrigajlov and Sonja as focal images in which he invests his own paradoxical demands for special meaning.

The emphasis here on Svidrigajlov and Sonja as functions of Raskol'nikov's symbol-making activity is important because it concentrates our attention all the more on the unconscious working of the hero's mind. It implies that any influence these characters might have on the hero is determined and organized essentially by his own unconscious. We are forced to examine all the more carefully the autonomous demand within him for transcendent meaning in his life and his inner willingness to manipulate his environment until this demand is met.

Raskol'nikov's special relation to Svidrigajlov and Sonja goes to the heart of the general issue of mythic action. He vacillates between them, approaches them, shakes free of his fascination with them, only to need their company again. His approach and flight relative to these characters is structurally that of traditional man's relation to his ritual masks. In both cases the individual is subject to the same archaic pattern of human thought: the demand for a concrete image to which one can attach sacral meaning and with which one can personally interact. As sacral value accrues to a mask in the savage's mind, it becomes the embodiment of some cosmic power and appears to exert independent authority over him.[27] Svidrigajlov and Sonja also appear to assume influence over the hero to the degree that they become more and more identified with his own urges toward power and confession. As suggested above, however, it is Raskol'nikov himself, the "wearer of the mask," who is both the source and the recipient of their power.

There is a rhythmically progressive quality to the mask experience that is basic to ritual. In the beginning the wearer maintains a measure of control over the mask and even appears not to take it seriously. At this point he both believes in its power (unconsciously) and does not believe (consciously). He relates to the mask in what can only be termed a "play-serious" or "as if" state of mind.[28] As the ritual continues, this condition gradually becomes more serious, i.e., the mystical value he invests in the mask grows. With time there is a slippage in the wearer's mind, and the power he wishes to see in the mask becomes real to him, overwhelms him, "possesses" him. Logic and objective reality are now fully bypassed in the wearer's mind, and he is free to commune directly with the mystical power he has projected into the mask. The ecstasy the wearer experiences at this moment is a form of epiphany, a spontaneous sense of integration felt between his own finitude and the cosmic absolute represented by the mask. This is perhaps the most sacral experience within the mythic mode. The process of increasing identification with the mask is also profoundly creative for the wearer because he feels himself qualitatively changed when in touch with it. It is as if he has lifted himself from the ground with his own hands.

The stages of the mask experience are instructive in understanding the development of Raskol'nikov's enigmatic relation to Svidrigajlov and Sonja. The hero's mental condition is especially open to the mask experience and its strong current of communion with mystical forces, for he seeks and expects the supernatural throughout the novel.[29] His sensitivity to extraordinary forces at work in his life prepares him to discern equally mystical significance in the figures he unconsciously chooses as masks in his adventures. Hearing about Svidrigajlov for the first time, before their initial meeting, Raskol'nikov seizes on the single characteristic in him that fits his own haunting preoccupations with power—Svidrigajlov's willfulness, as revealed in his calculated exploitation of his wife, his servant, and Raskol'nikov's sister Dunja. He raises Svidrigajlov to the superpersonal level of a principle very early, when he speaks of "the Svidrigajlovs of this world" (50). Again early in the novel, when he is angered by the wealthy lecher who stalks a drunken girl on the street, he hurls the epithet "Svidrigajlov" at him, thereby making the name fit a category of meaning. Even before he sees Sonja, he associates her with selflessness, the implied opposite of exploitative power: "Why, perhaps we should not refuse even Sonecka's fate! Sonecka, Sonecka Marmeladova, Sonecka the eternal, while the world lasts!" (49). Later he refers back to this early stage of Sonja's meaning to him by stating flatly, "I chose you ... I chose you long ago to tell this thing to; even then, when your father talked about you and Lizaveta was alive, I thought of this" (343). Thus, from the beginning Raskol'nikov is ready to attach the mutually implied values of ego-expansion and ego-dissolution to convenient concrete images. In this sense he unconsciously selects and fashions Svidrigajlov and Sonja to conform to his inner needs just as a savage selects and fashions raw material to make his mask. Both processes are based on the same mode of imagistic thinking and symbolic projection.

There are special physical characteristics about Svidrigajlov and Sonja that distort them into mask-like figures. Masks are usually carved with grotesque features to accentuate their awesome and mystical "differentness" from ordinary reality. The radical "differentness" Raskol'nikov attaches to these two characters is accentuated in the same way. Svidrigajlov's face, with its unnatural youthful and healthy appearance, strikes Raskol'nikov as "a mask." His eyes are "too blue" and "have too heavy and unmoving a gaze" (488). His artificial freshness contrasts jarringly with the long history of dissoluteness in the man, and the effect is grotesque. Sonja's physical appearance is childlike and frail (the diminutives used to describe her hands, arms, face, and overall figure are numerous). The contrast of this vulnerability is especially grotesque in relation to the perversion and degradation typical of ordinary prostitutes (as described in Raskol'nikov's street encounter in part 2, chapter 6). Sonja's street-walking regalia with its nocturnal sunshade, dowdy gaudiness, and outlandish red plume are also glaringly at odds with her sensitive naivete. Her "angular" face, which bears the stamp of what Raskol'nikov calls "insatiable compassion" and the flashing intensity of "religious mania," completes her extraordinary physical impression on him.

In addition to the physical distinctiveness of Svidrigajlov and Sonja there are several qualities that make them extraordinary to the hero. Both see ghosts, and he happens upon each when he is distraught and deep in thought about that person. Uncanny coincidence lies just beneath the surface when the hero learns that Sonja wears Lizaveta's cross. The same blurring of ordinary reality occurs when Raskol'nikov cannot decide whether Svidrigajlov had actually been in his room or whether he saw an apparition. The hero's general expectation of something supernatural in his life blends with the several bizarre associations that he sees clustering about these two characters. He is more than ready to dispense with logic and move to primitive, imagistic thinking.

As mentioned above, there are stages in the mask experience, beginning with a state of semi-independence from the object and ending with a mystical sense of absorption into the power attributed to it by the wearer. This archetypal ritual is also present in Raskol'nikov's relation to his chosen "masks" of Svidrigajlov and Sonja. At first he struggles to remain free of each while being irresistibly drawn to the special meaning he is prepared to see in them. Raskol'nikov's first interview with Svidrigajlov begins with Raskol'nikov's game of pretended sleep. He has an immediate aversion to his guest and is more than once tempted to terminate their conversation. Yet he is fascinated with pursuing apparently random questions that lead consistently to Svidrigajlov's egoistic exhibitionism (anecdotes about his past, his wife, and his views on eternity and ghosts). The effect is that on a conscious level Raskol'nikov dislikes Svidrigajlov and wishes to be rid of him. Unconsciously, however, Raskol'nikov is fascinated by his guest and is not at all eager for his departure. Guided by timely cues provided by Raskol'nikov, Svidrigajlov speaks to the very questions of control that preoccupy the hero. Svidrigajlov's demonstrated capacity to subordinate those around him to his own will, without regret and even with a flair for humor, corresponds like a template to the hero's own desire to be a scimitar-wielding Mahomet or a Napoleon "forgetting" an army in Egypt and "passing it off with a joke at Wilno" (284). Their dialogue is one of implication and selection on Raskol'nikov's part, which he adapts to his own situation in a most consistent manner.[30]

Such intermingling of conscious aversion and unconscious attraction is also apparent in Raskol'nikov's second intimate meeting with Svidrigajlov.

Realizing only vaguely that "some power over him lay hidden in the man" (482), that "for a long time he had felt a kind of need for Svidrigajlov for some reason" (483), Raskol'nikov seeks him out. The same play of pretending not to see Svidrigajlov initiates Raskol'nikov's conversation with him in the restaurant (part 4, chapter 3). As in their earlier interview Raskol'nikov tries to keep the conversation under his conscious control. He threatens Svidrigajlov in order to keep him away from Dunja and to stop him from informing on him as a murderer. He insistently tries to keep the conversation within logical bounds, reading Svidrigajlov moral lessons on debauchery as a dangerous disease. He tries to assert his independence from Svidrigajlov by challenging and taunting him, first with reference to his wife's ghost and then by charging him with boasting, lying, and cowardice. Through the entire interview Raskol'nikov keeps up his show of independence by expressing a conscious aversion to Svidrigajlov and the desire to irritate him. The unconscious aspect of their conversation is quite different, however. As in their first meeting Raskol'nikov prods Svidrigajlov into ever more detailed examples of his personal powers and calculated control over others. Each topic in their conversation articulates the question of Svidrigajlov's willful manipulation of others (e.g., cheating at cards, stories of debauchery, misuse of his wife and Dunja, the advantage he takes of children). Here Raskol'nikov is in an equivalent to the "as if" state of mind. He wishes to place a buffer between himself and his own gross egocentrism by condemning it in Svidrigajlov. At the same time he invariably heightens the effect of such willfulness on himself by provoking Svidrigajlov into his marathon display of just such egocentrism. Like a savage playing with his mask, Raskol'nikov approaches the unconscious identification of himself with Svidrigajlov, while trying to maintain autonomy from that very identification by pretending that it is neither important nor real to him.

Raskol'nikov's use of Svidrigajlov as a mask of power is never brought to the final stage of "possession" because of the latter's death. The archaic mythic mode of thought in Raskol'nikov, however, is one of implied opposites; his reduction to a clear form of one side of that tensive relation naturally calls forth its complement. Raskol'nikov responds to this binary pattern by symbolically raising the opposite of power (i.e., dissolution of ego) to the same level of a mask. That mask is of course Sonja. As with Svidrigajlov, Raskol'nikov chooses her to have a special meaning for him before they even meet. From their first encounters he proceeds into the "play-serious" state of mind which is found in the mask ritual. Raskol'nikov consciously taunts and provokes Sonja in order to prove his independence from her—just as he does with Svidrigajlov. He embroiders on her helpless position as a prostitute, her enslavement and probable end in sickness or crude debauchery, her inability to earn enough money for her desperate family, and her ill treatment at the hands of her manic stepmother. He persistently wears a mocking or cruel smile and attacks her last comfort, the existence of a compassionate God. But Raskol'nikov jeers at the very features of Sonja's self-abnegation that unconsciously attract him most. Her self-sacrifice is a point of reference around which he develops his own compulsion to confess. As he taunts Sonja, he "plays" with his own desire to step across the barrier by confession, bringing it into sharper focus for his own inner use. As with Svidrigajlov, the extent to which he exerts his supposed independence from her marks the degree to which he is unknowingly drawn to her.

Raskol'nikov soon passes beyond this tentative "play-serious" stage with Sonja and succeeds in transferring his own potential for ego-dissolution to her. His approach to the moment of transfer is indicated by identifying his own future with hers. He speaks of their destinies as bound together and of a journey somewhere together. He asks her to read him the story of Lazarus with its meaning of life that transcends temporal bounds, analogous to his mythic wish to overcome the limits of his own restricted life. His aggressive facade crumbles before the awe he experiences as he "steps over" by confessing to her and is "possessed" by the transcendent meaning this act holds for him. At this moment he succeeds in uttering the new word he seeks—in qualitatively redefining himself within the context of higher values. The mask experience now approaches the point of epiphany. Physical changes occur in him to denote the profound change he feels in his being. A sudden weakness along with absent-mindedness, a compulsion to act which "mastered him all at once, seized him body and soul" (530), crowd in upon him.

For traditional man the experience of uniting with the mask is akin to dying and being reborn simultaneously. The wearer's ordinary ego and his established identity are submerged in the greater meaning of the mask. He experiences the traumatic symptoms of death as he loses what he thought himself to be. So, as Raskol'nikov approaches the crossroads to confess, he is distracted by minor details in exactly the same way as a condemned man being led to his execution.[31] He shudders, feels crushed, and gives himself up to the sensation of profound change in his being: "It came upon him like a fit: a single spark was kindled in his spirit and suddenly, like a fire, it enveloped him entirely. Everything in him softened at once and the tears gushed out. He fell to the ground where he stood" (550).

In the mythic world rebirth is part of such death and carries with it a new sense of identity in which the wearer of the mask experiences the mystical exhilaration of full integration with something of cosmic significance.[32] This is the epiphany of the ritual, and it carries the sacral dimension of life which both savage and urban Russian seek. Raskol'nikov's new sense of integration is complete at the moment he sees Sonja and is inwardly assured that she will never leave him. Mask and man are now joined. It bears repetition here that Sonja is not essential as an autonomous person who influences Raskol'nikov by herself. He symbolically invests in her one possibility of experiencing a sense of transcending ordinary, oppressive reality with its limited range of choices. He projects his inner drive for higher significance onto her, submerges himself in the drive achieved through the mask experience, and is reborn into the special meaning he desires so intensely. This is the moment of special creativity which lies at the very center of the mythic mode of thought and behavior.

Notes

1. Vyacheslav Ivanov, *Freedom and the Tragic Life: A Study in Dostoevsky*, tr. N. Cameron (New York: Noonday Press, 1960). See part II, chap. 2.

2. Edward Wasiolek, *Dostoevsky: The Major Fiction* (Cambridge, Mass.: M.I.T. Press, 1964), 61.

3. See L. J. Kent, *The Subconscious in Gogol' and Dostoevskij, and Its Antecedents* (SP&R, 75; The Hague: Mouton, 1969), 120–22.

4. Alan W. Watts, *Myth and Ritual in Christianity* (London: Thames & Hudson, 1953), 7. The intent here is not to infer that Dostoevskij consciously develops Raskol'nikov as someone who grapples with mythic meaning but, rather, that the author is one of those seminal thinkers and artists who generates what S. E. Hyman has called "symbolic equivalents" to mythic forms "out of his own unconscious." (S. E. Hyman, "The Ritual View of Myth and the Mythic," *Myth: A Symposium*, ed. T. A. Sebeok [Bloomington, Ind.: Indiana Univ. Press, 1958], 94.)

5. See Joseph Campbell, *The Hero With a Thousand Faces*, rev. ed. (Bollingen Series, 17; New York: Pantheon Books, 1968), 11, especially his remarks on myth's value in "carrying the human spirit forward" into a special way of psychologically mastering an unresponsive environment.

6. Philip Wheelwright, "Poetry, Myth, and Reality," *The Modern Critical Spectrum*, ed. G. J. Goldberg and N. M. Goldberg (Englewood Cliffs, N.J.: Prentice-Hall, 1962), 319.

7. Renato Poggioli, *The Phoenix and the Spider* (Cambridge, Mass.: Harvard Univ. Press, 1957), 29.

8. See C. G. Jung, "The Spiritual Problem in Modern Man," *Civilization in Transition* (Bollingen Series 20, V. 10; New York: Pantheon Books, 1964) for a particularly cogent statement on modern urban man's sacrifice of spiritual identity to material progress.

9. William Barrett, *Irrational Man* (New York: Doubleday, 1958), especially pp. 21–22, stresses the individual's estrangement from a containing framework of traditional faith: "Man [has] lost the concrete connection with a transcendent realm of being; he [is] set free to deal with this world in all its brute objectivity."

10. S. R. Hopper, "Myth, Dream, and Imagination," *Myths, Dreams, and Religion*, ed. Joseph Campbell (New York: Dutton, 1970), 115.

11. Ernst Cassirer, *Language and Myth*, tr. Susanne K. Langer (New York: Harper, 1946), 26.

12. See Julian Huxley, *Religion Without Revelation* (New York: Harper, 1927), 274: "Primitive thought express[es] itself in images rather than in concepts, in forms which appeal to the senses and emotions rather than to the intellect, by means of symbolic rather than rational representation."

13. Mircea Eliade, *Cosmos and History: The Myth of the Eternal Return* (New York: Harper & Row, 1959), 100.

14. F. M. Dostoevskij, *Pis'ma*, ed. A. Dolinin, (4 vols.; M.: AN SSSR, 1928–59), II, 169.

15. Dmitrij Mere?kovskij, *Dostoevskij*, tr. G. A. Mounsey (London: Constable, 1902), 17.

16. M. M. Baxtin, *Problemy poetiki Dostoevskogo* (M.: Sovetskij pisatel', 1963), 7.

17. Northrop Frye, *Fables of Identity: Studies in Poetic Mythology* (New York: Harcourt, Brace & World, 1963), 31–38.

18. V. F. Pereverzev, *F. M. Dostoevskij* (M.: Gosizdat, 1925), 33.

19. For a discussion of *dromenon* and its basis in ritual action within myth see Hyman, 85. For an elaboration of the principle that action is integral to mythic cognition in the individual, see Campbell, 16–18.

20. See Claude Levi-Strauss, *The Savage Mind* (Chicago: Univ. of Chicago Press, 1969), 154–155. On pp. 217 and 224–227 of his *Structural Anthropology* (New York: Basic Books, 1963), he elaborates on what he terms "opposition and correlation," i.e., the existence of variable elements which, while superficially contradictory, perform a common function in the progression of the narrative or of a character's action. They mediate the same important change and so should be considered equivalent.

21. Konstantin Mochulsky provides a standard evaluation of Raskol'nikov's inner contest on moral and religious grounds in chap. 13 of his *Dostoevsky: His Life and Work*, tr. M. A. Minihan (Princeton, N.J.: Princeton Univ. Press, 1967).

22. See Baxtin, 338–339, especially his assertion that "two voices are the minimum of life, the minimum of being."

23. See C. G. Jung's treatment of inner dialectic in man's unconscious as a necessary prerequisite to psychic growth in his "The Transcendent Function," *The Structure and Dynamics of the Psyche* (Bollingen Series 20, V. 8; New York: Pantheon Books, 1960), and in his "Answer to Job," *Psychology and Religion: West and East* (Bollingen Series 20, V. 2; New York: Pantheon Books, 1958). In both essays he discusses the necessity of tension between moral opposites in the unconscious. Jolande Jacobi's commentary on Jung's theory of necessary duality as a factor in spiritual growth provides a helpful outline of this irreducible duality. See Jacobi, *The Psychology of C. G. Jung* (New Haven, Conn.: Yale Univ. Press, 1971), especially pp. 46, 54, 67.

24. All references to *Crime and Punishment* in parentheses in the text are to F.M. *Dostoevskij, Polno sobranie soănenij*, ed. L. P. Grossman et al. (10 vols.: M.: GIXL, 1956), V.

25. On p. 25 of his *F. M. Dostoevskij* Pereverzev refers to the Dostoevskian character who acts without knowing why and, in the process, touches a hidden or mystical potential in himself: "He [Dostoevskij] draws occurrences before the conditions that lead up to them; he draws relations between people before those people themselves, the deeds of his heroes before their characters. This is why deeds seem fantastic, relations [seem] confused, occurrences [seem] accidental."

26. See Nikolai Berdyaev, "Dostoevsky, the Nature of Man, and Evil," *Dostoevsky*, tr. Donald Attwater (New York: Meridian Books, 1957).

27. As David Bidney points out on p. 8 of his article "Myth, Symbolism, and Truth," *Myth: A Symposium*, "The mythopoeic mind does not regard myth as symbolic or a representation of some independent reality; the mythic symbols are identical with reality."

28. See Joseph Campbell's discussion of this play-serious aspect of the mask experience on pp. 22–24 of his *The Masks of God: Primitive Mythology* (New York: Viking Press, 1970).

29. Examples of Raskol'nikov's readiness to see supernatural influences in his life are rather frequent. Before the murder he wanders aimlessly about town and, "exactly as if fate had lain in wait for him" (66), he happens across the market place as Lizaveta is arranging with some peddlers to be gone from the house at a specified hour the next day. He is "struck with superstitious awe" (66) at the coincidence of hearing this particular conversation. Consistent with his broader pattern of seeing mystical forces at work in his life, he has this experience immediately after his dream about the horse which, he thinks, has freed him "from the evil spells, from the sorcery and fascination, from the temptation" (66) of his murder plan. We are told he has "recently become superstitious" (69) and that his behavior strikes him as governed by something strange and mysterious. Examples of his inference of supernatural forces in his life are legion. He finds an axe in the porter's shed and thinks, "'It was not my planning, but a devil that accomplished that!'" (79). When he despairs of living with the burden of his crime, desperately trying to pull himself together and live out the principle of the superman, he speaks aloud: "'Now we shall measure our strength'" (197). The moment is attended by the authorial remark that he speaks "as though he were addressing some dark power and summoning it up" (197). When he is explaining the murder to Sonja, Raskol'nikov again reads mystical agents into his motive and action: "the devil was pulling me along then .... it was the devil who killed the old hag, not I" (438).

30. See Baxtin's discussion of the interplay between verbal and psychological communication on p. 342 of his *Problemy poetiki Dostoevskogo*. His remark on Dostoevskij's characters that "in their dialog the remarks of one touch on and even, in part, coincide with the remarks of the inner dialog of the other" is a variation on the question of unconscious projection and selection within a conversation as discussed here.

31. Compare Raskol'nikov's psychological state of transition to Myškin's description of a condemned man's last minutes in part I, chap. 5, of *The Idiot*.

32. As in a mask ritual the deep personal sense of unity that Raskol'nikov experiences is transitory and, therefore, is open to repetition. For Dostoevskij's hero a virtual reenactment of this epiphany and sense of identity with Sonja (i.e., the special meaning he attributes to her) occurs in chapter 2 of the epilogue. In traditional societies the mask ceremony tends to be institutionalized in its repetition (religious celebrations, commemorations of seasonal or crop changes, etc.).

RAYMOND J. WILSON III

Raskolnikov's Dream in Crime and Punishment

In trying to understand Raskolnikov's apparently erratic behavior in *Crime and Punishment*, readers have often resorted to the idea that Raskolnikov has a "split personality" even before they find out his name comes from the Russian root *raskol* meaning schism or split. However, the simple notion of a two-way Jekyll–Hyde or emotional–intellectual split in Raskolnikov never proved completely workable in analyzing Raskolnikov's personality. Raskolnikov cannot be forced into so limited a mold. The implications of Raskolnikov's horse-beating dream provide more flexibility for analysis. Aspects of the dream reflect facets of Raskolnikov's complex personality. This very flexibility, however, causes problems in interpreting the dream, as W. D. Snodgrass demonstrates in his analysis:

> First of all, where is Raskolnikov in his dream? Is he the horse, the little boy, the father, or the brute Mikolka? The answer must be Yes. All of the characters of the dream are the dreamer. The problem is not who is who, but rather to understand the tenor of the dreamer's apprehension of the world, that is, of his mind.... For the horse, also, I have given what must seem disparate interpretations. Does the horse represent the teen-aged girl, Dunya and Sonia. Or does it represent the pawnbroker, the landlady and the mother. Or Marmeladov and Raskolnikov?

From *Literature and Psychology* 26, no. 4 (1976).

> Once again, the answer to all the questions is Yes. To miss the identity of all these characters as symbolized by the horse is to miss an essential texture of Raskolnikov's mind.[1]

Obviously needed is a way to select, from this wealth of material, the aspects of the dream which best help us explain Raskolnikov's actual behavior, without oversimplifying the character by denying that other aspects exist. Confusion in the novel over the painter Mikolka's name helps us do this.

At the moment Raskolnikov is about to confess his murder to a police examiner named Porfiry Petrovich, a painter bursts into Porfiry's office claiming the crime as "mine alone." The painter's name creates confusion. In Dostoevsky's own words, not attributed to any character, the painter is "Nikolay," the name used by both the police examiner (338)[2] and the master worker who reported Raskolnikov's return to the scene of the crime (344). Raskolnikov's friend Razumikhin calls the painter "Mikolay" (132) and "Nikolka" (427). In the painter's confession scene with Porfiry, Raskolnikov alone calls the confessing painter "Mikolka" (340). If we assume an error by the author, this confusion would be surprising. However, as Raskolnikov's mistake, the error provides a clue to our use of the dream material.[3]

The name "Mikolka" links the painter to the Mikolka of Raskolnikov's horse-beating dream (Part 1, Chapter 5). Raskolnikov dreams himself as a little boy feeling guilt and horror at his inability to prevent a drunken peasant named Mikolka from beating the animal to death. Like the painter, the dream Mikolka claims full responsibility for the crime, screaming, "You keep out of this! She's mine, isn't she? I can do what I like with my own" (54). Raskolnikov had been about to reveal his murderer personality, prompted—like the dream's Mikolka—by anger and hatred. When the painter confesses, Raskolnikov listens instead to a inner voice urging him to act as if the crime were none of his business. This detached attitude is in the dream by the little boy's father, an onlooker, who tells the little boy that the crime belongs to Mikolka and is none of the boy's business.

Each of the three main actors in Raskolnikov's dream—Mikolka, little boy, and onlooker—reflect ways of reacting that Raskolnikov consistently demonstrates in the novel. First the peasant Mikolka, who kills the horse, projects the Raskolnikov capable of a physically brutal axe-murder and of cruelly insulting those who love him. Second the little boy Raskolnikov, who cries agonized tears, represents Raskolnikov aiding the Marmeladov family and the one who impulsively prevents a well-dressed man from pursuing a confused young girl. Finally there is the little boy's father in the dream who urges him to continue their walk to the graveyard saying, "It is none of our business. Let us go." The father has the voice of the uninvolved onlooker Raskolnikov who says, "What business, is it of yours?" to the policeman he has just asked to aid the young, girl (47). The same onlooker operates when Raskolnikov tells himself how "stupid" he is to give his money to the Marmeladov family (24).

We see three personalities in Raskolnikov's three interviews with the police inspector. In the first interview, Porfiry mainly deals with Raskolnikov's onlooker personality. Raskolnikov maintains a "none-of-my-business" attitude and deals successfully with a trick question about the painters, one of whom Raskolnikov later calls by the dream nickname. Raskolnikov evades this trick. But later we discover that his hostile tone of laughter at the beginning has enabled the magistrate to guess "everything then" (434). Obviously Porfiry's trained ear detected the murderer's voice.

The murderer personality becomes even more important in the second interrogation, at the end of which Raskolnikov calls the painter by the dream nickname. On the way to Porfiry's office for this second examination, Raskolnikov "felt infinite, boundless hatred for him, and he even feared that his hatred would make him betray himself" (319). Whenever Raskolnikov is in one aspect of his personality and has to shift suddenly to another, it shocks his emotional system. Porfiry intentionally evokes Raskolnikov's murderer personality, the result being that "At moments" Raskolnikov "longed to throw himself on Porfiry and strangle him then and there" (327).

Porfiry's tactics make it difficult for Raskolnikov to keep from reacting like a murderer. At one point, he "fell suddenly into a real frenzy ... a perfect paroxysm of fury" (335). Alternately, Porfiry shocks Raskolnikov by reminding him that the crime is supposedly none of Raskolnikov's business, by saying variations of "Good Lord! What are you talking about? What is there for me to question you about?" (322). Such reminders progressively, upset Raskolnikov:

> As he had before, he suddenly dropped his voice to a whisper, instantly recognizing with anguish and hatred that he felt obliged to submit to the command, and driven to greater fury by the knowledge. (935)

Finally Raskolnikov "rushed at Porfiry" (336), who is quite delighted at this open display of murderous qualities telling Raskolnikov that he has already betrayed himself. But, before Porfiry can confront Raskolnikov with the implications of his actions, the painter bursts in to confess. The timing is pure coincidence. But Raskolnikov calls the painter "Mikolka" and this is not coincidence. For Dostoevsky employs the supposed error again.

In the third interview Porfiry no longer tries to provoke the murderer in Raskolnikov. Instead, he speaks in a mild paternal tone evoking the little boy personality, urging Raskolnikov to drop his onlooker pretense. Notably, here for the first time, Porfiry calls the painter by the dream character's nickname: "No, Rodion Romanovich, my dear chap, Mikolka isn't in this at all!" (437). Raskolnikov responds "like a frightened small child caught red-handed in some misdeed" (438). He smiles "meek and sad" and speaks "as if he no longer could conceal anything at all from Porfiry" (440).

In the sense we have been using, everyone has many parts to his personality. But in Raskolnikov's case important parts are alienated from each other. The onlooker cannot see how the old woman's death can possibly concern him. The murderer has sneering contempt for the little boy's acts of impulsive generosity. The little boy is totally horrified by the murderer's acts of brutality. This alienation gives meaning to the word "split" in the term "split personality." These are not postulated interior forces or images but overt ways of acting which the other characters recognize. The real test of the dream characters' explanatory value is whether they contribute to the reader's understanding of Dostoevsky's depiction of Raskolnikov. Eight important episodes demonstrate that they do.

(1) *Raskolnikov's reunion with his sister.*

On seeing his sister for the first time in three years, Raskolnikov brusquely denounces her marriage plans. Those present make allowances for the insult because of his "condition," which we can see as the temporary dominance of the Mikolka personality. Dr. Zosimov later recalls this in terms that could apply to Mikolka: A "monomaniac, who had been goaded almost to raving madness by the smallest word ...." (213).

But the next morning, Raskolnikov arises talking to himself the way that the dream's onlooker talked of those who tortured the animal. In the dream the onlooker implies: What business is it of ours? He says, "They are drunk, they are playing the fool" (56). And awake, Raskolnikov thinks:

> His most horrifying recollection was of how 'ignobly and disgustingly' he had behaved, not only in being drunk, but in taking advantage of a young girl's situation to abuse her fiancé in front of her, out of stupid and hastily conceived jealousy, when he knew nothing either of their mutual relationship and obligations or, properly speaking, of the man himself. And what right had he to condemn him so hastily and rashly? Who had appointed him the judge? (201)

The onlooker in the dream said: "It's none of our business. Let us go." Like him, Raskolnikov now says ...

> of course, I can't gloss over or efface all this nastiness, now or ever ... and so I must not even think of it, but appear before them in silence ... and not ask forgiveness, but say nothing. (202)

Yet, on seeing his mother and sister again, Raskolnikov makes all right again with the charm of a little boy—astounding the others present. Their mother's face "shone with pride and happiness as she notes "how simply and delicately" Raskolnikov achieved the reconciliation. And his friend Razumikhin thinks: "Now that's what I absolutely love him for!" (215).

(2) *The murder itself.*

Before the crime, the onlooker in Raskolnikov's personality tells him that he cannot possibly be serious in his plans—but not from any sense of moral outrage: rather, being split from the murderer, the onlooker feels no identity with the Raskolnikov who can be brutal. However, when the time comes, Raskolnikov, like Mikolka, strikes Alyona repeatedly with the blunt side of the axe. Raskolnikov then reacts in horror at his own crime just as the little boy of the dream reacts to Mikolka's cruelty. Lizaveta's arrival turns little-boy horror into terror, and as Raskolnikov flings himself forward with the axe "her lips writhed pitifully, like those of a young child when it is just beginning to be frightened ..." (76). Lizaveta, like the old mare, responds minimally and ineffectively. And, as a voice in the dream had urged (55), Raskolnikov mercifully finishes her off with one blow from the sharp edge of the axe. Again Raskolnikov first reacts like the little boy, with horror and repulsion for what he had done, rather than with "fear for himself."

In the dream the onlooker treats the crime as trivial: "'Come away,' said his father, '... Come away; don't look!'" (54). And "It is none of our business. Let us go" (56). After the crime, Raskolnikov turns more and more to this attitude.

> But a growing distraction, that almost amounted to absentmindedness, had taken possession of him; at times he seemed to forget what he was doing, or rather to forget the important things and cling to trivialities. (77)

Raskolnikov calmly washes his hands and cleans the axe, treating the bodies in the other room and the money in the bedroom as if they were none of his business. Near-discovery shakes him out of this mode. But as he escapes, we listen to an interior debate. One voice urges him to run, to hide in the doorway, to take a cab. The other, parallel to the dream's onlooker calms him and urges him to act as if nothing has happened.

(3) *Raskolnikov's meeting with Zametov.*

When he meets Zametov, the police clerk, at a bar called the "Crystal Palace," Raskolnikov tries to talk of the axe murder like an onlooker who can have only passing interest. But "in a flash he remembered, with an extraordinary intensity of feeling," the scene in the murder room. And he "was suddenly filled with a desire to shriek out, to exchange oaths with them, stick out his tongue at them, mock them, and laugh, laugh, laugh" (155). Raskolnikov's Mikolka personality makes Zametov shiver and recoil suddenly from Raskolnikov. Dostoevsky describes the result of the struggle between the Mikolka personality and onlooker in Raskolnikov's appearance:

> The latter's eyes were glittering, he had grown shockingly pale, and his upper lip trembled and twitched. He leaned as near as possible to Zametov and began moving his lips, but no sound came from them; they remained like this for half a minute. He knew what he was doing, but he could not restrain himself. (159)

Zametov's obvious recognition of the murderer brings Raskolnikov "to his senses." The onlooker emerges again, and Raskolnikov successfully acts as if the murder is none of his business.

(4) *Raskolnikov's return to the scene of the crime.*

When Raskolnikov leaves Zametov, the switches continue. Meeting Razumikhin at the door of the bar, Raskolnikov viciously insults him. Then he stands by, watching an attempted suicide, as if it were none of his business, never even wondering if he should try to help. He goes to the murder scene where he must pretend that the crime is no business of his. Suddenly switching to the horrified little boy, he asks to be taken to the police. People hesitate and the commotion of Marmeladov's accident distracts him. He tries to help the man and impulsively gives all his money to the widow for the funeral. This little-boy generosity stirs Raskolnikov to great joy, but then his onlooker takes control and misinterprets, reinforcing the theme that Raskolnikov can go on living as if the crime were none of his business: "... it had come to him suddenly, as to a man clutching at a straw, that even for him it was 'possible to live, that life was still there, that his life had not died with that old woman'" (182).

(5) *The confession to Sonya.*

In the dream the onlooker had urged the little boy on toward the cemetery, a dubious course. And another insight by the onlooker demonstrates the limited life open to Raskolnikov if he continues clutching at the straw that the onlooker off ed him at the Marmeladov's:

> 'Where was it,' Raskolnikov thought, as he walked on, 'where was it that I read of how a condemned man, just before he died, said, or thought, that if he had to live on some high crag, on a ledge so small that there was no more than room for his two feet, with all about him the abyss, the ocean, eternal night, eternal solitude, eternal storm, and there he must remain, on a hand's-breadth of ground, all his life, a thousand years, through all eternity—it would be better to live so, than die within the hour? Only to live, to live! No matter how—only to live!' (152)

In effect, the onlooker urges Raskolnikov to stay up on the cliff face, a disastrous choice. But Sonya urges him to try to climb down to the solid ground, as dangerous as that effort might be.

The little boy in Raskolnikov takes the first step down when he confesses to Sonya. Raskolnikov must overcome the onlooker's urging him not to confess. But when Sonya begins to guess his secret, Raskolnikov "looked at her and suddenly in her face he seemed to see Lizaveta" (30). The expression is that of a small child and Raskolnikov's little boy personality at last emerges. Dostoevsky supplies the italics to make this point more emphatic:

> Her fear suddenly communicated itself to him: the same terror showed in his face and he gazed at her with the same fixity and almost with the same *childish* smile. (394, Dostoevsky's emphasis)

Sonya's tender reaction brings tears to Raskolnikov's eyes and, "Long unfamiliar feelings poured like a flood into his heart and melted it in an instant" (395). But on her vow to follow him to prison, Raskolnikov "felt a sudden shock of the change of personality modes and "the old hostile, almost mocking smile played his lips" (395). In declining the offer, Raskolnikov no longer speaks as a little boy: "In his changed tone she now suddenly heard the voice of the murderer" (295).

(6) *Raskolnikov's impulse to murder Svidrigaylov and to commit suicide.*

As more characters learn Raskolnikov's murder—first Sonya, then Svidrigaylov, then Dunya—Raskolnikov finds the onlooker's indifferent position more difficult to maintain. The position erodes, leaving more and more the choice between murderer and little boy. At one point, the murderer seems dominant as Raskolnikov resolves "with cold despair" to murder Svidrigaylov (445). This proves unnecessary, but the murderer's most vulnerable victim may be Raskolnikov himself. The Mikolka part of him takes malicious pleasure in repeatedly striking a victim aspect of himself, just as the dream's peasant enjoys striking repeated blows. Raskolnikov even numbers his repeated psychological blows:

> '... Oh, aesthetically speaking, I am a louse, nothing more,' he added, suddenly beginning to laugh like a madman. 'Yes, I really am a louse,' he went on, clinging to the idea with malicious pleasure, burrowing into it, playing with it for his own amusement, 'if only because, first ... secondly ...: thirdly ... Finally, I am a louse because ... Oh, platitudes! What baseness!' (264)

The dreaded Mikolka killed the mare. There is a danger that Raskolnikov will kill himself. As Svidrigaylov puts it, "Rodion Romanovich has two ways open to him: a bullet through the brain, or Siberia" (484). Raskolnikov contemplates suicide on the canal at the very moment that Svidrigaylov actually kills himself.

(7) *Raskolnikov's last interview with his mother.*

Turning sharply away from suicide at the canal, Raskolnikov proceeds immediately to his mother where his "heart was all at once softened" just as at his confession to Sonya. Then Sonya had knelt at Raskolnikov's feet; now with his mother, Raskolnikov "fell down before her and kissed her feet, and they wept, with their arms about one another" (495). Her reaction makes clear that the little boy possesses his personality then:

> 'Rodya, my dear, my first-born,' she said, sobbing 'now you are just like the little boy you used to be; you would come to me just like this, and put your arms round me and kiss me.' (493)

Raskolnikov repeats this gesture a year later falling at Sonya's feet and accepting "resurrection into a new life" (526) at the feet of the woman whom the other prisoners called, "Little mother" (523). Like a little boy he is free to start a new life. That evening Raskolnikov for the first time combines the objectivity of the onlooker with the warm emotion of the child:

> Everything, even his crime, even his sentence and his exile, seemed to him now, in the *first rush of emotion*, to be something external and strange, as if it had not happened to him at all. (526–527, my emphasis)

The onlooker has never before been described as having strong emotions. This is a more whole, more complete feeling and indicates a process of reintegrating the split-off parts.

(8) *Raskolnikov's final confession to the police, and the eventual reintegration of his personality.*

The three parts of Raskolnikov's dream also explain Raskolnikov's confusing final confession scene, resolving it into the interplay of specific personality fragments. Raskolnikov has decided that he cannot act as if the crime were none of his business. First, too many people know about his guilt; and second, he cannot live like a man on a ledge of a cliff—he must confess to start a new life. But he has not repented. Saying goodby to his sister Dunya early in the very day of his confession, Raskolnikov repudiates her suggestion that he is "half atoning for your crime" by "advancing to meet your punishment." Raskolnikov's contempt for his victim still resembles the dream Mikolka's contempt for the old mare.

> 'Crime? What crime?' he cried, in a sudden access of rage. 'Killing a foul, noxious louse, that old money lender ... was that a crime? That is not what I am thinking of, and I do not think of atoning for it.' (498)

Raskolnikov feels sorry only for the stupidity of his failure. Thus even as he prepares to confess, Raskolnikov claims he still feels as if he had committed no crime. His sister's response indicates her frustration at his inability to grasp the implications of his own action. "'Brother, brother, why are you saying this? You really did spill blood!' cried Dunya, in despair" (498).

Raskolnikov then visits Sonya to bid farewell. He goes to her, as he realizes moments later, out of Mikolka-like cruelty. "I wanted to see her terror, and watch her heart being torn and tormented!" (504). But as Raskolnikov leaves Sonya's apartment, a desperate renewal of the onlooker wonders, "Is it really impossible to stop now and revise all my intentions again ... and not go?" (503).

Suddenly remembering Sonya's advice to "say aloud to all the world, 'I am a murder!'" Raskolnikov has a shuddering change "like a clap of thunder" and "tears gushed out." To admit the murder as his crime, while not in the murderer aspect of his personality, would be a step towards unifying the split-off parts. Raskolnikov "almost flung himself on the possibility of his new, complete, integral sensation" (505). Desire for completeness, for this integral sensation, brings the split parts close enough to allow Raskolnikov to fall on his knees in the Haymarket. But comments by bystanders, that he is a drunk or a pilgrim to Jerusalem, encourage the onlooker by acting "as a check on Raskolnikov" stilling "the words 'I am a murderer,' which had perhaps been on the tip of his tongue" (505).

Raskolnikov's need for a "complete, integral sensation," to be obtained by claiming the murder, suggests the importance of confession for Raskolnikov. It is not the act of confessing that is important but the consequences. By confessing Raskolnikov would publicly and irrevocably claim the murderer as part of himself. In addition to any good feelings the confession right give him, claiming the murderer would make it part of his public identity. His position as prisoner would give him the sustained public identity of "the axe murderer," making the shift to onlooker difficult. For a whole year after confessing, Raskolnikov will resent this identity. But the prison situation relentlessly forces Raskolnikov to accept the reality that he did murder the old lady; this being prison's main therapeutic quality. Only when Raskolnikov finally accepts this reality can the little boy's triumph pave the way for the slow emergence of a coherent personality.

But there is danger that Raskolnikov will not confess. For personality switches continue even after the Haymarket insight. When Raskolnikov enters the office of Ilya Petrovich, this police clerk chatters on treating Raskolnikov with such complete implicit assumption of innocence that the onlooker powerfully revives in Raskolnikov. The police officer does not even exactly remember Raskolnikov's name, creating a temptation to try again to act as if the murder were "none of his business." Svidrigaylov posed the greatest threat to reveal Raskolnikov's secret. News of his death removes another obstacle to the onlooker's position, further tempting Raskolnikov to turn back. Raskolnikov staggers out of the office, but the sight of Sonya renews the little boy personality that had sent Raskolnikov into the office. He returns and confesses.

Dreams can only be interpreted in the light of other elements of personality. With a literary character, we have only those elements which the author chooses to give us. In *Crime and Punishment*, Dostoevsky consistently describes Raskolnikov in terms of Mikolka, onlooker, and little boy, even providing the italics to indicate how we are to interpret his words; he gives us the discrepancy over the name of the painter Nikolay; and he indicates that Raskolnikov's salvation must take the form of a reintegration. Clearly, in Mikolka, the onlooker, and the little boy we have found the route by which Raskolnikov's dream carries us to a better understanding of his dilemma.

Notes

1. W. D. Snodgrass, "Crime for Punishment: The tenor of Part One," *The Hudson Review*, XII, No. 2, Summer 1964, p. 239.

2. Feodor Dostoevsky, *Crime and Punishment*, tr. Jessie Coulson, ed. George Gibian (New York: Norton, 1960, p: 338. All references in parentheses are to this edition.

3. I am indebted to Lee T. Lemon of The University of Nebraska–Lincoln for checking Coulson's rendering of the painter's name against the original Russian text. I also want to thank Professor Lemon for the generous time he spent reading this paper and offering suggestions.

FRANK FRIEDEBERG SEELEY

The Two Faces of Svidrigailov

The figure of Svidrigailov has fascinated some Western critics no less than it fascinated Dunia and Rodion Raskol'nikov. For Middleton Murry in 1916, Svidrigailov was the principal hero, the most striking figure in *Crime and Punishment*.[1] Philip Rahv, somewhat more cautiously, says that Svidrigailov "is so fascinating a character in his own right, exercising an appeal nearly matching that of the hero, that at times he threatens to run away with the story."[2]

Yet most critical appraisals of Svidrigailov are summary and/or neglect important parts of the evidence. It has become almost traditional to define him as the double of Raskol'nikov's dark self, as an extrapolation of the would-be superman in Raskol'nikov. But this not only leads to facile simplification of a complex character: it misses the fact that Svidrigailov is a fundamentally different type of "superman" than the type aspired to by Raskol'nikov.[3]

Any adequate account of Svidrigailov must pivot on an assessment of at least three capital facts of his career: the feelings he inspires in Dunia (and in his child-bride); his sparing of Dunia when he has her at his mercy; and his suicide. But before considering these facts directly, it may be useful to summarise the author's evidence—and Dunia's[4]—on his personality.

At his first meeting with Raskol'nikov Svidrigailov bursts into hearty

From *Canadian-American Slavic Studies* 12, no. 3 (Fall 1978).

and unreserved laughter[5]; if we bear in mind the significance which Dostoevskii attaches to laughter as an index of character, this should alert us to a positive side in Svidrigailov. Indeed, he laughs and smiles a great deal throughout the novel, and as often as not, good-humoredly; this bespeaks an affinity with Dunia and opposes him to Raskol'nikov, whose laughter is usually either forced or sardonic.[6] Moreover, as is implied by this laughter *naraspashku*, Svidrigailov is distinguished by a singular candor: he is always honest with himself and more than averagely honest about himself.

His intelligence is attested not only by the quality of his irony (which, incidentally, he turns against himself as readily as against others), but by his penetrating and just characterisation of other people (his wife, Dunia, Luzhin, Razumikhin and even, up to a point, Raskol'nikov).

He loves Schiller and appreciates Raphael; but this does not make him merely a Romantic. Though there are elements of Romanticism in his passion for Dunia and in his proclamation of illusion as the key to happiness,[7] he appears thoroughly realistic in regard to himself and other people.[8]

Unlike the materialist Luzhin and the rationalist half of Raskol'nikov, Svidrigailov believes in ghosts and in other worlds. Unlike Luzhin, who takes all his ideas from the West, and Raskol'nikov, whose dark self is imbued with Western values, Svidrigailov prefers Russia to all other countries and is bored by foreign travel. These are virtues in Dostoevskii's eyes.

He is as free from Raskol'nikov's drive to power as from Luzhin's greed for money: he leaves his wife's wealth to his children, reserving for himself only the competence she had herself given him. And on the testimony of Dunia as well as on his own, usually truthful testimony, Svidrigailov was, in the main, a good husband (though no sort of father) and a good landowner and master, loved by his servants and peasants.

So much on the credit side. On the other, he is a self-confessed voluptuary (*sladostrastnik*) and profligate (*razvratnik*). There are rumors (but only rumors) that by his sadistic baiting he caused his servant Philip to commit suicide; Dunia, who has lived under his roof, disbelieves this, although she admits it was believed by the servants. There is also the rumor that he was responsible for the suicide of the teenage ward of Mrs Resslich; but we are informed too, that she had plenty of other reasons to commit suicide: not only was she deaf and dumb and alone in the world but her guardian "hated her beyond measure, grudged her every morsel of food and even beat her inhumanly."[9]

It is commonly assumed that the second of Svidrigailov's three dreams on the night before his death is a confirmation of his guilt. This is a possible interpretation. But the settings of the two tragedies were quite different. And the girl in the dream had drowned herself, whereas Mrs. Resslich's ward hanged herself.[10] Besides, is it not rash to try to read Stavrogin back into Svidrigailov? Anyhow, if, for the sake of argument, one assumes that Svidrigailov was responsible for those two deaths, that would only level his crime-score with Raskolnikov's—although he had lived twice as long![11]

What this balance-sheet shows is that Svidrigailov belongs in Dostoevskii's category of *shirokie russkie liudi*, who are, according to Svidrigailov himself, *chrezvychaino sklonny k fantasticheskomu, k besporiadochnomu*.[12] Unfortunately for him, Svidrigailov (like Raskol'nikov) is clearly aware only of his negative self. His positive traits he recognises severally, but for him they don't add up to an alternate self: hence his complaint that he is nothing and his longing to be something—anything.[13]

In fact, there is a vein of dark poetry in Svidrigailov (expressed in his existentialist vision of hell, or of Dunia as an early Christian martyr or hermit).[14] And there is a capacity for heroism, which is first realised in his sparing of Dunia: surely it is nothing less than heroic to renounce of one's own free will what one has panted for, been haunted by, obsessively lived for during many months?

Such a synoptic view of Svidrigailov explains how he could be loved not only by his servants and by Marfa Petrovna but by his teenage fiancée—and by Dunia. For it is quite clear that Dunia has loved him, and perhaps more than she understood. Her relations with him, while she was living in his home, had by no means been confined to attempts to reclaim him. There had obviously grown up between them an intimacy of friendship: not only had she taken shooting lessons from him, but she had discussed with him Russia and life and even her beloved brother.

That so self-controlled and proud a girl as Dunia could wrestle for his soul with entreaties and tears—reveals how deeply her heart was involved. And this is evidenced further by her "excessive terror"[15] when she learns that he has come to Petersburg; by her use of *ty* at their last meeting; and by her final refusal to shoot him—even at the risk of being raped. If one asks why she could not acknowledge her own feeling even after the death of his wife, part of the answer must be that love had been overlaid by sheer horror of the animal passion in him: remember his musings on her "morbid" chastity.[16]

But, then, why did Svidrigailov let her go? To this there would appear to be only one possible answer. At the critical moment he discovered, he realised that not only could he not rape this girl but he could not bring himself to blackmail her into compliance—that he not only desired her excruciatingly, but he had come to love her. This was his vision on the road to Damascus—his moment of truth, analogous to Raskol'nikov's discovery that he had killed not the old woman, but himself.[17]

And this goes far towards explaining his suicide. Of course, he had toyed with the idea before: at least from the time when he hinted to Raskol'nikov that he might be going on a journey.[18] But his fear of death, new sexual adventures, not to mention the drag of inertia—might have postponed such a *dénouement* almost indefinitely. Now, however, all of a sudden, his whole philosophy of life had been shattered. Behind, or beside, the hedonist self, of which alone he had been conscious, there now loomed another self, which in the last resort had proved stronger than that with which he had identified. And he had wasted his whole life ignoring—when not flouting—that self: the self which loved Dunia and which her intuition had come close to loving. After encountering this second self, he could no longer live through his first self, but having lost Dunia irrevocably, he could not live by his second self either.

This is confirmed—for the reader, primarily—by his second and third dreams. The first dream is a fairly transparent anticipation of the immediate future: he has vermin running all over his body, as they will soon be doing in the grave. The second dream takes him back to the past; it represents a transfiguration of the death of Mrs. Resslich's victim. It does not indicate whether Svidrigailov had actively precipitated that death or had only contributed passively, by not intervening. What it does proclaim is that for him there is no escape from the past—the past will be with him always. And the implications of this are made explicit in the third dream (of the five-year-old turning, in his bed, into a French whore). This means that his pristine self will still be with him, to contaminate and denature all that his new self holds most sacred.

None of these dreams determines his suicide: that was determined at the moment when he picked up the revolver thrown away by Dunia.[19] What the dreams do is to keep him on course, while explaining that course to the reader.

But in the hours before sleep he does begin to live in and through his new self. His provision for Sonia and for his child-bride is disinterested and generous: he is going to meet the death he had so dreaded with a heart free from malice and full of charity. And this charity (in the Pauline sense) finds one more, heroic expression. In sending his last greeting, through Sonia, to Razumikhin, he is saying—to Razumikhin: "I am glad you will do for her what I could not"; and, through Razumikhin, to Dunia: "Take him and be happy." As Bazarov says of Odintsova's coming to his deathbed: "*Eto po-tsarski.*"[20]

Notes

1. J. Middleton Murry, *Fyodor Dostoevsky: A Critical Study* (London: M. Decker, 1916).

2. "Dostoevsky in *Crime and Punishment*," *Partisan Review*, 27, No. 3 (1960), 393–425.

3. What they have in common is the axiom: "To the superman all is permitted." But Raskol'nikov makes this license conditional on the ability to say a new word; Svidrigailov does not, and in fact, eschews philosophising. Moreover, their objectives are radically different: Raskol'nikov seeks power, Svidrigailov—pleasure.

4. Dunia is manifestly a witness of truth, though she may be uncertain on some points and mistaken on others. On the other hand, Luzhin is a rogue and a rival: Raskol'nikov is self. Dostoevskii himself warns us against swallowing Raskol'nikov's judgments uncritically.

5. Within half a dozen lines we read: "*vdrug raskhokhotalsia ... smejas'otkrovenneishim obrazom ... smcias' naraspashku....*" In his relations with Raskol'nikov Svidrigailov laughs more often than he smiles. His laughter is in almost all cases expansive, loud, sincere. His smiles are mostly slyly mocking, occasionally cunning. With Dunia he does not laugh; his smiles run the whole gamut from condescension through mockery and rage to despair.

6. Another trait opposing him to Raskol'nikov is his refusal to judge others (p. 378: *ia nikogo reshitel'no ne obviniaiu*). But this smacks of Laodiceanism rather than Christian charity and may even imply a certain complacency; Raskol'nikov is harsh in his judgments on people whose failings he cannot admit in himself.

7. *Prestuplenie i nakazanie*, p. 370: *vsekh veselei tot i zhivët kto vsekh luchshe sebia sumeet nadut'*; cp. Pushkin (*Geroi*): *T'my nizkikh istin mne dorozhe / Nas vozvyshajushchij obman*. Svidrigailov's version is parodic, but none the less Romantic for that. Citations from *Crime and Punishment* in this and the preceding and in all following notes are from: F. M. Dostoevskii, *Polnoe sobranie sochinenii* (Leningrad: Nauka, Leningr. otenie, 1972–), VI.

8. Cf. his characterisations of his wife (pp. 363–64) and of Dunia (pp. 365 *et seqq.*). On himself, cf. such candid self-revelations as: *iia redko lgu* [p. 220], *otchego zhe i ne pobyvat' poshliakom ... osobenno esli k tomu i natural'nuiu sklonnost' imesh'* [p. 217]; *Deistvitel'no, ia chelovek razvratnyi i prazdnyi* [p. 222]; *Da i kakoi is otets!* [*ibid.*]; *Net, kakol ia igrok. Shuler ne igrok* [p. 359]; the apologia for his womanising (pp. 359, 362); etc.

9. Rumor charges Svidrigailov with responsibility for the death of his wife as well as of Philip and of the deaf and dumb girl. But it is plain that his quarrel with Marfa Petrovna was only a tangential factor in her death, and Svidrigailov is quite ready to talk about it and indeed to claim that his conscience is clear on that score. Whereas his habitual candor fails him in regard to the other two deaths: he shrinks from Raskol'nikov's questions about them. Is there any significance in the fact that Marfa Petrovna, of whose death he is innocent, and Philip, of whose death Dunia believes him to be innocent, both appear to him as ghosts, whereas the girl appears to him only in a dream, not as still living but as still dead?

10. There is conflicting evidence about the manner of the girl's suicide. Luzhin asserts that she hanged herself (p. 228). In the dream she had drowned herself. But Svidrigailov only adds to the confusion when he says (p. 368): "*... Resslikh ... vot to samaia, pro kotoruiu govoriat, chto devchonka-to; v vode-to zimoif-to....*" So Svidrigailov believes, whether awake or asleep, that the girl drowned herself. But when awake, he places the suicide in winter; in his dream it happens in May or June (Whitsuntide: p. 391). And if the girl died in winter, one wonders where she would have found water to drown in, with every lake, river and

pond frozen over? One wonders, too, whether, if he had been the prime cause of the death, Svidrigailov could have been in any doubt as to the season (or the manner).

11. This, needless to say, is not to equate Svidrigailov with Raskol'nikov: it is to indicate that Svidrigailov does not kill himself because he is a greater criminal than Raskol'nikov.

12. *Prestuplenie i nakazanie*, p. 378. He adds (*ibid.*) with devastating clearsightedness: *no beda byt' shirokim bez osobennoi genial'nosti.*

13. *Ibid.*, p. 359: *Verite li, khotia by chto-nibud' bylo; nu, pomeshchikom byt', nu, otsom, nu, ulanom, fotografom, zhurnalistom ... n-nichego, nikakoi special'nosti....*

14. *Ibid.*, p. 365.

15. *Ibid.*, p. 237: *chrezmernyi strakh.*

16. *Ibid.*, p. 365: *Avdot'ia Romanovna tselomudrenna uzhasno, neslykhanno i nevidanno.* (*Zamet'te sebe, is vam soobshchaiu eto o vashei sestre kak fakt. Ona tselomudrenna, mozhet byt', do bolezni, nesmotria na ves' svoi shirokii um, i eto i provredit.*) Of course, we are not bound to accept Svidrigailov's conception of morbidity; perhaps his singular temperament would have required a mate of similarly uncommon disposition. However, Dunia is no average girl; but her emotional and her sexual constitution deserve to be studied on their own.

17. Raskol'nikov kills the old woman: he is wrong in thinking that he has killed his (true) self, but he has come as close as he can to doing so. Svidrigailov spares Dunia and so sets his (true) self free, but can find no way to run two such selves in double harness.

18. When Svidrigailov arrives in Petersburg, he finds himself, whether he realises it or not, at a crossroads. His main, conscious purpose is to capture Dunia—at any cost and on any terms. Meanwhile he has to kill time, and the girl-bride is both a distraction and a blind. If Dunia had foiled him, or he had won and then tired of her, his hedonist self might have settled for marriage (to this teen-ager) and/or a further round of sexual adventures. Meanwhile, his hidden self wants Dunia no less—but only in freedom and love. It has already condemned life without her on these terms as empty and unendurably boring; and the corollary to such an assessment must have been: Better put an end to it.

19. Symbolically: he had given Dunia life and freedom; she leaves him to die. She had been prepared to kill him; he executes the judgment in her stead.

20. In my 1974 paper "On Suicide in Dostoevsky's Later Works" I took a more clinical look at Svidrigailov in terms of the psychiatric concept of "ontological insecurity." The two approaches can be regarded as complementary.

GERALD FIDERER

Raskolnikov's Confession

At the end of *Crime and Punishment*, while Raskolnikov stands trembling at the bureau in the police station, the assistant superintendent enters in high spirits and addresses him:

> "You here? What can I do for you?" (He seemed to be just a trifle intoxicated.) "If it's business you're a bit early. I'm myself here quite by accident. However, I'd be glad to be of any help ... I confess, Mr. ... Mr. ... Excuse me...."
>
> "Raskolnikov."
>
> "Of course, Raskolnikov! You surely couldn't suppose I had forgotten! Please don't think me that sort of person.... Rodion Ro .... Ro ... Rodionovich, isn't it?"
>
> "Rodion Romanovich."
>
> "Yes, yes, yes! Rodion Romanovich, Rodion Romanovich! I had it on the tip of my tongue."

He had forgotten, as we say, Raskolnikov's name, both surname, and patronymic. What are we to make of this trivial lapse of memory? The assistant superintendent himself behaves as most of us would in such an embarrassing moment; he simply denies it. "You didn't think I'd forgotten

From *Literature and Psychology* 30, no. 2 (1980).

did you?" he insists, as he goes on to misremember the patronymic.

If asked to explain an error of this kind from everyday life, most of us fall back on some commonsense reason: the fellow is a bit drunk, we point out, and he is so surprised to see Raskolnikov that his memory is 'naturally' impaired. And why bother with such a petty detail anyway? But when the word 'naturally' is invoked to explain an error like this, the actual intention is to deny any causation for it, just as the assistant superintendent himself does. Attributing his lapse to alcohol is like attributing a dream to indigestion; it fails to account for the specific nature of the dream or slip of the tongue, and as common sense usually does, simply begs the question.

Why should the assistant superintendent make just this error and not some other, is the question we must continue to ask. From a formalist point of view, we need have no recourse to such common sense. We assume that there are no accidents in the work of art, and notice that the forgetting of Raskolnikov's name has an organic function in the scene. Indeed, it sets the tone for the entire interview, because the literary point of it is that just at the moment of Raskolnikov's self-exposure, he is most safe, farthest from the mind of the police official whose suspicions were earliest and decisive. This is simply an instance of irony of situation, for it contrasts expectation and response, appearance and reality. The ironic heightening lends the episode its poignance, tension and interest. And when we look further at the assistant superintendent's word of apology, we smile with received pleasure from the irony of statement: "Good Lord!" the assistant superintendent says, "What literary chap or—er—scholar did not start off by doing something—er—original?" What the assistant superintendent means by original (the Nietzschean essay Raskolnikov has published) is in striking contrast to the "original" deed he has come to confess; the perception of this contrast between what the assistant superintendent says and what the reader knows is a source of literary pleasure, of complication, of understanding of reality. This account is a good deal more than common sense dismissal. But is it enough?" Is it entirely accurate to say that the assistant superintendent's lapses of memory indicate that Raskolnikov is the farthest thing from his mind? Or is this what we have come to call a Freudian slip, or parapraxis in the technical language of depth psychology?

A parapraxis means something. It represents unconscious anger, resentment, envy and suspicion. It embodies the hostile wish to forget, as we all secretly know when we forget someone's name. We, too, say we have it "on the tip of the tongue," simultaneously knowing we know the name, yet not knowing it. His hostility accounts for his embarrassed and very apologetic tone. He had, in fact, hated Raskolnikov at first sight. Raskolnikov had provoked him into a rage by staring long and hard at his red moustaches which stuck out horizontally from the side of his face; Raskolnikov had publicly attacked him for smoking a cigarette; the assistant superintendent momentarily displaced his rage onto a prostitute, who was standing nearby, shouting at her, "... you dirty slut. What was going on at your house last night ... you old Jezebel?" But when Raskolnikov faints, the assistant superintendent turns back to him shouting:

> "Have you been ill long?"
> "Since yesterday," Raskolnikov murmured in reply.
> "And did you go out yesterday?"
> "I did."
> "Though ill?"
> "Yes."
> "At what time?"
> "About eight in the evening...." Raskolnikov, white as a sheet gave his replies ... jerkily. The superintendent interrupted, "He can hardly stand on his feet, and you—"
> "Never mi-i-nd!" the assistant superintendent said in a rather peculiar voice....
> Everybody fell silent suddenly. It was odd.

The effect is uncanny because Raskolnikov has here made his first confession (we should say unconsciously) and everyone in the room understands. In that intense silence of the police station we recognize the experience of unconscious communication as another instance of Dostoevsky's pressure on our deepest susceptibilities. The time of the murder was known to be about eight in the evening, yet Raskolnikov admits that that is the time he went out. Even more peculiar, he lies about his illness—in order to incriminate himself. He had been sick for weeks, and yet he insists that he has been sick only "since yesterday." There can be no doubt that the assistant superintendent—cruel, philistine and even stupid—is completely attuned to the unconscious communications Raskolnikov makes, or that a mysterious bond is here established between them.

If we now turn to Raskolnikov's last confession at the end of the novel, we recognize with shock "the figure of the assistant superintendent flashing through his mind. 'Ought he really to go to him? Couldn't he go to someone else? At least it would all take place in private. No! No! To Gunpowder! To the assistant superintendent! If he must drain it, then let him drain it at one gulp!'" So he insists on a masochistic self-immolation. Remember that Porfiry the superintendent is a far more interesting, indeed sympathetic and imaginative character, with whom Raskolnikov has had a decent and humane relationship. That is precisely why he won't do. Raskolnikov requires a brute for his particular psychic need.

But Gunpowder isn't there. "Isn't anyone in?" Raskolnikov plaintively asks. Suddenly he gives a start. The assistant superintendent stands before him. "It's fate!" thought Raskolnikov. "Why is he here?"—as if he had summoned up his tormentor by the magical power of his thoughts.

II

Rene Wellek says Raskolnikov's crime is "inadequately motivated."[1] Pisarev wept uncontrollably when he finished reading the book; and then sat down to write his classical essay showing that Raskolnikov's crime was due to malnutrition. Joseph Frank denies that there even was a crime: "... his crime—if one can really call it a crime."[2] Murder? Double murder—with a hatchet? Raskolnikov himself makes no such denial. That is his interest. Joseph Frank thinks the murder had its origin in the Russian radical ideology of the mid-1860's, and offers a "dramatic illustration of how Raskolnikov's ideas twist and distort his feelings." Can we actually believe that Raskolnikov, or anyone, commits murder because of an abstract idea—even if it is Nietzschean or Nihilist?

If these critics who disclaim the problem of guilt and motivation are right, so too is Fred Crews right in his repudiation of depth psychology on the ground that it lacks "falsifiability." I wish to suggest that we may have a means for the verification or falsification of depth psychological theory better than case histories, better even than verbatim protocols of therapy sessions, in the evidence which lies before us in the literary work. It is the very best data, for it comes close to fulfilling the laboratory science criterion of reproducibility. Unlike the analytic session where nuance, context, suggestion all have hidden distorting and subjective roles—the evidence of the text is objective and absolute, before each reader to confirm or deny.

As a matter of fact, the historical and sociological critics (including the Soviet critics) are of further value, because they enunciate the "null hypothesis" for the test of psychological theory which Professor Crews called for. If they are right, all the psychodynamic implications of the novel are wrong. Crews disclaims the unconscious; Pisarev, Frank and Wellek disclaim Raskolnikov's guilt. He himself thinks of his mother and sister and says: "Oh, the low creatures! They even love as if they hated. Oh, how I hate them all!" When he asks Sonia's forgiveness, which is instantly forthcoming, he is overcome by "a strange and startling sensation of bitter hatred of Sonia. As though himself surprised and frightened by his sensation, he quickly raised his head and looked intently at her...." And then he realized: "It was not hatred at all; he had mistaken one feeling for another.... To his mind that moment vas uncannily like the moment when he stood behind the old woman and disengaged the hatchet...."

Can we still deny (Crews, the Soviets, Frank and others to the contrary) the deep, deep truth of the fusion of Eros and Thanatos? After the Romantic myth of Liebestod, the hundreds of Renaissance puns on killing and dying, from Wagner to Woody Allen, isn't it too late in the history of culture to shut our eyes to that particular fact? Even neurophysiologists have abandoned their behaviorist straitjacket to use the concepts of instinctual drive, sexuality, and aggression, ambivalence and emotion—because their new data from limbic system researches demand it. Does not the fact of Raskolnikov's ambivalence demand that we too entertain the concept of unconscious motivation, the dual theory of erotic and aggressive drives, the invariable fusion of libido and destrudo?

When the hatchet just appears to Raskolnikov by the power of his thoughts, whenever the coincidences occur, his dreams bring back the eternal return of images, feelings, and experiences which have been estranged from consciousness, but nevertheless emerge with uncanny effect. They are eternal and ineradicable. The dualism of conscious–unconscious, love and hate, sadism and masochism, murder and sexuality, pain and eroticism is most fully represented by the doubles in Dostoevsky's fiction. Dunya and Mrs. Raskolnikov (sister and mother) are congruent with Lisavetta and the old hag he murders; Raskolnikov with Svidrigaylov; Mrs. Raskolnikov with Mrs. Marmalaydov (both mothers die) and his landlady; Raskolnikov with Razumikhin; Marmalaydov the masochist with Svidrigaylov the sadist. Indeed, every character seems to have his double, his opposite, his mirror-image.

The relationship of Raskolnikov the prude with Svidrigaylov the sensualist is the most complicated, extended, baffling and mysterious of these dualities. Svidrigaylov is the corrupter of young girls, the shameless voluptuary who has left a swath of human wreckage in his past. It is hinted that he is responsible for the suicide of a fourteen-year-old girl and the murder of an old woman money lender. Raskolnikov appears maddeningly prudish. When Luzhin suggests that he might have a sexual interest in Sonia, who is after all a beautiful young prostitute, it drives him into a self-righteous frenzy. When Sonia enters his room he offers her a place on the sofa; but it so characteristically occurs to him that the sofa "was too *familiar* a place and served him as a bed"; so he hurriedly points to a chair instead. He is obsessed with saving fallen women, who all appear to be obscurely related to his own sister.

One of the most telling of Raskolnikov's attempts to save women occurs just after he received the letter from his mother announcing the marriage of his sister. While walking aimlessly, torturing himself with the thought of her marriage, his attention was fixed on a young girl. "He could not help noticing her ... reluctantly at first and, as it were resentfully, and then more and more intently. She was wearing a silk dress that seemed to be scarcely fastened and that was torn open behind." She seemed to be drunk and vulnerable to the advances of a corpulent, thick-set, red-lipped man who was watching her: When this pretty sixteen-year-old staggered to a seat, crossed her legs and revealed her charms to the man standing nearby, Raskolnikov goes mad with rage: "Hey you, Svidrigaylov! What do you want here" he shouts. He finds a policeman and entreats him: "The main thing is not to let her fall into the clutches of that scoundrel! I'm sure he intends to rape her! It's easy to see what he wants!" It is easy for Raskolnikov to see because the fat lecher is the representative of his own desires. But how peculiar to call him Svidrigaylov. The instant before he had been thinking of his sister Dunya's marriage to Luzhin and of Svidrigaylov's attempt to seduce her. Now he sees another young girl about to be sexually assaulted and by an unconscious act of condensation behaves as if she were his own sister and the man his sister's seducer. This is so far a summary of his words and actions. How can we make sense of it without the concepts of the unconscious, condensation, symbolism and projection? That his blind rage is not the result of a reasoned morality, but of his own guilt and repressed sexual wish is clear from his ambivalence; for almost his very next words to the policeman are "leave them alone! It's not your business! Let them be! Let him ... have his fun!" Much later, when Raskolnikov finally vanquishes his rival Luzhin, he seems again to subside into his characteristic ambivalence: "He who had more than anyone else insisted on breaking off his sister's engagement now seemed least of all interested in what had happened."

What are we to make of this? After browbeating Dunya continuously, repeating "Luzhin or me" interminably, he is suddenly uninterested. This is the typical behavior inexplicable by the literary historian's recital of nineteenth century radical debates. We must have recourse to conceptual tools from the language of depth psychology—dynamic ideas like ambivalence, rationalization, condensation, projection—in order to gather even a literal sense of the action. Readers have intuitively done so all along. It seems fatuous to insist that Dostoevsky is a psychological writer and that the modern constructs of defense mechanisms should be appropriately and cautiously applied. What is not so obvious is the corollary: that the psychological ideas are given meaning, concretion and indeed verification by the rough, grainy, complex texture of Dostoevsky's world.

Luzhin, the corpulent seducer, Svidrigaylov—all three represent the sexual possession of Dunya which Raskolnikov himself unconsciously desires. The greater the unconscious desire, the more powerful the force of repression and the intensity of projection. It is in this way that we understand Svidrigaylov's role in the novel, for he it not merely Raskolnikov's double; but his mirror-image or reciprocal. He consciously does what Raskolnikov unconsciously wishes. The complexity and complemetarity emerge when we recognize that Raskolnikov's surface and prudery and guilt form the substance of Svidrigaylov's unconscious. Think of his dream just before his suicide. It is a nightmare of sexual revulsion and terror; recall his horror and disgust when he hallucinates something warm and furry darting across his leg under the blanket. How strange for the voluptuary who permits himself everything sexual to have the same anxiety dream of impotence and failure as Raskolnikov, who permitted himself nothing sexual. But even Svidrigaylov's surface behavior is ambiguous and complicated. Though a murderer and philanderer, he is also a benefactor and savior. Before his death he dispenses three thousand roubles to everyone in sight. His suicide is the reciprocal of Raskolnikov's murder. For just as surely as Raskolnikov must declare: "was it the old hag I killed; no, I killed myself"; so is Svidrigalov's suicide with Dunya's three-chambered little revolver, the murder of her introjected image. If Svidrigaylov's particular nightmare is of a provocative, mocking, shameless little girl who literally laughs him to death, Raskolnikov's third dream is of a provocative, mocking, shameless old woman who laughs him to terrified flight. Both are anxiety dreams of the deepest masculine fears, of impotence and failure.

When Raskolnikov wakes he sees Svidrigaylov for the first time: "Surely this is not the continuation of my dream?" he thought, as if Svidrigaylov had arisen from his unconscious. The last time he sees Svidrigaylov he is again terribly surprised, shocked by the apparent coincidence which turns out to be just a memory lapse—the result, as Svidrigaylov tells him of "the strange, harsh and gloomy things which influence a man's mind." Svidrigaylov insists that they have everything in common. They are both ghost-ridden, and their conversations are invariably eerie and baffling:

> "When I came in here a few minutes ago," Svidrigaylov said, "and saw you lying with closed eyes ... I said to myself at once 'that's the very man!'"
>
> "What do you mean—that's the very man?" cried Raskolnikov.
>
> "Well, as a matter of fact, I'm damned if I know," Svidrigaylov muttered ... as though puzzled himself.

The fusion of the roué and prude; murderer and suicide, form a unity of opposites around the axes of sexuality and violence. But the connection of sexuality and murder is even more deeply embodied in Raskolnikov's identification with Sonia, the redemptive whore. "Haven't you, too, done the same thing?" he asks her, "You too stepped over—you had the strength to step over...." The murderer and prostitute whose crimes seem to meet and fuse are tied together by the transgression they have in common—by the raising of Lazarus, the uncanny phallic return of what was long ago estranged from consciousness—our primal sexual and homicidal wishes. The way in which these wishes are indissolubly joined is clear from the language and tone of Dunya's disavowal of marriage: "I haven't murdered anyone yet," the worthy sister tells Raskolnikov. He himself breaks through the Nietzschean rationalizations and speaks with the final truth of the unconscious when he says: "If only ... no one had loved me and I, too, had never loved anyone! There would *have been nothing of all this!*" However it contradicts the disclaimers of guilt (like Wellek, Pisarev, Frank) or the disclaimers of the unconscious like Crews, we must confront Raskolnikov's own declamation. We cannot escape the conclusion that murdering for Raskolnikov was a distorted way of loving.

Listen to his stream of associations:

> "Mother, sister—how I loved them! Why do I hate them now? Yes, I hate them. I hate them physically. I can't bear them to be near me.... Oh, how I hate that old hag now! I could have killed her again if she had come to life! Poor Lisavetta! Sonia! Why did she have to turn up just then? Lisavetta! Sonia! Poor meek creatures with meek eyes."

The innocent he murders and the whore he marries undergo the same startling condensation as did the masculine, sexually threatening figures of Svidrigaylov and Luzhin. In Raskolnikov's third dream, immediately following this monologue, he is terrified because he lacks the power to kill the old woman. He identifies with his victims, the poor meek creatures, with meek eyes. He embraces the little mare of his first dream; kisses it on the eyes and muzzle, is beaten himself as he becomes one with it.

From the point of view of Raskolnikov's ambivalent identifications, we apprehend his terror of the open door of his landlady as the introductory image of the novel; from the viewpoint of his dependency needs we can understand his impotence, ambivalence, sadomasochism and sexual renunciations: why he gives up his father's watch and his little gold ring "with three red stones," why he cannot even fit the keys to any of the locks in the old woman's room, why he is continually fainting and being fed by women throughout, why his murder is primarily a death wish directed against himself, why he hates Svidrigaylov as the representative of sexuality. And finally, why he is liberated into maturity by the death of his mother, and his passional love for a saintly whore.

Mrs. Raskolnikov is jealous of Sonia. As far as she can tell, Sonia "is the cause of all the trouble." Like the archetype of the Jewish mother, she gets sick and takes to her bed while she keeps complaining that Raskolnikov won't visit her, but has "plenty of time for *his girl.*" With this nuclear constellation it is not surprising that all Raskolnikov wishes to do is to hand them over to the care of Razumikhin.

He had wished to be like Napoleon, "the man to whom everything is permitted," heroic, erect and stiff like bronze; he only wanted to dare, but he had always known that he was impotent, passive, dependent and, suffering, enjoying his masochistic agony, like his spiritual father, the jelly-like Marmeladov. While torturing himself over his mother's letter he had realized that it was an

> "old, old question which had entered his heart. Long, long ago, his present, feeling of utter desolation and despair had arisen in him, and it had accumulated and grew until in the last few months it had become concentrated and come to a head, assuming a form of a fearful, wild, and fantastic question ... how his mother's letter had burst upon him.... It was clear that he ought not now to brood or to suffer passively.... He had to make up his mind at all costs, do something, anything, or ... forever give up every right to act, to live, and to love.
>
> 'Do you realize, do you realize, sir, what it means when you have nowhere to go?' He suddenly recalled the question Marmeladov had asked the night before ...
>
> Suddenly he gave a start. A thought flashed through his mind.... He knew he *felt* that it would most certainly cross his mind and was already waiting for it ... a month ago—and even yesterday for that matter—it was only a dream, but in a new terrifying and completely unfamiliar guise, and he himself suddenly realized it. The blood rushed to his head and everything went black before his eyes."

He had been brooding over his sister's marriage. This was the moment when his incestuous, homicidal and masochistic wishes return from the repressed and overwhelm him with their uncanny terror. Now they are conscious and real. The decision to act them out in reality floods him with the excitement of his orgiastic death wish, and he faints away. When he comes to himself again, he will see that disheveled young girl with the torn dress whom he saves from the fat man he calls Svidrigaylov.

What is crucial in these associations is the way they cut through the levels of Nietzschean and Napoleonic rationalization to reveal the infantile dependent needs: the desolation of having nowhere to go, the fear of abandonment to Siberian wastes, with no one to care, to feed, to love. At the end of the novel this fear of separation from Sonia breaks out in naked form. "Why is she taking leave of me, like my mother or Dunia? My future nurse!"

Paradoxical as it seems, the murder of the old woman and Lisavetta represent an orgiastic union with them, aimed at preventing the loss of his incestuously loved objects. The reality of such a counterphobic act brings about the very thing that is most feared. But Raskolnikov's unconscious aim is, nevertheless, to fulfill sadomasochistic desires for union with them. Concomitantly there is an enormous burden of guilt.

Strange to say, Raskolnikov's guilt was antecedent to his crime. Indeed, the crime is a means of expiating guilt and bringing about the feared and wished for punishment. "Long ago," he tells Sonia, when he makes his confession to her, "long ago I chose to tell you this, when your father told me about you and when Lisavetta was still alive." So the innocent he murders and the saintly whore he marries became unconsciously condensed and doubled even before he meets Sonia, even before he committed the criminal act. After the act, during one of his dialogues with the superintendent of police Raskolnikov felt a new kind of terror: "the thought that Porfiry thought him innocent, began to alarm him suddenly."

In an essay called "Criminality from a Sense of Guilt," Freud writes of patients who commit transgressions precisely because they are forbidden. The criminal act seems to mitigate the guilt which was present prior to the transgression. Freud says: "The invariable result of analytical work is that this obscure sense of guilt derives from the Oedipus complex and the two great criminal intentions of killing ... and having sexual relations with the mother. In comparison with these two, to be sure, the crimes committed in order to account for this sense of guilt were comparatively light ones for the sufferer to bear. (A kind of plea bargaining, whereby the neurotic pleads guilty to, the lesser intrapsychic crime.) We must remember in this connection that parricide (or matricide) and incest ... are the two greatest crimes man can commit, the only ones which in primitive communities are avenged and abhorred as such." Indeed, Freud speculates, this may explain the origin of mankind's universal sense of guilt. Maurice Beebe[3] has demonstrated that of Raskolnikov's three motives, the critical one is the masochistic need to suffer. How can we account for the ambivalence and neurotic guilt? It seems to have its origin according to the law of the talion in Oedipal and incestuous desires.

III

Freud's best and most famous case history is that of the Wolfman—another Russian ex-student of twenty three—who was so dependent that he was unable to dress and feed himself when he was brought to Freud in 1910. He had been diagnosed as incurably manic depressive by the leading psychiatrists of that day, Kraepelin and Ziehen. In recovering the history of his infantile neurosis, memories of a passive sexual relation with his father came up. As a little boy he would throw temper tantrums in order to provoke punishment and beating which would simultaneously palliate his sense of guilt and gratify his masochistic sexual desires. But at the same time as these passive sexual wishes appeared, active and sadistic ones accompanied them—tormenting small animals, fits of rage, fantasies of beating large animals (horses, in particular). Very early in the analysis the patient offered the following dream:

> I dreamt ... that I was lying in my bed. In front of the window there was a row of old walnut trees.... Suddenly the window opened of its own accord and I was terrified to see that some white wolves were sitting on the big tree in front of the window. The wolves were quite white and like foxes or sheep dogs, for they had big tails like foxes. In great terror, evidently of being eaten up by the wolves, I screamed and woke up.... I had had such a clear and life-like picture of the window opening and the wolves sitting on the tree.

After four years of analysis the dream was deciphered. Its meaning became clear and the neurosis was resolved. The solution surprised Freud himself. "Many details of the analysis seem, even to me, so extraordinary that I have felt some hesitation in asking other people to believe in them." The patient emphasized the lasting sense of reality and Freud took this as his starting point, because the sense of actuality in the dream means that some part of its content is claiming to possess the quality of reality—that is, of an occurrence that really took place. The dreamer was five years old but he was reminded of something that must have belonged to an earlier period. In one session he offered the interpretation for the part of the dream which said that, "suddenly the window opened of its own accord...." He said it must mean, "my eyes suddenly opened." I was asleep, therefore, and suddenly woke up, and as I woke up I saw something: "the tree with the wolves." By the technique of free association what was next recovered was a scene of the most violent motion. That is to say, he suddenly woke up and saw in front of him a scene of the most violent movement at which he looked with strained attention. It was the primal scene: when he woke up he was a horrified small witness to the coitus and genitals of his parents. The white wolves were the parents, in white underclothes.

Obviously such an event creates a state of great excitement in a child. Surrounded by an aura of shame as "secrets of adults," appearing to be violent and assaultive, real experiences of this kind are wrongly interpreted. If a small child observes sexual scenes between adults he misinterprets them as sadistic, cruel, and destructive acts. In the emerging Oedipus complex everything the child learns about the parent's sexual life, especially anything experienced suddenly, is implicated in the development of the Oedipus complex and gives it its unique coloration and texture. Furthermore, the frenzied excitement creates the impression that sexuality is dangerous. An experience like this establishes a connection between the ideas of sexual excitation and danger which may last for life. When uncanny sensations come up in adults they are experienced not as something totally new and strange, but on the contrary as the return of something old and disgusting which had been repressed long ago. When uncanny feelings arise the analysts like to say "primal scene material is approaching."

Let us now consider the uncanny dreams of the other young Russian ex-student in his twenties. In his first dream of the beating of the little mare he identifies with the mare, "embracing her blood stained muzzle, kissing her on the eyes, on the lips" in images that seem very much like Oedipal love. Like Freud's Wolfman, who also had obsessive fantasies of beating a horse, Raskolnikov's Oedipal feeling is colored with sadistic and masochistic impulses. Like the Wolfman's, Raskolnikov's dream is presented ambiguously, as if it really happened. The Wolfman's window suddenly went up; Raskolnikov's mother cannot now take him away from the window. Recalling Freud's dictum that such ambiguity does, in fact, indicate an event from real life, we recognize that the dream event from the age of seven may be a screen memory of a still earlier event from the real life of childhood. It is this event, the primal scene, which is represented by Raskolnikov's second dream of cruelty and violence:

> He was awakened in the dead of night by a terrible scream ... never in his life had he heard such unnatural sounds. Such howls; such shrieks, sobs, blows and curses. He could not imagine such

> brutality, such frenzy. He raised himself in terror and sat up in bed panting with agony.... He suddenly recognized the voice of his landlady ... beseeching someone to stop beating her ... suddenly Raskolnikov shook like a leaf. He had recognized the voice; it was the voice of the assistant superintendent ... and he was beating the landlady!

We have now come full circle and returned to the man Raskolnikov made his confession to: the man who miscalled him "Rodion Ro—Rodionovich," forgetting his patronym with the uncanny implication that Raskolnikov is his own father. Participating in Raskolnikov's dreadful terror, we recall Svidrigaylov's question—"am I a monster or myself the victim?"—the question which applies to every character in the novel. As we enter Raskolnikov's dream we recognize that all the peasants took part in the beating of the old mare, perhaps those serfs who in 1839 beat Dostoievsky's father to death. Since the whole town participates in the guilt, it is clear that murder is a shared and collective act. As Raskolnikov's last dream of the epilogue foretells, the whole world becomes ravaged in the illimitable future. Men become mad and kill each other, in senseless fury, raising armies against each other, devouring each in the name of political convictions and creeds they take to be infallible. This is terribly close to a prophetic vision of the tragedies we have recently witnessed. Feeling our own complicity, we ask ourselves Svidrigaylov's question: Are we monsters or ourselves the victim? Tragic pity and terror are not inspired by the idea that the hero is ill-fated, star-crossed, or simply unlucky; nor is it coincidence and fate which cause the murder of innocents like Lisavetta. The conflict is within our own nature, psychically divided against itself, dual and destructive. The crime and punishment must be our own.

Notes

1. Wellek and Warren, *Theory of Literature* (New York, 1942), p. 87.
2. "The World of *Crime and Punishment*" in the *Norton Critical Edition* (New York, 1975), p. 569.
3. "Raskolnikov's Three Motives," in the *Norton Critical Edition* (New York, 1975), p. 586.

R.E. RICHARDSON

Svidrigailov and the "Performing Self"

At the beginning of part 6 of Fedor Dostoevskii's *Crime and Punishment* the protagonist Raskol'nikov, having committed a double ax murder for profit, is disturbed by a nagging thought, namely that he must soon decide on a future course of action. He symbolizes his choice by two names: "Better Porfirii ... or Svidrigailov?" Porfirii Petrovich is the police magistrate who in Raskol'nikov's mind represents the way of confession, punishment, and expiation. Porfirii is the path to a return to conservative law and order and normal social contact with ordinary humanity. Svidrigailov is the profligate gentleman whose example, if followed, would further and finally isolate Raskol'nikov from humanity and turn him into a sinister and self-willed Man of Bronze. In his own formulation, Svidrigailov describes Raskol'nikov's choice thus: "Rodion Romanovich has two ways open to him: a bullet through the head, or Siberia" (PSS 385; C 463).[1] Ultimately Raskol'nikov chooses Porfirii and a Siberian prison term, but the battle in his mind proves tortured and difficult.[2]

Traditional criticism makes Svidrigailov an evil character. As one popular interpreter has it, Svidrigailov is "a monster of wickedness" who "leads the camp of Evil in *Crime and Punishment*."[3] Yet because of the complexity and expansiveness of his portrait in the novel we must see Svidrigailov as more than a melodramatic villain. It is not by chance that Dostoevskii spends so much energy and ingenuity in making Svidrigailov the

From *Slavic Review* 46, no. 3/4 (Autumn–Winter 1987).

wittiest, most whimsical, ironic, and paradoxical character in the novel. We may have difficulty imagining Arkadii Svidrigailov as a comic hero, but it is just as hard to see him as a "wholly serious character."[4] Raskol'nikov calls him a "vile, disgusting, salacious creature" (PSS 371; C 463). Yet no sooner does he leave the company of "that hardened scoundrel, that debauched, licentious brute" than he begins to reconsider, for "there was something about Svidrigailov that was at least out of the ordinary, if not mysterious" (PSS 374; C 467).

Svidrigailov suffers from numerous flaws in his character, but the two most pronounced are his excessive sensuality and existential boredom. It is these twin stalking horrors that dominate Svidrigailov's life in the novel and give him his special role.

It is an understatement to say that Svidrigailov is a mysterious man.[5] At first glance his outward appearance is above average and even attractive (PSS 188; C 234):

> He was a man of about fifty, rather tall, stout, with wide sloping shoulders that gave him a round-shouldered look. He was stylishly but comfortably dressed, and had an air of a great gentleman. He carried an elegant cane, with which he tapped the pavement at every step, and his gloves were newly cleaned. His broad face, with its high cheekbones, was pleasant enough, and his complexion had a fresh color that did not belong to St. Petersburg. His hair, which was very fair, was still thick, and had only the merest touch of grey in it; his thick, wide, spade-shaped beard was even lighter in color than his hair. His blue eyes had a cold, watchful, considering look; his lips were very red. He was altogether remarkably well-preserved, and looked much younger than his years.

There are in this portrait of Svidrigailov obvious elements of theatricality. Svidrigailov is theatrical in his bearing and he uses tricks of the theater to create a self-conscious and dramatic image of himself. His stylish clothes, elegant cane, and newly cleaned gloves represent his credentials and give him an image of superficiality that is later shown to be false. These symbols of foppishness tilt the reader toward a purely intellectual apprehension of the character of Svidrigailov, but these first impressions will later be contradicted.

Although the relevant issues remain disguised, Raskol'nikov nonetheless discerns another and less innocent and less neutral feature of Svidrigailov's handsome appearance. Svidrigailov had "a rather strange face, almost like a mask: red and white, with a very light-colored beard and still quite abundant fair hair. The eyes seemed somehow too blue, and their gaze too massive and unmoving. There was something terribly unpleasant in the handsome face, so extraordinarily young for its years" (PSS 357; C 449).[6]

This mask allows Svidrigailov to play his assigned role as an incarnation of evil and a vulgarian. Svidrigailov has, in a sense, become the victim of exaggerated and distorted reports, which, as is typical in Dostoevskii, degenerate into rumors. Like so many other characters, especially women, in Dostoevskii's novels, Svidrigailov has been slandered irrevocably; he decides to play the role to the hilt, engaging in gestures of self-dramatization. This, of course, is not the sole logical response to his position in society, but it is the one that seems to suit him best. He even admits to playing a role, but one in tune with his "natural tendencies" (PSS 217; C 272). His self-image is projected through symbols of decadent elegance: his fancy cane, his clean gloves, his "foppishly elegant" linen, his large ring set with a valuable stone.

Svidrigailov is largely absent from the plot of the novel. His involvement in the story takes place largely at some remove in time, and in the main we learn about him only tangentially in others' accounts of past events. Arkadii Ivanovich Svidrigailov enters the text indirectly through Raskol'nikov's mother's letter to her son in part 1. Raskol'nikov's sister, Dunia, had been the object of indecent proposals from Svidrigailov while she was in the employ of him and his wife, Marfa Petrovna. The ensuing scandal ended in Marfa Petrovna's complete indictment of her husband and his lecherous ways. One rumor leads to another, half-truths are inflated out of proportion, and Svidrigailov becomes "mad, bad, and dangerous to know."[7]

Svidrigailov's reputation as an odious and evil man is the product of a rather primitive provincial mythmaking on the part of the vulgar and superstitious inhabitants of the Russian countryside where his wife's estate is located. Svidrigailov's arrival as a rank stranger among the bored and gossipy rural vulgarians must have sparked lively and imaginative speculations about his past, present, and future. Why does a sophisticated, healthy, handsome, and relatively young man who has a professed preference for a life of freedom in the city agree to marry a definitely older woman with bad breath ("she was always chewing a clove or something" [PSS 363; C 453]) and move to her country estate to live on a very short tether? The incongruity of Svidrigailov's surrender to such circumstances cannot fail to generate creative and outrageous gossip. After all, this small, circumscribed, and petty world fed on rumors and scandal, and was always hungry for more nutrition. Someone like Svidrigailov who comes into their midst with no professional or civil responsibilities immediately arouses fear and envy in small minds.

The ground in these Russian backwaters is fertile for the seeds of slander, and inevitably Svidrigailov becomes the target of loose tongues.

Typical of the grossly exaggerated and inflated responses to Svidrigailov are the circumstances surrounding his "extravagant passion" for Dunia Raskol'nikov which resulted in his "dishonest proposals" to her (Dunia's mother's words).[8] Marfa Petrovna overhears a conversation in which her husband asks Dunia for certain favors. Jumping to conclusions Marfa Petrovna dismisses Dunia and sends her away. The reaction, according to Dunia's mother (PSS 29; C 30):

> The whole town talked of the scandal for weeks, and things got to such a pitch that Dunia and I could not go to church because of the contemptuous looks we got, and the whispering, and even remarks made aloud in our presence. None of our acquaintances would have anything to do with us, they even cut us in the street, and I learned for a fact that some shop assistants and junior clerks planned to insult us in the basest manner by smearing the gates of our house with tar, so that the landlord began to press us to leave the flat.

The chief source of overheated rhetoric about Svidrigailov's conduct is his wife ("she is rather garrulous and likes to talk about her domestic affairs and complain about her husband to all and sundry" [PSS 29; C 30]). In this case she spends a month going about the town and district disseminating details about the scandal between her husband and Dunia (PSS 29; C 30).

Petr Petrovich Luzhin, a distant relative of Mrs. Svidrigailov and a suitor of Dunia, is "a wretched scandal-monger" (to use Dunia's words) who also loses no opportunity to malign Svidrigailov. Luzhin has followed with gleeful interest all the accusations against Svidrigailov and is particularly anxious to embellish these rumors and harden them into facts. Luzhin's motives in discrediting are often just another manifestation of his paranoia that Raskol'nikov, Dunia, and Svidrigailov are plotting against him (PSS 230; C 288). Constantly on guard to avoid "exposure" (of what?) and "denunciation" (by whom? to whom?) Luzhin spends much of his energy trying to besmirch the reputations of others, including Svidrigailov, Lebeziatnikov, and Sonia Marmeladova.

Another minor source of misinformation about Svidrigailov is Raskol'nikov's mother, Pul'kheria Aleksandrovna. Like so many other characters in the novel she has a definite "passion for trivial gossip" (Raskol'nikov's phrase for his mother), a good portion of which is directed at Svidrigailov whom she has never met.[9]

Since Svidrigailov does not actually appear until half way through the novel, the reader rather expects to know him only from a distance. But unexpectedly he shows up in St. Petersburg and for reasons that are unclear decides to visit Dunia's brother. He is supposed to have driven to his death a serf on his wife's estate, and widespread public opinion has implicated him in the untimely death of his wife. It is, therefore, understandable that at their first meeting Raskol'nikov is surprised to find Svidrigailov "almost excessively amiable" (PSS 217; C 272), not at all what he had expected, given Dunia's evaluation: "He's a horrible man? I can't imagine a worse" (PSS 175; C 219).

Svidrigailov is friendly, even cheerful, and frank about his personal life; so much so that Raskol'nikov feels free to press him for details about his past. Svidrigailov admits candidly that he drank and gambled to excess and that these vices put him into a position of dependency on his wife, who was, he stresses, considerably older than he, and whom he had married as part of a bargain involving her payment of his gambling debts.

Svidrigailov seems eager, even relieved, to discuss the circumstances surrounding his wife's death: He has concluded that he in no way contributed to the death of Marfa Petrovna. "The medical inquiry revealed apoplexy, as a result of bathing immediately after a heavy meal accompanied by almost a bottle of wine, and indeed there was nothing else it could have shown" (PSS 215; C 270).

As for the rumors that he beat Marfa Petrovna, he admits that he gave her a couple of blows with a riding switch ("Marfa Petrovna may even have been pleased at this evidence of passion, so to speak" [PSS 216; C 270]), but the incident does not resemble the tyrannical sadism it was made out to be. In this account the real tyrant in the relationship seems to have been the wife, who imposed strict controls and rules on his behavior and activities. Later, in a third and final conversation with Raskol'nikov, Svidrigailov reveals the details of a verbal contract between himself and his wife, a contract comprising six points. Like so much else about Svidrigailov, his marriage arrangements were a parody of what one would expect of the institution in an Orthodox society. Only the first point resembles usual marriage vows, since it pledged him never to leave Marfa Petrovna. The other five points spell out in detail the terms under which Svidrigailov could indulge in limitless infidelity. The final point was a promise to disclose to Marfa Petrovna any "great and serious passion" (PSS 363; C 453). Within this framework the Svidrigailovs continued their uneasy, but far from stormy, marriage for seven years and through the births of a couple of children.

In spite of the aura of mystery and alleged sadism that surrounded Svidrigailov's life, there is little corroboration of extraordinary events in the family. Even Dunia Raskol'nikova, whose pleasure at revenge on Svidrigailov would likely be great, is quick to set straight the record against her attempted seducer. Svidrigailov exhibited no undue aggression in her presence, she says. As for Marfa Petrovna, "He was always very patient and very polite with her. There were many times when he was even too indulgent with her, during those seven years" (PSS. 175; C 219).

Lest his reputation as a mystic flag, Svidrigailov, during his first meeting with Raskol'nikov, is anxious to relate how Marfa Petrovna's ghost has appeared to him on three separate occasions. In Gothic novels ghost stories are a natural part of the trappings and usually function to increase the atmosphere of evil and danger, to warn of impending personal disaster. Svidrigailov's ghost stories are, however, trivial and humorous. On her funeral day Marfa Petrovna comes as a wraith to her husband to remind him to wind the dining-room clock. Her second appearance is with a deck of cards in her hands; she offers to tell his fortune for his trip to St. Petersburg. Svidrigailov prattles on: "She was very good at telling fortunes. I shall never forgive myself for not letting her tell it. I took fright and hurried away; it is true that the bell went just then" (PSS 220; C 276). The third encounter with Marfa Petrovna's ghost is no less absurd. She comes to ask his opinion of an new green silk dress with a long train. This time Svidrigailov becomes more assertive and asks for an explanation: "What makes you go to all the trouble of coming to me for such trifles?" She replies whimsically: "Good gracious, my dear, it's getting impossible to disturb you about anything!" (PSS 220; C 276). Svidrigailov continues by teasing his dead wife about his plans for marrying again, but she warns him of the folly of such an undertaking, adding, "and nice people will laugh at you" (PSS 220; C 276).[10] Not surprisingly, Raskol'nikov is unimpressed by Svidrigailov's tales of the macabre and remains skeptical of this travesty of the supernatural, even suggesting that Svidrigailov may be making it all up.[11]

Svidrigailov promulgates an image of himself as eccentric by expressing provocatively and in great detail odd views of traditional historical institutions. He sees foreign travel, even to a setting as romantic and picturesque as the Amalfi coast of southern Italy, as boring and contemptible (PSS 218; C 274):

> I don't know why, but you look at the dawn breaking, the bay of Naples, the sea, and you are sad. The worst of it is, you know, that you really do grieve for something. No, better stay in your own country; here at least one can blame somebody else for everything and find excuses for oneself.

His *goûts particuliers* run more to the truly exotic and potentially dangerous. "Perhaps I might go on an expedition to the North Pole.... They say Berg is going to make an ascent in a great balloon on Sunday in the Yusupov Gardens, and that he will take passengers up for a consideration. Is that true?" (PSS 218; C 274). Svidrigailov likes to underscore his experimental and hypothetical view of things, throwing out whimsical and imaginative challenges to those around him. When offering his own thoughts on life after death during a conversation with Raskol'nikov, he eschews the traditional images of heaven and hell (PSS 221; C 277).

> Eternity is always presented to us as an idea which it is impossible to grasp, something enormous, enormous! But why should it necessarily be enormous? Imagine, instead, that it will be one little room, something like a bathhouse in the country, black with soot, with spiders in every corner, and that that is the whole of eternity. I sometimes imagine it like that you know.

His "What if?" proposition about eternity has a kind of Dostoevskian estrangement about it. But there is also a reverse process to Svidrigailov's hypothetical afterlife. Instead of elaborate Dantesque images of physical torture he suggests—with comic bathos—that eternity might offer a worse fate than bodies racked with pain and corporal suffering—it might be unspeakably boring!

As an amateur psychologist Svidrigailov has developed strong and bizarre opinions about human behavior, particularly about that of women. He suggests, even insists, that women are more vulnerable to affrontery, pity, and flattery. As weapons to manipulate human female conduct, these are failure proof: "it sometimes happens that women are highly gratified at being outraged, in spite of their apparent indignation. It happens with everybody: mankind in general loves to be affronted, have you noticed? But especially women. You might almost say it's their only amusement" (PSS 216; C 271). But if "the amusement of affrontery" does not work in a given situation, Svidrigailov goes on to say that pity will almost always turn the trick (PSS 365; C 455):

> when a girl's heart begins to feel pity for a man, then of course she is in the greatest danger. She begins to want to save him, and make him see reason, and raise him up, and put before him nobler aims, and awaken him to a new life and new activities—well, everybody knows what can be dreamt of in such circumstances.

For Svidrigailov the usual and normal emotions of human relations are merely stakes in a no-limit game, cards to be played and trumped recklessly and with bluff and bravado if possible. According to him the most useful card and the one surest of winning is flattery, for which he has worked out an elaborate and cynical theory (elaborate because of its subtlety and cynical because of the use to which he puts it). In fact flattery is "the greatest and most reliable means of subjugating a woman's heart, which never disappoints anybody and always produces a decisive effect on every single woman, without exception" (PSS 366; C 456).

Svidrigailov cannot refrain from relating to Raskol'nikov how he used gross and outrageous flattery (more role-playing) to seduce a virtuous lady who was devoted to her husband, to her children, and to her virtue. "What fun it was, and how little trouble! ... And how angry she was with me when at long last I told her that in my honest opinion she had been seeking satisfaction just as much as I had" (PSS 366; C 457).[12]

Much of Svidrigailov's exaggerated bravado ("I like my sewers filthy" [PSS 370; C 462]) is directed toward potential sexual targets; but, like so much else about Svidrigailov, his sexual tastes and habits are more in the realm of theory and hypothesis than in the realm of reality. Consequently, they are much less nefarious than Raskol'nikov's idea. He laughs when relating to Raskol'nikov a strange encounter with a thirteen-year-old girl and her mother at a dance. The mother and daughter had just arrived in St. Petersburg and had showed up at the dance by mistake, thinking it was really a dancing class. It turned out to be "a horrible den ... and, of course, there was a cancan of a unheard-of kind, such as there never was in my day. Yes, sir, there has been progress there," says Svidrigailov sarcastically (PSS 370; C 462). The young girl becomes confused and embarrassed by the suggestive and insulting activities to the point that she begins to cry. Svidrigailov is amused by the consternation of the newcomers and offers them help by paying for lessons in French and dancing, an offer which they accept. The whole affair has become a kind of elaborate practical joke.

Svidrigailov leaves it to Raskol'nikov to divine the motivations for his actions, as well as the implications for the outcome of their relationship ("a very curious story, that is not finished yet" [PSS 370; C 462]). He frankly admits to Raskol'nikov that he is telling him such stories on purpose, "to hear [Raskol'nikov's] outcries" (PSS 371; C 463). The details are so elaborate and realistic—even naturalistic—that Raskol'nikov does protest, and Svidrigailov achieves the reaction he was seeking. A large part of the effect comes from Svidrigailov's style of speech, which is witty, inventive, and engaging.

It is difficult to know just what Raskol'nikov's real feelings are toward Svidrigailov's breezy "confessions" about the young girls in his life. He listens patiently and probably with a certain fascination, and his protests are trite and stock. At any rate he apparently begins at this point to believe the stories and accuses Svidrigailov of indulging his sensual appetites and of behaving monstrously. The obvious irony here is that Raskol'nikov's appetites are, while purely intellectual, even more monstrous. How dare Raskol'nikov accuse anyone of self-indulgence?

The centerpiece of Svidrigailov's "debauchery" is his impending marriage to a sixteen-year-old girl from a poor family in need of financial help. Svidrigailov implies that the idea of marriage and a second family does not really appeal to him, but the young girl is too great a temptation. Still in short skirts, with fair hair, rosy lips, and tiny feet, this "unopened bud" creates in Svidrigailov an uncontrollable desire to fantasize. In fact, he asserts that his "present condition, of being betrothed, is perhaps really better than marriage" (PSS 369; C 461).

In spite of Svidrigailov's lurid account of how this nameless Nabokovian "nymphet" blushed and wept when he unceremoniously took her on his knee, the relationship, if not in the narration at least in fact, is proper and even avuncular for his part. Svidrigailov's lechery is playful, with the quality of a game about it. He is simply enjoying vicariously what Vladimir Nabokov was later to call "the perilous magic of nymphets."[13] He has no intention of taking advantage of the girl and is more interested in the situation and the reaction of the parents. It seems to amuse him to watch these simple but burdened people grovel and scramble for a rich man's patronage. It excites him to think of the *potential* (not *actual*) power he exerts over a young, intelligent, but melancholy, girl.

The nameless girl is confused and nervous, saddened by the thought of future events that she cannot understand and for which she is not prepared. But all comes to nothing when Svidrigailov shows up at their apartment in the rain the night before he kills himself. To make up for the anxiety he has caused the girl he leaves her 15,000 rubles in silver. The entire anticlimactic extent of Svidrigailov's corrupting influence has included, besides some uncertainty, some mystery, and a little tension, a legacy of jewelry, and a small fortune in negotiables. The whole episode is a kind of elaborate practical joke; Svidrigailov comes in the guise of a seducer and corrupter, but he leaves as a benefactor, bestowing enough money so that the girl can in the future avoid unwelcome attention from men with more sinister and less whimsical designs. His action is an ironic parallel to Raskol'nikov's plans for philanthropy. Svidrigailov at least used his own money.

Svidrigailov's joke is a prelude to another kind of parody, his suicide. Almost all commentators agree on this point of Svidrigailov's place in the novel. The suicide is stylistically Gogolian, suggests Donald Fanger, for example:

> His suicide ... is described in comic terms, and the purity of comic effect is preserved by closing the scene with the pulling of the trigger: we do not hear the shot or see the body fall; his death is no more meaningful or real than his life; he can as it were, vanish but not die. In other words, this figure, inaccessible to any hope of spiritual redemption, is presented as also inaccessible to any large degree of sympathy from the reader—in accordance with the demands of the comic.[14]

It is difficult to say for sure whether suicide for Svidrigailov is a nonsensical gesture of metaphysical despair or an attempt at archaic heroics. He spends the early part of his final evening making the rounds of various brothels and taverns, where he buys drinks for all, including two little clerks. His taste for the absurd is still acute, since his generosity toward them is explained by his fascination with their noses: "They both had crooked noses, one twisted to the right and the other to the left. Svidrigailov was much struck with this circumstance" (PSS 383; C 478). In either case, Dostoevskii meets "the demands of the comic," especially and particularly in the preparatory scenes.

Eventually, Svidrigailov seeks out a squalid, down-at-the-heels hotel, very likely a brothel. He is given a cramped and stuffy room under the stairs; a ragged and seedy waiter brings him an odd meal of tea and veal. Before drinking the hot tea to warm himself, Svidrigailov cannot refrain from engaging in a little eavesdropping on his neighbors in the adjoining room. As he looks through a crack in the wooden walls he studies a scene that is Gogolian in its comic irrelevance to everything that is happening in his life. There are two guests in the room (PSS 389; C 484):

> One, in his shirt sleeves, a man with extraordinarily curly hair and inflamed red face, stood in the post of a public speaker, with his legs wide apart to preserve his balance, and pathetically, beating his breast, reproached the other for his beggary and lack of social standing, and reminded him that he had plucked him out of the gutter and could drive him back there when he would, and that only the finger of God sees everything. The object of the tirade sat on the chair with the expression of a man with an irresistible desire to sneeze which he cannot gratify. He glanced occasionally at the orator with a dull and sheepish eye, but he plainly had no idea what the trouble was and it was even doubtful whether he heard anything that was said. On the table, where the candle had nearly burned down, stood an almost empty decanter of vodka,

> glasses, bread, cucumbers, tumblers, and a long-emptied tea service.

Like characters from a Gogolian story the two *louche* gentlemen in the next room provide Svidrigailov and the reader with a momentary diversion and the opportunity to speculate further on the circumstances and biographies of two gratuitous and totally extraneous characters. The wealth of detail increases and there is a feeling of curiosity about a scene that proves to be irrelevant to the future focus of the chapter and its story, again underscoring the incongruity of Svidrigailov's immediate position and state of mind.

The depressing and absurd wretchedness of his surroundings begins to annoy Svidrigailov ("the room felt stuffy, the candle burnt dimly, the wind howled outside, a mouse scratched somewhere in a corner, and the whole room smelt of mice and some kind of leather" [PSS 389; C 484–485]) as he concentrates on what to do next: "You would think I ought to be quite indifferent to all these questions of aesthetics and comforts now, and here I have grown as particular as a wild animal fastidiously choosing a place ... He, he! Are pleasant sensations so nearly essential to me" (PSS 389–390; C 485).

The remainder of the night Svidrigailov tries to sleep and suffers nightmares, one about a young girl of about fourteen who has drowned herself and another about a cold and frightened little girl of no more than five whom he helps to bed after bringing her in from the rain. But Svidrigailov's dream of a sentimental gesture of help proffered to a suffering child quickly and dramatically becomes a nightmare of perversion—the child's, not Svidrigailov's (PSS 393; C 489–490):

> Suddenly it seemed to him that the long black lashes stirred and fluttered as though they were about to lift, and from under them looked, with an unchildlike wink, a shy, sharp eye, as though the child were not asleep, but only pretending. Yes, it was true; her lips parted in a smile; the corners of the mouth quivered, as if she were still restraining herself. But now she had ceased to control herself at all, and it was a laugh, a downright laugh, an impudent invitation gleamed from that unchildlike face; it was corruption, it was the face of a courtesan, the brazen face of a mercenary French harlot. Now without further concealment, both eyes were open, enveloping him with their shameless, burning glance, inviting him, laughing.... There was something monstrous and infinitely offensive in that laugh, in those eyes, in all that nastiness in the face of a child.

The sequence is ironic and reverses the normal expectations. No good deed goes unpunished, and, for his sentimental and compassionate involvement with the little girl, Svidrigailov is subjected to an attempted seduction by a five-year old. Listening to some inner moral tuning fork Svidrigailov curses the little girl and raises his arm to strike her. But why? Why is Svidrigailov ready to punish her brazenness? Is it perhaps that he is highly sentimental and not a brutal scoundrel? Perhaps the "French harlot's" smile is Dostoevskii's as he takes away the final challenge, the final layer of Svidrigailov's quest for escape from boredom and banality.

Fully awake now, Svidrigailov faces the difficult problem of how to find an appropriate death. His plan includes going to the Petrovskii Island, but, as he makes his way past run-down and depressing wooden houses, he sees here a dirty, shivering dog, there a drunk, face down on the pavement, and concludes: "This is a good enough place; why go to Petrovskii" (PSS 394; C 491). In what Robert Payne calls Svidrigailov's "last contemptuous bow to conformity,"[15] he decides—almost smiling—to shoot himself in front of a tall watchtower ("At least there will be an official witness," he reasons [PSS 394; C 491]). This official witness turns out to be a Jewish fireman wearing a copper helmet that makes him look like Achilles from the *Iliad.*

Svidrigailov's final dramatic gesture is to make a private joke about going to America. "If you are asked, say I said I was off to America," requests Svidrigailov, while Achilles dully and mechanically repeats in broken Russian "This is not the right place" [*zdesia ne mesta*] (PSS 394; C 491). "America is [Svidrigailov's] bleak private fancy, the loneliest of witticisms."[16]

One recent critic sees Svidrigailov's death as a kind of parody of his military background and regimental past.[17] A subtler, more Dostoevskian irony, however, exists in Svidrigailov's confrontation with Achilles. "And what could more graphically illustrate the utter inanity of existence merely for the sake of existence than his meeting with the Jew who for centuries has been leading a shadow-like existence, the Wandering Jew![18]

In an earlier conversation with Raskol'nikov's sister, Dunia, Svidrigailov offered his own characterization of the Russian mind, implying that the analysis was particularly applicable to himself. "the minds of the Russian people in general are broad, Avdotia Romanovna, like their country, and extraordinarily inclined to the fantastic and the chaotic; but it is disastrous to have a broad mind without special genius" (PSS 378; C 472). The ironic paradox of the Russian mind—expansive, but without particular ambition or ability—is arguably the source for much of Svidrigailov's unexplained and enigmatic laughter throughout the novel.[19] Like Raskol'nikov, Svidrigailov never engages in true social laughter. His is a private laughter of internalized vision, based on irony; Svidrigailov's laughter is not humane. It is generated by compulsive hostility and underscores his scorn and contempt for those around him. Normally social laughter brings relief from tension and invites a gesture of shared triumph or victory. Svidrigailov's laughter is never infectious, first because it is private (to outsiders there is nothing, objectively, to laugh at), and second because spectators are not invited to participate. There is, furthermore, a cruel intellectual quality about Svidrigailov's laughter. He is often witty, but it is a wit that increases tension and torment. Believing in Raskol'nikov's "Russianness," for instance, Svidrigailov can only laugh at his clumsy attempts to rescue others (in fact, it is Svidrigailov who actually saves the Marmeladov children through charity), and it amuses him to deflate in whatever way he can Raskol'nikov's heroic claim on the world. Like Raskol'nikov, Svidrigailov is ready to use the world and its material comforts. Unlike Raskol'nikov, he perceives the irony of his position, for he sees no way the world might use him. Svidrigailov never suggests that his type is outmoded; he just makes fun of any effort to verify it. As he watches and measures his own participation in extraneous events, what he somehow fears most is the charge of banality. Not uncontaminated by human contrivance, Svidrigailov tries to avoid indictment on this score by creating an artificial and theatrical "performing self,"[20] a kind of self-parody.

In only one scene in *Crime and Punishment* is Svidrigailov's sensuality displayed in action and without fatuity. It is a most serious, intense, and carefully constructed scene in part 5, chapter 5, as Svidrigailov tries to seduce or, if it should come to that, rape Dunia Raskol'nikova. The plan is to blackmail Dunia into submission, using knowledge of her brother's crime. Svidrigailov's plot is well planned, and at first luck is on his side. Against her better judgment, Dunia accompanies Svidrigailov to his rooms alone. Once inside Svidrigailov talks in an uncharacteristically agitated and disjointed manner. So much is riding on this meeting (he realizes that it is his last chance to clarify his relationship with Dunia), and he has so much to think about that his strategy is almost self-defeating. Moreover, both Svidrigailov and Dunia have aces hidden up their sleeves: He has locked the door and pocketed the key; she has brought a loaded gun.

Svidrigailov wastes little time in confronting Dunia with the evidence that her brother is a double ax murderer, but he somehow tries to soften the blow with an exceptionally articulate and almost convincing summary and defense of Raskol'nikov's "theory" and motives. Shocked by what she has heard, Dunia wants to leave but now finds the door locked. Svidrigailov remarks that he only wanted privacy. "After all, we couldn't shout the subject of our conversation all over the place" (PSS 379; C 473). The next minute

Svidrigailov loses all control. "He was almost raving. It was as if something in his mind had suddenly given way" (PSS 380; C 474). Svidrigailov exclaims (PSS 380; C 474):

> You ... one word from you and he is saved! I ... will save him. I have money, friends. I will get him away at once, and I will get a passport, two passports. One for him, the other for me. I have friends, practical people.... Would you like me to get another passport for you ... for your mother? ... What need have you of Razumikhin? I love you so ... I love you infinitely. Let me kiss the hem of your dress, let me. Let me! It is more than I can bear to hear it rustle. Say to me, "Do this!" and I will do it. I will do anything. I will do the impossible. Whatever you believe in, I will believe in too. I will do anything, anything. Don't look at me like that, don't! I tell you, you are killing me.

Svidrigailov's lust for Dunia has flared and he can no longer conduct himself with his usual urbanity born of disinterest. Frightened by Svidrigailov's aggression and fearing force, Dunia pulls out the revolver and threatens her captor, who is only stimulated and titillated by this welcome new dimension to the action. Ironically, Svidrigailov recognizes it as his gun, which he had actually taught Dunia how to use. At such moments the mind focuses on strange priorities, and Dunia insists on pointing out that the gun really belonged to Svidrigailov's wife: "There was nothing of yours in her house" (PSS 381; C 475).[21]

Finishing this "wild-west" scene "with more melodramatic exaggeration than artistic measure,"[22] Dostoevskii has Dunia shoot, grazing Svidrigailov slightly, pull the trigger again and misfire, and finally throw down the weapon. She is left to the tender mercies of her tormentor, who becomes more interested in spiritual rather than sexual love. "'So you do not love me?' [Svidrigailov] asked softly. Dunia shook her head. 'And ... you cannot? ... Not ever?' he whispered in despair. 'Never!' whispered Dunia" (PSS 382; C 477). Svidrigailov gives Dunia the key and recommends that she leave quickly. He looks out the window the whole time and "there was a strange smile on his face, the weak, pitiful, mournful smile of despair" (PSS 383; C 478). He takes the gun Dunia left behind, having decided to finish what she could not do.

In spite of the overheated action of the scene, there is an atmosphere of scrupulous realism and irony. Once again, the arch-villain Svidrigailov fails or refuses to live up to his reputation and press his strategic advantage over a female victim. Even his trump card, lust for Dunia, has failed him.

Svidrigailov's talk of love has been desperate and disjointed. After all, he can hardly know Dunia well enough to make a meaningful offer of marriage or permanence. Viacheslav Ivanov is probably right when he states that Svidrigailov is "incapable of love."[23] Svidrigailov is simply unable to fit into the convention of mutual love.

In the final analysis incongruity defines Svidrigailov, the disparity between appearance and reality. He is a man who arouses fear in those he comes in contact with, but in fact he is a man who is controlled by those who fear him. He leads a double life, seeming to exude evil, debauchery, and self-gratification, but in fact performing the only genuinely effective acts of charity and good will in the novel.[24] Finally, there is the incongruity of Svidrigailov, so easily condemned and hated, who, by the end of his role in the novel, has earned the respect and perhaps even gratitude of the reader who comes to know this Faustian character, a distant relation to the one Goethe called "part of that Power which eternally wills evil and eternally works good."

NOTES

1. Citations from *Crime and Punishment* are from volume 6 of F. M. Dostoevskii, *Polnoe sobranie sochinenii* (Leningrad, 1972–) and the Coulson translation, edited by George Gibian (New York; Norton, 1964). References are given in the text in parentheses as PSS and C followed by the page numbers.

2. The relationship between Raskol'nikov, Porfirii Petrovich, and Svidrigailov is emphasized structurally by the fact that Raskol'nikov has three substantial conversations with each of the other men.

3. Ronald Hingley, *The Undiscovered Dostoevsky* (London, 1962), pp. 97 and 93.

4. Ibid., p. 92.

5. Even the name *Svidrigailov* is ambiguous and unclear in its significance. There have been several elaborate attempts to make sense of this Russianized Lithuanian surname (cf. Richard Peace, *Dostoevsky: An Examination of the Major Novels* [Cambridge, 1971], p. 45 and p. 315n, as well as Charles E. Passage, *Character Names in Dostoevsky's Fiction* [Ann Arbor, 1982], pp. 61–62), but Sidney Monas is probably right when he says that "(Svidrigailov's) name does not yield to allegorical interpretation, although it suggests Polish-Lithuanian ancestry, like 'Dostoevsky,' and might hint at some hidden identification" (p. 539 of Monas's translation of *Crime and Punishment* [New York: Signet, 1968]). The Soviet editors of Dostoevskii's works note (PSS 7:367–368) that the name appears in some articles published in *The Contemporary* in 1861 and that the character is mischievous and from the provinces.

6. Perhaps Svidrigailov's ironic vision of life keeps him youthful. The mask image as it relates to Nikolai Stavrogin in Dostoevskii's novel *The Devils* is discussed by Joseph Frank in his essay "The Masks of Stavrogin," *The Sewanee Review* (Autumn 1969), pp. 660–691.

7. As is usual in Dostoevskian scandals facts are unimportant; the event is the thing. When Marfa Petrovna finally learns from a certain letter that Dunia is completely innocent ("Mr. Svidrigailov had a change of heart and repented" [PSS 29; C 31]) she loses no time in going public with the news. Mrs. Raskol'nikov reports (PSS 30; C 31-32) that she went

> to every house in the town and everywhere ...; she showed everybody Dunia's letter to Mr. Svidrigailov, read it aloud, and even allowed people to copy it (which seems to me to be going too far). She spent several days in going the rounds in this way, and some people began to complain that preference had been shown to others, and so turns were arranged, so that people were already waiting for her in each house, and everybody knew that on such-and-such a day she would be in such-and-such a place to read the letter. To every reading people came who had already heard both in their own homes and in other people's as well.

By one turn of the cards Dunia's position in society changes from public condemnation to universal respect.

8. "My information is exact ... [Svidrigailov] is the most depraved, the most completely abandoned to vice, even of people of his own kind.... Such, if you wish to know, is the sort of man he is" (PSS 227–228; C 285–286).

9. Mrs. Raskol'nikov is an interesting example of Dostoevskii's portraits of middle-aged nervous provincial women. She for instance has "presentments" that make her afraid that her son will fall into a well in St. Petersburg and drown like a certain Lieutenant Potanchikov whom she heard about in the provinces (PSS 173; C 216) or that she and Dunia will be crushed by a pianoforte being moved in the street as they are walking along (PSS 185; C 231).

10. Svidrigailov also admits to having been visited by the ghost of Filip, a servant of his who died under mysterious circumstances some years before (PSS 220; C 276). Luzhin is eager to implicate Svidrigailov in the man's death and insists that Filip "died of brutal ill-treatment," "driven, or rather persuaded, to his violent end by the ceaseless systematic persecution and punishment of Mr. Svidrigailov" (PSS 228; C 286). Curiously, Dunia quickly comes to Svidrigailov's defense in this case: "I only heard a very strange story about this Filip's being some sort of hypochondriac, a kind of home-grown philosopher, who, the servants said, 'read himself silly,' and about his having hanged himself more because of the mockery than because of the beatings of Mr. Svidrigailov" (PSS 228–229; C 286–287). Again, accusations against Svidrigailov remain vague and unconfirmed.

11. This and other trivial babble are reminiscent of the Gogolian narrator in Gogol"s humorous stories, maybe of the fatuity of Khlestakov.

12. What a nice foil to Raskol'nikov's totally serious preoccupation with ideas that Svidrigailov's schemes are totally superficial.

13. Vladimir Nabokov, *Lolita*, part 1, chapter 29. "I am not concerned with so-called 'sex' at all. Anybody can imagine those elements of animality. A greater endeavor lures me on: to fix once for all the perilous magic of nymphets."

14. Donald Fanger, *Dostoevsky and Romantic Realism: Study of Dostoevsky in Relation to Balzac, Dickens, and Gogol* (Cambridge, Mass., 1967), p. 233.

15. Robert Payne, *Dostoevsky: A Human Portrait* (New York, 1961), p. 209.

16. John Jones, *Dostoevsky* (Oxford, 1983), p. 222.

17. A. D. Nuttal, *Dostoevsky's "Crime and Punishment": Murder as Philosophic Experiment* (Brighton, 1978), p. 128.

18. A. Z. Steinberg, "Dostoevsky i evreistvo," *Versty* [Paris], no. 3 (1928), pp. 104–105. Translated and quoted by David I. Goldstein, *Dostoevsky and the Jews* (Austin, Texas, 1981), p. 53.

19. Smiling and laughing are characteristic gestures for Svidrigailov. For instance, he smiles sixteen times and laughs eighteen times during the novel. Both Svidrigailov's smiles and laughs are almost always qualified grammatically. The smiles are described as "strange," "vague," "mocking," "malicious," "condescending"; while he is shown laughing

"candidly," "heartily," "shortly," "uproariously," and "loudly." Contrary to Bergson's claim that "true" laughter is laughter of a group, implying a complicity with other laughers, Svidrigailov's laughter, though hearty and spontaneous, is private and never shared with or by those around him.

20. This term was coined and used by Richard Poirier in his indispensably original study, *The Performing Self* (New York, 1971). Characters in this performing self made have, according to Poirier's theory, three common aspects in their social behavior and in their perceptions of themselves as social beings. First, they treat any occasion as a scene or a stage to dramatize the self as performer. Second, their participation in social situations is superficial and only on the level of rendition rather than commitment or understanding; it is performance that matters—pacing, tone, juxtapositions. Finally, their performance becomes a curious exercise of power, as Poirier puts it, "curious because it is first so furiously self-consultive, so even narcissistic, and later so eager for publicity, love, and historical dimension" (p. 87).

21. At this point Dunia suddenly drops the formal, polite *you* pronoun and addresses Svidrigailov in the familiar *thou* form.

22. Ernest J. Simons, *Dostoevsky: The Making of a Novelist* (London, 1940), p. 181.

23. Vyacheslav Ivanov, *Freedom and the Tragic Life: A Study in Dostoevsky* (New York, 1952), p. 82.

24. Svidrigailov offers 10,000 rubles to Dunia (PSS 223; C 279); he pays Mrs. Marmeladov's funeral expenses, makes arrangements for the Marmeladov orphans, and settles a substantial amount on each of them, as well as on Sonia (PSS 334; C 418). As mentioned above, his sixteen-year-old betrothed gets a "trifling present" worth 15,000 rubles (PSS 386; C 482).

GILES MITCHELL

Pathological Narcissism and Violence in Dostoevskii's Svidrigalov

"It was fear, the ultimate fear of death, that made men mad."
—D. H. Lawrence

"He would willingly make of the Earth a Ruin of Lies / And swallow the World in one tremendous Yawning. / He is Ennui!"
—Baudelaire

I
EGO-IDEAL, APATHY, AND FEAR OF DEATH

Studies in the psychology of narcissism in its relation to fear of death have only recently begun,[1] but they provide the basis of a new analysis of Dostoevskii's most complex image of evil.[2] Svidrigalov is present in only about fifty-three pages of the novel, but "his shadow lies over *Crime and Punishment* long before he makes his actual appearance,"[3] and "he is so fascinating a character ... that he threatens to run away with the story."[4] By the time he appears, the reader knows that Svidrigalov has recently attempted to seduce Dunia while she is employed as governess in his house, thus causing her to lose her job. Later we learn from Svidrigalov and others that he is a sexual predator; that he may have caused the deaths of several people, including two children; that he has visual and auditory hallucinations

From *Canadian-American Slavic Studies* 24, no. 1 (Spring 1990).

of apparitions; and that he probably regards himself as a victim of women and thus innocent. We learn also that Svidrigalov is chronically bored and that he is still obsessed with Dunia, whom he plans to possess sexually either through seduction with money or coercion with the threat of revealing to the police his knowledge of Raskol'nikov's confession of murder to Sonia. Dunia rejects Svidrigalov's attempt at seduction, shoots at him twice, and then puts the gun down. Feeling pity for her momentarily, Svidrigalov asks her if she cannot give herself to him willingly. When she replies that she cannot, he rushes her out of his room in order to keep himself from seizing her. He pockets the pistol which Dunia has dropped and goes to Sonia to give her the ten thousand roubles with which he has tried to seduce Dunia. He has earlier performed similar acts of seeming generosity. He then goes to the house of his fiancee, where he leaves the last of his money, and then eventually to bed in a hotel, where he has nightmares until daybreak, when he shoots himself, although he is afraid of death. In the following essay I will discuss (1) his fear of death and his apathy; (2) his lust for Dunia and his role as victim; (3) his rage, his dream of innocence, and his suicide; (4) and finally, his pathologically omnipotent manipulation of time and eternity.

Before discussing death fear and apathy in Svidrigalov, it will be necessary to describe the typical ego-ideal of the narcissist. Pathological narcissism is a personality disorder characterized by intense, excessive, and sometimes fatal devotion to the ego-ideal. In the normal person, the ego is nourished by the ego-ideal, for it provides self-esteem and meaningfulness and supports a realistic moral sense. However, in pathological narcissism, aspirations and ideals become images of "perfection and omnipotence"[6] which weaken the ego so that in extreme cases such as Svidrigalov's, "one dies for one's ego-ideal rather than let it die."[6] This implacable and deadly allegiance to the ego-ideal is the core of Svidrigalov's psychology. Because the narcissist believes the ego-ideal to be more real and more powerful than the object world (the external world), the ego-ideal overwhelms the ego with its inordinate needs and demands. Thus the narcissist is "exploitive and sometimes parasitic," assuming the right "to control and possess others and to exploit them without guilt feelings."[7] The narcissist assumes the right to be "overtly violent and dangerous to other people's physical integrity."[8] The narcissist may present, as Svidrigalov does, "a surface which very often is charming and engaging," in order to conceal from self and others a "coldness and ruthlessness."[9] The emotional life of the narcissist "is shallow," containing "little empathy for the feelings of others."[10] However, the narcissist's grandiosity involves an "inordinate need for tribute from others,"[11] possibly a clue to the motive of some of Svidrigalov's seeming generosity.

I will attempt to show that Svidrigalov's narcissism is a flight from his humanness into grandiosity and omnipotency, that it is a flight from mortality and vulnerability, from "being in the world."[12] Narcissism is primarily "a flight from death."[13] For Svidrigalov, escape into narcissistic omnipotence justifies exploitiveness and allows, on the unconscious level, "a sense of being in control of death."[14] The narcissist's sadism may provide the "psychological safety [of] being beyond the fear of death."[15] In this regard Svidrigalov is atypical, for he is quite aware of his fear of death: "I am afraid of death and don't like to hear it spoken of."[16] I will argue that fear of death is the basic motive for Svidrigalov's sadistic version of eternity, and that his suicide, like the typical narcissistic suicide, is motivated by the wish to be "master of life and death."[17] Considering the universality of narcissism as a subject in literature, it is interesting to note that many twentieth century thinkers believe that death fear is the core fear, that "underneath all fears, fear of death is universally present,"[18] that "the anxiety of death is the source of all anxiety,"[19] and not, as Meyer points out, "a derivative of other anxieties."[20]

It is not surprising that Svidrigalov frequently refers to his boredom, for the narcissist is "chronically bored."[21] Greenson defines boredom as "a state of apathy,"[22] and "Apathy," like narcissism, "is a defense against the anxiety of death."[23] To put it another way, apathy is a way of avoiding an "overwhelming feeling of annihilation," to live "*as though dead* in order to avoid death"[24] (emphasis added). Apathy is a descent "into a vortex of non being in order to avoid being."[25] Svidrigalov believes that he lives, partially, in the world of the dead—the eternity of his apparitions. He says that when he dies he will enter "fully into that world" (244). The fact that Svidrigalov lives as though partially dead gives particular force to Singer's statement that apathy is "equivalent to a death experience"[26] and to Simmons' idea that Svidrigalov "gives one the eerie feeling of coming to grips with a human phantom."[27] In Petersburg, while waiting for a chance to possess Dunia, he is "bored to death" (240). The purpose, then, of sinking into apathy while waiting for a chance at Dunia is to delay or "to prevent ego dissolution and suicide," as Singer says in reference to his patients.[28]

The narcissist cannot overcome chronic apathy by engaging in empathic interests with other people,[29] for people are not sufficiently real. They are "devalued, shadowy images."[30] Svidrigalov has no social life. About his friends he says, "I won't go to see them. I was bored with them before" (240). To the narcissist the only reality is the ego-ideal. There is no place that Svidrigalov wants to be, for place is as unreal as people. His wife, Svidrigalov says, "suggested that I go abroad, seeing that I was bored," adding, "I had been abroad before, and I always hated it" (240). He then tells Raskol'nikov,

"There is nothing left for me to do" (240). Because of his boredom, Svidrigalov's consciousness is extremely narrow, so much so that Svidrigalov, like the typical narcissist, might be accurately described as being "partly unconscious"[31] in order to reduce the pain of being. For all people, "the final terror of self-consciousness is the knowledge of one's own death,"[32] but for the narcissist, consciousness is particularly difficult to tolerate. To deaden consciousness with apathy is to become increasingly haunted by feelings of annihilation and "intense feelings of emptiness."[33] One of the suicidal elements involved is that the narcissist intends for apathy to *disguise* emptiness, but when it is disguised it intensifies itself. It is "the exquisite fear of emptiness that accounts for its suicide potential."[34] Fear of death leads to apathy, and apathy leads to and tries to disguise emptiness. When Svidrigalov says, "There is nothing else left for me to do" (240), he reveals an almost unbearable feeling of emptiness. However, he is lying; he still plans to debauch Dunia, for "apathy provokes violence,"[35] and Svidrigalov hopes to renew his life by filling up his emptiness with Dunia's innocence.

III
SEDUCTION, COERCION, PITY, AND DESIRE

Svidrigalov has a pathological need to idealize his debauched predations in order to see himself as victim, as innocent. Debauchery, he says, is "something constant, based on nature, indeed, and not subject to fantasy, something that exists in the blood as an eternal flame, always ready to set one on fire, and not to be readily extinguished, for a long time to come, perhaps for many years" (397). Svidrigalov depends upon debauchery to keep himself alive: "If it were not for it, one might have to shoot oneself without more ado" (398). However, Svidrigalov wants more than mere existence; therefore, he invests his predations with the image of himself as a "romantic" (401)[36] and as a victim. At the back of Svidrigalov's need to see himself as a romantic victim is his equation between innocence and life itself, for Svidrigalov equates innocence with fullness of being. He equates emptiness with death. He believes that he loves Dunia; he desperately needs the power of innocence as a possession taken from a beautiful and highly moral virgin, for in his despair he cannot change himself and *become* innocent. Because he believes that he loves Dunia "infinitely" (417) and that he is therefore her victim, he cannot see his wish to seduce or to coerce her as a morally monstrous thing.[37]

Greenway says that in his confrontation with Dunia, Svidrigalov develops a moral sense so powerful that he "becomes incapable of seducing her."[38] He also becomes incapable of remaining alive: his "suicide confesses unbearable guilt."[39] I will argue that Svidrigalov lets Dunia out of his clutches for two reasons. One is that for a few seconds he pities her, and in this he shows only the *potentiality* for developing a moral sense. The other is that physical coercion would violate his image of himself as the innocent victim of a woman whose beauty has forced him to fall in love with her. To Svidrigalov, "the whole question" of his life is, "am I a monster or am I myself a victim?" (237).[40] Svidrigalov tells Dunia that she has victimized him in that if he did murder his wife, Dunia is "the cause" (419). Svidrigalov believes that she has victimized him simply in that he is attracted to her. This is the meaning of his telling her, "even in the country you did me more harm than I did you" (412), an accusation that ignores the fact that he caused her to lose her job as governess, thus exposing her to the depredations of Peter Luzhin. He blames her beauty for his behavior: "why was she so pretty? It was not my fault" (402), he says to Raskol'nikov. Never does he explicitly admit to the murder of his wife. The murder does not matter to him, partly because he regards Dunia as the real murderer. Therefore, about the death of his wife he can say, "my conscience is perfectly clear" (238). He feels about this murder as he does about the ones committed by Raskol'nikov, that to feel guilt over the murders he committed is "a lot of nonsense" (427). He says this *after* his confrontation with Dunia; therefore, it is difficult to agree with Greenway that Svidrigalov has developed a powerful moral sense as a result of that confrontation.[41] When speaking of the floggings he gave his wife, he says, "I am quite aware that I behaved atrociously and so on and so forth" (238), but he also says that some women enjoy being flogged and are "highly gratified at being outraged." That, he says, is "the truly humane view" (239). It follows, he believes, that he has "behaved atrociously" because he is a victim of his wife's wish to be flogged and of his own humanity. It is not likely that Svidrigalov is being facetious in describing his behavior as "humane," for he idealizes his innocence by idealizing his destructiveness, as the narcissist typically does, by "idealization of the omnipotent destructive parts of [the] self."[42]

In short, what Svidrigalov considers innocence is really sadism, hence his need to idealize and to vindicate his innocence. (The equation between sadism and innocence is not complete in Svidrigalov. If it were, he would be a psychopath who could not feel guilt on the unconscious level, and I will argue later that on this level Svidrigalov does feel guilt. As a psychopath, he would be incapable also of feeling pity for Dunia.) Innocence is also life to Svidrigalov, as I have suggested. The logic involved here is that sadistic human sacrifice (e.g., taking Dunia's life/innocence) would serve to assure Svidrigalov of "victory over death."[43] When he tells Dunia that if she refuses him sexually he will inform the police about Raskol'nikov's confession to

Sonia, she fires a pistol at him and wounds him slightly. When she attempts to shoot him a second time, the pistol misfires, and she flings it down. By refusing to kill him, she puts herself at his mercy, and it is at this point that he feels pity for her. So brief and so ambivalent is his pity that Svidrigalov hurries Dunia out of the room because he knows, and she knows—"Dunia understood" (420)—that he cannot control himself for more than a moment. Pity, for a moment, reveals what Merezhkovskii describes as a "potentiality for kindness"[44] in Svidrigalov, but it does not redeem him. Thinking about it later that night, he rejects it: "Oh, to the devil with it" (428). Furthermore, in thinking of his pity for Dunia, he does not feel it; he only remembers it. Svidrigalov will not nurture or transform himself with his pity because unresolved fear of death leads inevitably, in May's words, to rejection of "the human emotions of pity and love."[45] For Svidrigalov to rape Dunia would probably contradict the self-image he most favors, that of the charming sybarite who coolly, innocently, and even benevolently exploits women. A few critics have referred to Svidrigalov as a rapist, and perhaps rightly so, but there are only "rumors," according to Luzhin, who hates Svidrigalov, and no actual evidence of rape. Svidrigalov has always believed that any woman, even a "vestal virgin" (402), will yield to flattery. If he were able to seduce the infinitely desirable Dunia, he could then perceive her as having given up her innocence to him, an act which would enhance his idealization of his sadism as innocence. On the other hand, if he can succeed in inducing her to kill him he will have shown himself to be the innocent victim of a woman who is so murderously, "morbidly chaste" (402) that she would rather kill than love him. In any case, his moment of pity for Dunia is the one thing about Svidrigalov with which one's sympathies can actively connect. His pity, brief though it is and tainted with other feelings, enriches Svidrigalov's characterization and makes possible a complex response to him on the part of the reader, who is aware of Svidrigalov's desire to be loved and of his ignorance of what love is.[46]

Kiremidjian says that at the end of the novel Svidrigalov seems to realize that "only the gift of love will in fact regenerate him."[47] There may be some truth in this statement, as Svidrigalov's capacity for pity could indicate, but not much. Kiremidjian's idea is presumably based on Svidrigalov's saying that Dunia "might indeed have re-moulded me somehow ..." (428). However, to Svidrigalov love means the reciprocally dependent relationship of predator to prey; therefore, Dunia's love would have merely salved, as it were, the narcissistic wounds in his infantile images of power. The dreams that Svidrigalov has on the last night of his life make it quite clear that suicide is far more important to him than love. Unlike Raskol'nikov, Svidrigalov is incapable of considering the logical alternative to suicide: giving up the grandiose, idealized image of his destructiveness. He realizes that Dunia finds him so morally repugnant that she has tried to kill him in order to keep from being touched by him sexually. Therefore, in order to escape Dunia's crushing negation, he will give up his bodily life in order to preserve his narcissistic ego-ideal.

III
RAGE AND THE DREAM OF INNOCENCE

I will now attempt to show that Svidrigalov feels a terrible rage against Dunia, not only because she rejects him, but also because he needs her; and further, that this rage is unacceptable to him, that he must deny it. He denies it, I will argue, by splitting the image of Dunia into the two children of whom he dreams on the night before he commits suicide. These dreams deal with the central question of whether he is monster or victim. They show his unconscious knowledge of, as well as his distortions of, the truth.

In the first dream he is *victimizer*, in the second, *victim*. The first dream is set in a flower-filled garden in which there is a house, also filled with flowers, including white narcissi. In an upstairs room of this house, on tables shrouded with white satin, Svidrigalov finds a coffin lined with white silk and surrounded by wreaths of flowers. In the coffin lies a fourteen-year-old girl in a white tulle dress, her face "full of infinite unchildlike grief and immense bitterness" (429). Although Svidrigalov obviously sees this look on her face, he does not react to it in any way. The account of the dream merely says that "Svidrigalov knew her.... She was a suicide, drowned.... savagely wounded by the outrage that had horrified her young childish conscience" (429). We know that she is the girl sold to him by Madame Resslich. In the second dream Svidrigalov finds outside his door a five-year-old girl who is cold and wet, and who is crying out of fear of punishment for breaking a cup. Svidrigalov carries her to his bed, puts her into it, and wraps her in blankets. Suddenly he feels "heavy anger." "Here I am," he says, "getting myself involved!" (430). As he starts to leave the room, he notices that she is looking at him seductively, that she has the face of a "French courtesan" (431). When she raises her arms to put them around his neck, he raises his hand to strike her, calling her an "accursed creature!" (431). He then awakens, feeling "jaded and angry" (431).

In order to unlock the pathological content of these dreams, I should like to work with the tentative assumption that the two girls in these dreams represent the splitting of Dunia (and probably womankind) into "all good" and "all bad," for such "splitting is a major narcissistic defensive strategy."[48] Defensive splitting here has the purpose of *denying* anger and hatred against

Dunia. In dealing with the motives of the narcissist, it is crucially important to understand the function of unconscious anger, for the narcissist has "a hungry, enraged, empty self, full of impotent anger at a world which seems as hateful and revengeful as the [narcissist] himself."[49] In fact, the narcissistic personality consists "largely of defenses against this rage."[50] Svidrigalov dream-wishes to justify his unconscious anger. To do so, he uses the technique of projection, for he must show himself in his dream that Dunia, like the "all bad" child-prostitute, is corrupt and that she wishes to victimize him. Such "projection of oral rage ... is central in their [narcissists'] psychology."[51] Svidrigalov has depended upon Dunia to keep him alive, to make him believe that life is worth living; and he is not exaggerating when he tells her that by rejecting him she is denying him life: "You are killing me" (417). Such dependency makes the object (Dunia) "intensely hated."[52] Svidrigalov can keep this unacceptable hatred and anger unconscious by splitting it off from the innocent "all good" part of Dunia and displacing it onto an "all bad" part. In brief, splitting is a method of disguising rage.

Anger is typically a severe threat to the narcissist's self-esteem because narcissistic anger chronically expresses itself in "the extreme form of envy."[53] Envy is a threat to the narcissist because it is such a tormenting reminder of emptiness and need that it "can in extreme cases lead to suicide."[54] Like anger, envy always involves "hatred of the object"[55] because the object "seem[s] to have things they [narcissists] do not have."[56] It may seem odd to say that Svidrigalov feels envy, because there is no explicit evidence that he does. However, I will suggest that he envies Dunia her fullness of being, her life, which he equates with her innocence, as opposed to his emptiness, which he equates with death. It is certainly the innocence of his fiancee that attracts him to her: She is "an unopened bud" (405). She has a "little Madonna face ... like a Raphael Madonna's ... blushing with maidenly shame" (406). Her face, he adds, is also like that of the "Sistine Madonna" (406). Furthermore, the beginning of Svidrigalov's dream of the "good" Dunia (the girl whose death he caused) strongly indicates a buried and unbearable envy. I say this because before the girl enters this dream, Svidrigalov attempts to associate *her* symbol of innocence, whiteness, *with himself*. The setting of the dream is Whit Sunday, a day for wearing white, hence the name. Svidrigalov feels a sense of "longing," and "his mind began to dwell persistently on flowers" (428), among which he wishes to remain. "He particularly noticed great bunches of delicate white narcissi in jars in the window .... He was reluctant to leave them" (428–29), but he does leave them and go into the house, where he sees the dead girl, her coffin lined with white and placed on a table covered with a white cloth. The presence in the dream of Whit Sunday, the last Sunday of the Easter season, seems to indicate Svidrigalov's anguished and twisted longing for resurrection in an innocence[57] which he has possessed only by violating it.

A further reason for believing that the two girls in Svidrigalov's dreams are split images of Dunia is that the night's pre-dreaming begins with images of her which pervade and disturb Svidrigalov's mind: "Little by little the image of Dunechka as he had last seen her began to glimmer before him" (427). "I must," he says, "think of something else" (427), and what he thinks about is his conscious but self-deceptive belief that he has never felt much anger or hatred in his life—"I never greatly hated anybody" (427). His dream of the child-prostitute explicitly belies this statement. In this dream he is "heavy with anger," for getting "involved" (430). This anger erupts from the dream into consciousness when Svidrigalov awakens feeling "jaded and angry" (430). Immediately he goes outside and up the street and kills himself.

A crucial question to be considered next is how the narcissist's anger works in the unconscious logic of suicide. In narcissistic suicide, rage is ultimately turned against the self. Freud says that one reason for this action is "to control aggressiveness toward the outer world,"[58] an important consideration for Svidrigalov, for he wishes to preserve his image of innocence. This rage becomes suicidal when the more one checks aggressiveness "towards the exterior [world] the more severe—that is aggressive—he becomes in his ego ideal," which increases its "aggressiveness against his ego."[59] Such a situation "often succeeds in driving the ego into death."[60] Freud's statements do not, however, tell enough about the dynamics of this process. It is important to note that the narcissist has internalized (incorporated) the desired and hated objects (people, world) that have rejected him or her.[61] Then, because the objects of rage and desire have been internalized, the narcissist can destroy them by committing suicide.[62] The result is "the disappearance of the entire world";[63] thus the narcissist rebels against an existence made miserable by the fear of both death and life. For the narcissist, suicide is "the obvious way of taking revenge."[64] Paradoxically, then, rage will become the "internal saboteur" by which the narcissist will "love (himself) to death."[65]

On the conscious level, Svidrigalov has only a modicum of conscience (unlike Peter Luzhin, who seems to have none), but it is enough to allow him to formulate the central question of his life: whether he is victim or monster. The dream of the drowned girl originates in Svidrigalov's conscience, but he *rejects* its most obvious meaning with the dream of the child-prostitute, a dream in which he denies that he is guilty of victimizing the drowned girl and Dunia. More importantly, the dream of the child-prostitute obliquely expresses a wish to believe that Dunia has betrayed him and is therefore corrupt. However, the dream of the drowned girl reflects an almost explicit admission of guilt.

The next question is, then, how does this guilt manifest itself in narcissistic suicide? The answer is that the narcissist atones for the guilt of murdering the internalized people by killing the self.[66] Therefore, in killing the hated internalized people (Dunia, especially) *and* himself, he sacrifices them, and his body, to his ego-ideal—the ideal of himself as victim. Thus, according to the logic of both pathological narcissism and scapegoat sacrifice, he achieves his "victory over death."[67] Obviously, in Svidrigalov's act of atonement there is no redemption, for making atonement by killing the self requires the simultaneous killing of his internalized victims. Svidrigalov's suicide is not, therefore, a consciously considered act of moral judgment upon an evil life. It is an act of despair, an expression of the very emptiness which makes his fear of death so acute. The narcissistic ego-ideal demands that such emptiness *not* be confessed and used as a guide to life, but instead requires total allegiance to itself. In the hour of his death, Svidrigalov turns altogether away from life in rejecting his memory of and his capacity for pity: "These thoughts again! I must throw them all off, throw them off!" (428). Likewise, in his second dream he rejects pity by seeing the frightened and abused five-year-old girl as a prostitute, an "accursed creature" (431) whom he raises his arm to strike as he awakens. In rejecting pity for his victims, he rejects his humanity and prepares to make the final narcissistic gesture of sacrificing his life to himself.

IV
OMNIPOTENCE, TIME, AND ETERNITY

Being "terrified of aging and death,"[68] the narcissist will use various strategies for dealing with time's implacable movement toward death. One of these strategies is to create a sense of repetition "of the same experience [as] a narcissistic means of keeping control."[69] The most obviously repetitive behavior one finds in Svidrigalov is his preying on young virgins, especially girls in their mid-teens. Svidrigalov seeks to renew his life by possessing the innocence of these girls and in perhaps two instances taking, indirectly, their lives. Svidrigalov seems to think that if he cannot avail himself of the virtue, i.e., the strength, of Dunia, he can turn to his fifteen-year-old fiancee, but he does not do so because his wish for vengeance through suicide has become greater than his wish to continue his predations. Svidrigalov's nymphophilia and his fixation on youth are reflected symbolically in his face. Although Svidrigalov is well into his pre-senum, his face is "extraordinarily young" (395). It is "almost like a mask" (395), and what it masks is a fear-ridden and moribund psyche.

Another strategy the narcissist uses for dealing with the terror of time is to have the illusion of entering a "limitless extension" of time[70] so that one can "blend into eternity"[71] and make temporal "boundaries disappear."[72] Svidrigalov uses precisely this strategy with the visual and auditory hallucinations of his apparitions, which are his contacts with eternity as he conceives it to be. Svidrigalov's apparitions are his evidence for the existence of this eternity:

> Apparitions are, so to speak, shreds and fragments of other worlds, the first beginnings of them.... As soon as he [a sick man] falls ill ... the possibility of another world begins to appear, and as the illness increases, so do the contacts with the other world, so that at the moment of a man's death he enters fully into that world. (244)

Beebe says that Svidrigalov "insists" that "the ghosts that plague him rise ... from his own illness," that Svidrigalov "recognizes no spiritual force outside himself."[73] However, Svidrigalov makes quite clear his belief that he has "contact with the other world" (244). Svidrigalov can see fragments of this world because he "is disturbed," he says (244). "There is, of course, no reason why a healthy man should see them," he adds, because "a healthy man is mainly a being of this earth," and "he must live only this earthly life" (244). Svidrigalov thus elevates what he regards as an illness into a condition of omnipotence which allows him to live both on the earth and partially beyond it. Svidrigalov makes clear his belief that he lives partially beyond the earth in contrasting himself to the healthy man, who is restricted to living "only this earthly life" (244).[74] By creating his own eternity in this way, out of shreds and fragments—the apparitions which imply the existence of a world beyond death—and by putting some of his victims into it, Svidrigalov can control the thing he most fears: death. Svidrigalov's manipulation of time and eternity apparently prevents him from being dead for any longer than the "moment" when "he enters fully into that world" (244). Svidrigalov calls this vision of eternity "an argument" (244), but he obviously believes it because he believes that he has spoken with the apparitions of his wife, Marfa Petrovna, and his servant, Philip. In creating his own eternity, Svidrigalov presents a deific image of himself that reveals what Sugerman calls the "egotheism" of pathological narcissism.[75] The omnipotency theme implicit in Svidrigalov's way of transcending death is clear. By committing suicide Svidrigalov can enter fully into his eternity when he wishes to do so. Therefore, for Svidrigalov, suicide is what Slochower calls a "rebellion against death"[76] and what Eissler calls a proof that the ego (specifically, the ego-ideal) is "almighty."[77]

It may be significant that Marfa Petrovna and Philip apparently do not suffer in Svidrigalov's eternity. The reader cannot be certain about this matter, however, for this eternity is dreadful. "What if," Svidrigalov wonders aloud to Raskol'nikov, "there is nothing there [in eternity] but spiders or something like that?" (244). "Eternity," he continues,

> is always presented to us as an idea which it is impossible to grasp, something enormous, enormous! But why should it necessarily be enormous? Imagine, instead, that it will be one little room, something like a bathhouse in the country, black with soot, with spiders in every corner, and that that is the whole of eternity. I sometimes imagine it like that, you know. (244–45)

When Raskol'nikov protests in horror against this vision, Svidrigalov says that such an eternity "may be just" (245). The point is that this is the kind of eternity Svidrigalov would create; therefore, it may be the one which contains his apparitions and in which he partially lives even now: "I would," he says, "certainly make it like that" (245). To create such an eternity for himself, and others, would paradoxically enhance Svidrigalov's sense of omnipotency. That is, such an eternity would give the narcissist the power to be, in Kernberg's words, "victim and victimizer in one."[78]

The relevance of this pathological omnipotence to the meaning of *Crime and Punishment* as a whole may be indicated by comparing Svidrigalov's conception of egotheistic power over time and death to Raskol'nikov's Great Man theory, in which the Napoleonic man made "of bronze" (232) lives above the natural world, impervious to human fears and needs. Raskol'nikov's commitment to this narcissistic ego-ideal is extreme, but his agonizing self-questioning about this commitment is also extreme. Raskol'nikov gradually allows his suffering to guide him to the heroic Christian ideal of humility, so that his final vision is of a world of eternal love, "of endless springs of life" (463). Raskol'nikov's spiritual transformation dramatizes Dostoevskii's anguished belief in the "the saving and healing forces ... contained in the Russian soil and in a Russian national character imbued with the ideal of Christ."[79] Svidrigalov's damnation—much more fully than the ruin of Stavrogin or the elder Karamazov—shows Dostoevskii's anxious concern with, and understanding of what Frank calls the "psychology of decadence."[80] Svidrigalov's vision is a hell which he himself creates. In it he rules over an eternity filled with spiders and apparitions, narcissistically creating his own punishment.

Notes

1. "It is no accident ... that at the present time the dominant events in psychoanalysis are the rediscovery of narcissism and the new emphasis on the psychological significance of death." See C. Lasch, *The Culture of Narcissism: American Life in an Age of Diminishing Expectations* (New York: W. W. Norton, 1978), p. 42.

2. Over forty years ago R. P. Blackmur said that, "like Stavrogin, Svidrigalov was not *meant* to be understood." See Blackmur, *Eleven Essays in the European Novel* (New York: Harcourt, Brace & World, 1943), p. 137. Most critics have either agreed with Blackmur or assumed that Svidrigalov is all too easily understood, for there is to my knowledge no sustained in-depth study of Svidrigalov.

3. R. Curle, *Characters of Dostoevsky: Studies from Four Novels* (New York: Russell & Russell, 1966), p. 37.

4. P. Rahv, "Dostoevsky in *Crime and Punishment*," *Partisan Review*, 27 (1960), 407.

5. M. Jasovic-Gasic, J. Vesel, "Fear of Death and Narcissism," *Psychology Today* (Prague), 4 (1981), 371.

6. E. Menaker, "The Ego-Ideal: An Aspect of Narcissism," *The Narcissistic Condition: A Fact of Our Lives and Times*, ed. M. L. Nelson (New York: Human Sciences Press, 1977), p. 259.

7. O. F. Kernberg, *Borderline Conditions and Pathological Narcissism* (New York: Jason Aronson, 1975), p. 228.

8. O. F. Kernberg, *Severe Personality Disorders, Psychotherapeutic Strategies* (New Haven: Yale Univ. Press, 1984), p. 296.

9. Kernberg, *Borderline Conditions*, p. 228.

10. *Ibid.*

11. *Ibid.*

12. Heidegger as quoted by Ernest Becker, *The Denial of Death* (New York: The Free Press, 1974), p. 53. "He [Heidegger] argued that the basic anxiety of man is anxiety about being-in-the-world. That is, both fear of death and fear of life, of experience and individuation."

13. N. O. Brown, *Life Against Death: The Psychoanalytic Meaning of History* (New York: Random House, 1959), p. 116.

14. Kernberg, *Severe Personality Disorders*, p. 257.

15. *Ibid.*, p. 280.

16. F. Dostoevsky, *Crime and Punishment*, tr. J. Coulson, ed. G. Gibian (New York: W. W. Norton, 1976), p. 398. Hereafter page numbers will be cited in text.

17. K. Menninger, *Man Against Himself* (New York: Harcourt, Brace and World, 1938), p. 63.

18. Becker, *Denial of Death*, p. 16.

19. R. May, *Love and Will* (New York: W. W. Norton, 1969), p. 301.

20. J. E. Meyer, *Death and Neurosis* (New York: International Universities Press, 1975), p. 4.

21. Lasch, *The Culture of Narcissism*, p. 40.

22. R. W. Greenson, "The Psychology of Apathy," *Psychoanalytic Quarterly*, 18 (1949), 299.

23. May, *Love and Will*, p. 301.

24. Greenson, "The Psychology of Apathy," p. 300.

26. R. D. Laing, *The Divided Self* (New York: Pantheon Books, 1960), p. 99.

26. M. Singer, "The Experience of Emptiness in Narcissistic and Borderline States: The Struggle for a Sense of Self and the Potential for Suicide," *International Review of Psychoanalysis*, 4 (1977), 472.

27. E. J. Simmons, *Dostoevsky: The Making of a Novelist* (New York: Alfred A. Knopf and Random House, 1940), p. 165.

28. Singer, "The Experience of Emptiness in Narcissistic and Borderline States," p. 473.

29. Kernberg, *Borderline Conditions*, p. 229.

30. Lasch, *The Culture of Narcissism*, p. 39.

31. Greenson, "The Psychology of Apathy," p. 229.

32. Becker, *Denial of Death*, p. 70.

33. Lasch, *The Culture of Narcissism*, p. 31.

34. Singer, "The Experience of Emptiness," p. 477.

35. May, *Love and Will*, p. 30.

36. What Svidrigalov actually says is that other people apparently see him as a romantic figure, thus twisting to his own advantage Raskol'nikov's comments on his sadism.

37. One of Svidrigalov's functions as Raskol'nikov's double is that whereas Raskol'nikov's moral sense is highly developed, and he wishes to destroy it, Svidrigalov has almost no moral sense at all, although he believes that he does.

38. J. L. Greenway, "Kierkegaardian Doubles in *Crime and Punishment*," *Orbis Litterarum*, 33 (1978), p. 54.

39. *Ibid.*

40. Jackson suggests that Svidrigalov is implying in this question that moral laws are illusion, that people are "simply creatures of nature." R. L. Jackson, *The Art of Dostoevsky: Deliriums and Nocturnes* (Princeton: Princeton Univ. Press, 1981), p. 193. I argue that Svidrigalov's illusion is that *he* is moral by virtue of being a victim. Frank says that the notorious criminal, Pierre-Francois Lacenaire, who was a cultured, intellectual and an exceptionally vain man, "set himself up as a victim of his century." Lacenaire "helped to provide some features for ... Svidrigalov." J. Frank, *Dostoevsky: The Stir of Liberation, 1860–1865* (Princeton: Princeton Univ. Press, 1986), pp. 72–73.

41. In defense of the notion that Svidrigalov develops a moral sense after Dunia rejects him, Greenway says that Svidrigalov begins doing "ethically positive deeds," i.e., giving away money ("Kierkegaardian Doubles," p. 54). In fact, Svidrigalov performs several acts of charity *before* the confrontation with Dunia, and he does so partially because he wants Dunia to know of them; he asks Raskol'nikov to tell her (368). It may be that he continues these acts of charity because the confrontation fails to vindicate his innocence. There is very little upon which to base speculation regarding these acts. Svidrigalov himself says only one thing about them, and that is a reference to his having instructed Sonia to entrust Razumikhin, who loves Dunia, with the money which Svidrigalov has given to her. Svidrigalov has urged Sonia to tell Razumikhin that Svidrigalov wants him to keep the money for Sonia. When Svidrigalov reflects upon this matter later that night, he says that his motive was "mostly to torment myself (427). Svidrigalov is not, of course, a two-dimensional character. His acts no doubt reveal "the potentiality of kindness," in Merezhkovskii's words. See D. Merezhkovskii, "Dostoevsky," *Vechnye sputniki* (1897), quoted in V. Seduro, *Dostoevsky in Russian Literary Criticism, 1846–1856* (New York: Columbia Univ. Press, 1957), p. 45.

42. Kernberg, *Severe Personality Disorders*, p. 180.

43. In the passage cited, Becker discusses the logic of scapegoating in general. He does not refer to Svidrigalov. See E. Becker, *Escape From Evil* (New York: The Free Press, 1975), p. 108.

44. Merezhkovskii, quoted in Seduro, *Dostoevsky in Russian Literary Criticism, 1846–1856*, p. 45.

45. May, *Love and Will*, p. 30.

46. Kernberg says that "the search on the part of some patients for a primitive sense of goodness, happiness, fulfillment, and well-being via alcohol, drugs, or fragmented types of sexuality may be considered to contain the seed of what might become a search for love." See Kernberg, *Severe Personality Disorders*, p. 301.

47. D. Kiremidjian, "*Crime and Punishment*: Matricide and the Woman Question," *American Imago*, 33 (1976), 418.

48. V. D. Volkan, *Primitive Internalized Object Relations: A Clinical Study of Schizophrenic, Borderline, and Narcissistic Patients* (New York: International Universities Press, 1976), p. 239.

49. Kernberg, *Borderline Conditions*, p. 223.

50. Lasch, *The Culture of Narcissism*, p. 37.

51. Kernberg, *Borderline Conditions*, p. 228.

52. Kernberg, *Severe Personality Disorders*, p. 50.

53. Kernberg, *Borderline Conditions*, p. 170.

54. N. Schwartz-Salent, *Narcissism and Character Transformation: The Psychology of Narcissistic Character Disorders* (Toronto: Inner City Books, 1982), p. 87.

55. Schwartz-Salent, *Narcissism and Character Transformation*, p. 87.

56. Kernberg, *Borderline Conditions*, p. 228.

57. Considering the fact that Svidrigalov and Raskol'nikov are doubles, it is significant that during the Easter season, in Siberia, Raskol'nikov gives up his corrupt ego-ideal and affirms the innocence of humility.

58. S. Freud, "The Ego and the Id," tr. and ed. J. Strachey, *SE* 19 (London: The Hogarth Press, 1961), p. 54.

59. *Ibid.*, p. 53.

60. *Ibid.*

61. R. Klussman, A. Wallmuller-Strycher, "Beitrag zur psychogenen Polydipsie-Suizid ale Losung einer narzisstischen Krise," *Zeitschrift für Psychosomatische Medizin und Psychoanalyse*, 27, No. 4 (1981), 166.

62. *Ibid.*

63. Kernberg, *Severe Personality Disorders*, p. 293.

64. S. Sugerman, *Sin and Madness: Studies in Narcissism* (Philadelphia: Westminster Press, 1964), p. 131.

65. *Ibid.*, p. 22.

66. "Kann diese Phantasie nicht aufrecht erhalted bleiben—wie es bei unserem Patienten so deutlich ist—dann bricht die Absehrformation zusammen; das narsisstische object hat gleichsam versagt, es wird deshalb—im Selbstmordet" (Klussman, Wallmuller-Strycher, "Beitrag zur psychogenen Polydipsie-Suizid," p. 166).

67. Becker, *Escape From Evil*, p. 108.

68. Lasch, *The Culture of Narcissism*, p. 38.

69. M. E. Stern, "Narcissism and the Defiance of Time," *The Narcissistic Condition: A Fact of Our Lives and Times*, ed. M. L. Nelson (New York: Human Sciences Press, 1977), p. 90.

70. Stern, "Narcissism and the Defiance of Time," p. 186.

71. Menaker, "The Ego-Ideal: An Aspect of Narcissism," p. 250.

72. Stern, "Narcissism and the Defiance of Time," p. 189.

73. M. Beebe, "The Three Motives of Raskolnikov: A Reinterpretation of *Crime and Punishment*," *College English*, 17 (1955), 157.

74. Rahv's interpretation regarding this point is in accord with my own: "Svidrigalov

believes in ghosts ... who appear only to people whose psyche is prepared to receive them." See Rahv, "Dostoevsky in *Crime and Punishment*," p. 408.

75. Sugerman, *Sin and Madness*, p. 24.

76. H. Slochower, "Suicides in Literature: Their Ego Function," *American Imago*, 32, No. 4 (1975), 395.

77. K. R. Eissler, *The Psychiatrist and the Dying Patient* (New York: International Universities Press, 1971), quoted in Slochower, "Suicides in Literature," p. 395.

78. Kernberg, *Severe Personality Disorders*, p. 292.

79. Frank, *Dostoevsky*, p. 375.

80. *Ibid.*, p. 87. Frank also notes that Stavrogin and Karamazov show Dostoevskii's continuing interest in the psychology of decadence.

LAURA A. CURTIS

Raskolnikov's Sexuality

The use of doubles in Dostoevsky's fiction is generally acknowledged. Golyadkin in his 1846 novel, *The Double*, is only the first of a number of characters endowed with doubles, ending with Ivan Karamazov in Dostoevsky's last novel, *The Brothers Karamazov* of 1880. Perhaps his most complex treatment of the theme occurs in *Crime and Punishment* of 1866, where several characters serve at different points in the novel as doubles of the protagonist, Rodion Romanovich Raskolnikov.

Dostoevsky began *Crime and Punishment* as a story of "the current problem of drunkenness,"[1] and as such, featured in the first part of the novel the confession of the protagonist of what soon became the subplot, Semen Zakharovich Marmeladov, an ex-government clerk. As Dostoevsky developed the drunkard Marmeladov, striking similarities to Raskolnikov, on the surface an entirely different type, began to appear. Marmeladov's suitability as a double of Raskolnikov has not been a matter of contention. This is not the case, however, with the character Arkady Ivanovich Svidrigaylov, who enters the novel in person only in the second half, but who is generally accepted as the chief Raskolnikov double of *Crime and Punishment*.

Indeed, one of the most puzzling questions about *Crime and Punishment* is why Dostoevsky selected Svidrigaylov for this role.

Superficially, the choice of an aging minor aristocrat, a blasé man of the world dedicated to the pleasures of sensuality to mirror an impoverished middle class student, an ascetic intellectual torn between his theory and his emotions, seems odd. Differences of age, of class, of interests, of philosophy of life, and of temperament seem to separate the two characters irrevocably. It is true that there is a link between them in that both reject the moral codes of their society, Svidrigaylov partly because he is amoral, partly because a man of his position had the sanction of custom behind his mistreatment of social inferiors, and Raskolnikov, consciously at least, because he deliberately enacts, in defiance of strongly felt religious beliefs, a Napoleonic theory inspired by the infiltration of Western ideas into Russia of the 1860's. On the other hand, if Dostoevsky had been committed unambivalently to the discrediting of utilitarianism, nihilism, and Utopian socialism in favor of a conservative form of Russian Orthodox Christianity, would it not have been more effective to develop as Raskolnikov's chief double a person more clearly representative of Western ideology, a Luzhin or Lebeyzyatnikov, for example? What in a novel as much psychological as ideological, is the deepest connection between a roué who derives pleasure from debauching and humiliating young girls and an ascetic intellectual who inflicts suffering on himself by taking the lives of an old pawnbroker and her sister?

One way of approaching these questions is by looking for clues in part one, where Dostoevsky introduces the elements of the puzzle before making his protagonist take his decisive action. Here the reader learns about Raskolnikov's ideology: he is attracted by the idea that it is permissible to commit murder for the purpose of robbery, on the condition that the victim is evil and that the proceeds of the robbery are devoted "to the service of humanity and the good of all" (p. 84).[2] The reader also learns that Raskolnikov's lack of money has forced him to leave the university and his sister has contracted a loveless marriage primarily in order to help him. Furthermore, not only is Raskolnikov acquainted with a potential victim of robbery and murder; he has actually engaged in a rehearsal of the crime. Theory, necessity, and opportunity thus concur. In addition, Dostoevsky bends fate itself to Raskolnikov's more or less tentative plan; having relinquished his design as the result of a terrifying nightmare, the protagonist fortuitously overhears a conversation that informs him precisely when his prospective victim will be alone in her apartment, her younger sister away on a business appointment, and decides, after all, to go ahead with his crime.

Were this the total information provided to the reader in the first section of *Crime and Punishment*, it would be almost impossible to determine why Dostoevsky chose Svidrigaylov to represent an important side of

Raskolnikov. One would be forced to content oneself with the two alternatives offered in the epilogue: the superficial psychological formula of temporary mental derangement (all participants in Raskolnikov's trial recognized that the criminal had manifested a total lack of interest in his plunder, failing even to count the money in a purse before he hid it under a large stone) or Raskolnikov's own sociological and moral explanation—environmental influences, need, and a bad character. Or, accepting in the main the powerful polemic of Dostoevsky in favor of a conservative form of Russian Orthodox Christianity that argues that one must court suffering in order to be reborn, one would concur with Joseph Frank, a biographer of Dostoevsky. Frank is opposed to Freudian readings of the author, asserting that in his major works he repeatedly dramatized "the inner conflict of a member of the Russian intelligentsia torn between his innate feelings and his conscious ideas," and goes on to insist that these feelings, "the irrational," are "never Freudian in Dostoevsky but always moral as in Shakespeare."[3]

My own understanding of Raskolnikov's motives, however, is more in line with the approach of W.D. Snodgrass and other critics, through Edward Wasiolek, who writes, "If we are to take Dostoevsky's words in the *Notebooks* literally that Svidrigaylov is supposed to represent one side of Raskolnikov and that Svidrigaylov is an overt expression of what is unexpressed in Raskolnikov, then it would seem that we would have to look at Svidrigaylov's sexual aggressiveness as in some way an externalization of what is hidden in Raskolnikov's unconscious."[4]

Part one of *Crime and Punishment*, specifically, Dostoevsky's descriptions of Marmeladov and of Raskolnikov's nightmare about the horse, suggest additional motives for Raskolnikov's crime. Insofar as these motives are related to his sexuality they illustrate that his psychological makeup is irrational in a Freudian way, and that he has complementary sexual affinities with Svidrigaylov. Such affinities were perhaps never consciously recognized by Dostoevsky and therefore never stated explicitly or enacted overtly in the novel.

Dostoevsky introduces Marmeladov to the reader in a manner designed to suggest certain resemblances between the drunken ex-civil servant and the impoverished student. Both men wear poor, dirty clothing, Marmeladov's eyes "seemed to glitter with a kind of exultation—there was perhaps some understanding and intelligence in them, but at the same time there was also something that looked very much like madness" (p. 28), and, like Raskolnikov, seems to have spoken to nobody for a long time. Other resemblances are mentioned: Marmeladov says he married Katrina Ivanovna out of compassion, "for I could not bear to see such suffering" (p. 33); Raskolnikov is first attracted to Sonya by her suffering, and he later admits that he thinks what attracted him originally to an invalid, his deceased fiancée, was that "she was always ill" (p. 248); both Marmeladovs, husband and wife, have a penchant for kissing feet, an old-fashioned practice, as Marmeladov points out, offensive to enlightened men of advanced ideas (p. 36), and in spite of being a modern intellectual, Raskolnikov later kisses the feet of his mother and then of Sonya.

Raskolnikov shares the drunkard's self-destructive surrender of will and masochistic tendencies as well as his compulsion to confess. Marmeladov, finally employed again after a long period of drunkenness, experiences the peace and love of his home "as if I'd found myself in the Kingdom of Heaven" (p. 37). A month later, after "the whole of [a] heavenly day" spent dreaming about all the things he would do for his family, he suddenly stole the household money from his wife and went off on a five day drunken binge, sacrificing his job, his family, and his self-respect.

In an analogous gesture, Raskolnikov, renouncing his plans for murder as the result of a terrible nightmare and exulting in his newfound freedom, "now free from all those obsessions, magic spells, delusions, witchcraft" (p. 79), almost immediately afterwards throws his freedom away when he accidentally overhears the sister of his intended victim making plans to be away from home the next evening. He lets himself resume his plan, entering his room "like a man sentenced to death. He thought of nothing, and indeed he was quite incapable of thinking; but he suddenly felt with all his being that he no longer possessed any freedom of reasoning or of will, and that everything was suddenly and irrevocably settled" (p. 81). This surrender to a self-destructive compulsion experienced as a devilish external force is made clear in his later confession to Sonya: "The devil," he says, "had dragged me there, and ... it was only afterwards that he explained to me that I had no right to go there because I was the same kind of louse as the rest" (p. 433). Raskolnikov disguises his surrender to an inner compulsion by resorting to his theory of Napoleonic voluntarism to explain his action, both at the time of the crime and later in the very same confession to Sonya mentioned above, when he tells her, "It was something else I wanted to find out, it was something else that goaded me on: I had to find out then, and as quickly as possible, whether I was a louse like the rest or a man. Whether I can step over or not" (p. 432–33). Yet in spite of this later assertion that he was deliberately testing out his theory, Raskolnikov partially recognizes he was not acting freely as a kind of psychological experimenter on himself when he confesses to himself, much before he confesses to Sonya, that all along he hated himself, knew he was a louse worse than the pawnbroker, since "I knew *beforehand* that I would say that to myself *after* killing her!" (p. 292). The perceptive police inspector Porfiry later describes in an apt simile how circumscribed the element of will was in Raskolnikov's crime: "Here we are faced with a determination to take the first step, but it is a special kind of determination: he made up his mind to do it, and then it was as though he had fallen down a mountain or flung himself off a belfry, and he appeared on the scene of the crime as if he had been brought there against his will" (p. 467).

In addition to sharing with Marmeladov a self-destructive impulse, Raskolnikov also shares his masochism. Marmeladov's is unmixed; he says over and over that his alcoholism is really a thirst for affliction and weeping, that he drinks in order to multiply his sufferings, and that he wishes to be crucified. The blows of his wife are "a real pleasure" to him; he "can't do without them" (p. 41). Raskolnikov's masochism is more complex. A perfect illustration is when, returning to the scene of the crime, he pulls three times at the doorbell of the pawnbroker's apartment, "listening intently all the while and trying to recall everything as it happened then" (p. 191). Dostoevsky writes, "The appalling and agonizingly dreadful sensation he had felt then was coming back to him more and more palpably now, and every time the bell rang it sent a shiver down his spine, and he was getting a greater and a more and more delicious thrill out of it" (p. 192). Porfiry later analyzes Raskolnikov's emotions at that moment: "And it was not enough for him to have gone through those moments of terrible agony behind the door while people were battering at it and the doorbell was ringing—no, he had to go back to the empty flat in a state of semi-delirium, to recall the ringing of the bell and to experience again the chill down his spine" (pp. 467–68).

Attracted by Marmeladov's masochism and self-destructiveness, the protagonist is attracted too by Marmeladov's compulsion to confess his sins. Raskolnikov tells Sonya, during his first visit to her apartment, that he intends to tell her next time who killed Lizaveta. It is at this point in the novel (part 4, chapter 4) that he avows to her, "Long ago I chose you to tell you this, when your father told me about you and when Lizaveta was still alive" (p. 345). Aside from Sonya, however, Raskolnikov is ambivalent about particular auditors for his confession, and he vacillates between his desires for secrecy and for self-exposure.

A central symbolic image for Raskolnikov's drama expresses this ambivalence. It appears first when the young man is standing outside the pawnbroker's door, waiting for her to answer: "Someone was standing very quietly close to the very lock of the door and, as he was doing on the outside, listening carefully, lying low inside and, it seemed, also with an ear pressed to the door ..." (p. 94). The image is repeated upon the sudden arrival of two clients of the pawnbroker right after the murders, and Raskolnikov stands quietly, holding his breath, this time on the inside of the door (p. 101). From then on the image is invoked by the repeated psychological action each time someone (usually police inspector Porfiry) tries to get inside Raskolnikov's mind to divine his thoughts, and each time he himself is tempted to confess. His teasing of the chief police clerk, Zamyotov, is described in a simile that illustrates the metamorphosis of the door image into a mental action:

> He bent down as close as possible to Zamyotov and his lips began to move, but no sound came from them. This went on for half a minute; he knew what he was doing, but he could not control himself. The terrible words trembled on his lips, like the bolt on the door that day: another moment and out it would come, another moment and he would utter it!
>
> "And what if it was I who murdered the old woman and Lisaveta?" he said suddenly and—recovered his senses (p. 184).

Raskolnikov himself appears to be psychic, easily entering the minds and divining the secret thoughts and desires of most of the other characters, Razumikhin, Zosimov, Dunya, Mrs. Raskolnikov, Sonya, Porfiry, even, at times, Svidrigaylov, on one eerie occasion actually confessing the murder to his friend Razumikhin through mental telepathy:

> It was dark in the corridor; they were standing near the lamp. For a minute they looked at each other in silence. Razumikhin remembered that minute all his life. Raskolnikov's burning and piercing look seemed to become more and more intense every moment. It seemed to penetrate into his soul, into his consciousness. Suddenly Razumikhin gave a start. Something strange had passed between them. An idea seemed, as it were, to have slipped out, a kind of hint; something hideous and ghastly, something that both of them suddenly understood. Razumikhin turned as white as a sheet.
>
> "Understand now?" Raskolnikov said suddenly, with a painfully contorted face (p. 329).

Marmeladov confesses to obtain, along with the chastisement he feels he deserves, compassion. The former he receives in abundance from the onlookers in the tavern; the latter he receives from Raskolnikov. Marmeladov is hardened to the jeers of onlookers, telling them, "I'm not at all downcast by the general shaking of heads, for all this has long been common knowledge, and all the hidden things have been brought to light" (p. 31). The publicity of Marmeladov's confession disgusts Raskolnikov, who exhibits a hatred of crowds of mocking and inquisitive spectators throughout *Crime and Punishment*, telling Sonya that the worst thing about confessing his crime to the police is that "all those stupid brutes will crowd round me, glare at me, and put their silly questions to me, which I shall be forced to answer—point their fingers at me" (pp. 533–34). His forebodings prove accurate; when he obeys Sonya's instructions, bowing down and kissing the ground, even though he feels pleasure and joy at "this new and overwhelming sensation" (pp. 536–37), his action provokes mocking exclamations that prevent him from proclaiming aloud, as he had intended to, "I am a murderer." When he is finally able to utter the words to the police officer, instantly "people came running from all directions" (p. 542).

Raskolnikov's is a private confession, to a special type of auditor represented by his former fiancée and now by Sonya. To his former fiancée, "the strange girl who had wanted to enter a nunnery," (p. 531) he had talked about his Napoleonic ideas, presumably even about the prospective murder: "'I used to talk a lot to her about *that*, only to her,' he said pensively" (p. 531). Before he confides in Sonya, intruding on her privacy the way he provokes others to intrude on his, he prods her into admitting explicitly what he suspects to be the source of her strength in enduring her terrible life, her faith in God:

> Raskolnikov realized to some extent why Sonya could not bring herself to read to him, and the more he realized it, the more peremptorily and irritably he insisted that she should read. He realized too well how hard it must be for Sonya to betray and expose her *inmost* feelings. He realized that those feelings were indeed her present, and perhaps, her old *secret*, a secret she had probably cherished since she was a child, while she still lived at home with her family, her unhappy father and her stepmother, gone mad with grief, among the starving children and in the midst of disgraceful shrieks and reproaches. But at the same time he knew now, and he knew it for certain, that, though she might feel upset and worried and be terribly afraid of something, when she had begun to read, now, she herself was most anxious to read to *him*, and to him alone, and to make sure that he *heard*, heard it *now* ... (p. 341).

The two girls thus share an intense piety. They are both charitable: the fiancée liked to give alms to beggars; Sonya has gone to the extreme of prostitution in order to give charity to her family. Both girls are young and physically immature; Sonya looks even younger than her age: "In spite of her eighteen years, she looked almost a little girl, much younger than her years—almost a child, indeed ..." (p. 255). Both are further decorporealized by poor health, the fiancée having always been ill (Raskolnikov tells his mother, "If she'd been lame or a hunchback I believe I'd have loved her better still") (p. 248), Sonya being painfully thin. Finally, both girls are essentially uneducated, totally unacquainted with the kind of ideology that possesses the mind of the intellectual Raskolnikov.

In spite of the consistency Raskolnikov demonstrates in choosing simple and deeply pious young girls as recipients of his confessions, his underlying purpose in confessing to them, unlike Marmeladov's in confessing to a crowd, is relatively complicated. One of the main reasons is certainly the guidance we witness him seeking from Sonya of a deeply felt religion, and this is the motive emphasized by Dostoevsky throughout *Crime and Punishment*. But, although the author sustains a polemic in favor of Russian Orthodox Christianity, this explicit theme is by no means the whole secret of the hidden psyche of Raskolnikov that continues to fascinate readers of the novel.

One feature of this secret seems to be associated with sexuality—at least, with the curious lack of it in Raskolnikov. I have mentioned above the decorporealization of both the girls he confides in. Dostoevsky himself writes in his notebooks about the relation between Sonya and Raskolnikov: "Capital and Main Thing. Never even a word was spoken about love between them.... He, not speaking to her about love, saw that she is necessary to him like air...."[5] For no reason organic to her story, Dunya, the sister portrayed as Raskolnikov's temperamental double in her quick temper and pride, is described by Svidrigaylov as "quite morbidly chaste" (p. 487). The same type of displacement can be observed in Dostoevsky's apparently aimless digression in describing Razumikhin's fascination with Raskolnikov's landlady. The reader is startled to learn from Razumikhin how attractive "Pashenka" (Praskovya Pavlovna Zarnitsyna) is: "I tell you, old chap, she almost baffles me. She must be forty at least, I should say. She says she's thirty-six, and of course she has every right to say so. I assure you most solemnly, however, that my interest in her is more of an intellectual nature" (p. 142). Razumikhin fears (accurately, says the narrator of *Crime and Punishment*) Pashenka will be jealous of Dunya and of Mrs. Raskolnikov, whose face, even at forty-three, "still preserved traces of its former beauty" (p. 223). When Zosimov must spend the night in the apartment of the landlady in order to be on call for his patient, Razumikhin warns the young doctor, whom he accuses of being a "rake" (p. 255), to behave himself with Pashenka, who is "modest, silent, bashful, quite alarmingly chaste, and at the same time, sighing and melting like wax, poor creature" (p. 225). He goes on to describe what life with her would be like: "the real feather-bed principle ... the quintessence of pancakes, luscious pies, an evening samovar, soft sighs and warm fur-lined coats, hot, comfortable low stoves to snooze on ..." (p. 227). Zosimov asks Razumikhin why he tried to make a conquest of her, and Razumikhin explains: "But I haven't led her on. Most likely it was I who in my folly allowed myself to be led on. But it won't make the slightest difference to her whether it's you or me, so long as there's someone sitting beside her and sighing." Razumikhin suggests Zosimov go through integral calculus with her—

> it won't make any difference to her: she'll go on looking at you and sighing for a whole year, if you like. I myself talked to her for ever so long—oh, for two days, I think—about the Prussian Upper Chamber (I had nothing else to talk to her about, you see), and she just sat there sighing and sweating. (p. 226)

From this description we learn that the landlady, who seems to be simply an object of embarrassment and fear to Raskolnikov, is soft and stereotypically feminine, enjoys and suggests to men the sensuous comforts of life, tends to become jealous of possible rivals in beauty, and has a penchant for the attentions of young men. Razumikhin tells Raskolnikov, who has been called up to the police station because of the back rent he owes to his landlady, "It's a great pity, old chap, you didn't set about it in the right way from the very beginning. That wasn't the way to deal with her at all" (p. 142). The ascetic Raskolnikov apparently is unable to recognize what his fellow student with more direct susceptibilities to women, and in spite of a less manipulative personality than Raskolnikov's, sees right away: a flirtation with the landlady would have kept her from demanding the money Raskolnikov owed her.

A footnote to Raskolnikov's true attitude toward his landlady is provided by his second nightmare, which takes place in part two of *Crime and Punishment*, after he has returned from the police station where he had been summoned because of the money he owes to Mrs. Zarnitsyna. Here he imagines the tempestuous police lieutenant, Ilya Petrovich (who in the real encounter at the station house was insolent to the poorly dressed Raskolnikov and poured a stream of verbal abuse on Louisa Ivanovna, a fat, overdressed brothel madam) as administering a long, ferocious and sadistic beating to his howling and shrieking landlady, while crowds of spectators pour out of their rooms to watch. As natural as the transference may be when Raskolnikov uses the police lieutenant as a surrogate for his own anger at his landlady for having taken legal measures against him, the fact is that he is substituting her figure as the object of abuse for that of a prostitute. Thus, his nightmare suggests that Raskolnikov is not simply ascetic; he associates normal female sexuality with prostitution and wishes to see it punished violently by a surrogate for himself.

In addition, Raskolnikov's apparent lack of sexuality is contradicted by his interest in women who have been sexually abused. Difficult as Dostoevsky makes it to remember, because of his decorporealization of Sonya, she is after all a prostitute. The saintly and gentle Lizaveta whom he links firmly with Sonya by their childlikeness and other traits is envisioned as physically mature enough to be pregnant.

One aspect of Raskolnikov's hidden psyche is thus suggested by his choice of a special type of young girl—childlike, simple, uneducated, sickly, and saintlike—as the recipient of his disturbing confidences. The choice appears to be mirrored and distorted on a physical level by the 50-year-old Svidrigaylov's choice of a sixteen-year-old girl for his fiancée and the object of his sexual attentions. Svidrigaylov is attracted by the same childlikeness, piety, and simplicity as is Raskolnikov. In describing her, he says, "You know, her face reminds me of Raphael's Madonna. The Sistine Madonna has quite a fantastic face, the face of a sorrowful religious half-wit" (p. 492). Neither the fiancée nor Sonya is prepared temperamentally or educationally to encounter the intellectual and emotional complexities of a Raskolnikov, who torments himself and the girls with his spiritual self-exposure in a manner reminiscent of the protagonist's in *Notes from the Underground*.

Another aspect of Raskolnikov's sexuality—his attitude toward men and women, fathers and mothers—is revealed by his nightmare about the flogging to death of an old mare. The setting of the dream is in the country, or at least, on the outskirts of the town Raskolnikov lived in before he came to Petersburg. Beyond the last gardens of the town, but three hundred yards before a cemetery, is a tavern filled with its habitual crowd of boisterous and drunken peasants. Raskolnikov is a boy of seven, accompanying his father on their annual holiday visit to hear a requiem at the church in whose cemetery his grandmother lies buried.

As father and son pass the tavern, they witness a dreadful scene: a thick-necked, red-faced peasant called Mikolka invites companions into his huge dray, harnessed to a decrepit old mare instead of the appropriate and usual massive dray horse. In defiance of the laughter of these people, who refuse to believe so frail an animal can draw so heavy a load, Mikolka vows to make the mare gallop. The rest of the nightmare is a graphic description of how, trying to carry out his word, the driver and his friends whip the horse to death, Mikolka finishing her off first with a thick wooden shaft, and then with an iron crowbar.

Counterpointing Mikolka's shouts that the horse is his property, so he is entitled to do as he likes with her, are protests from one or two of the peasants in the name of Christianity as opposed to bestiality or heathenism, the futile efforts of Raskolnikov's father to draw his son away from the scene while explaining that the peasants are drunk and insisting, "It's not our business" (p. 78), and the hysteria of the seven-year-old boy, who first tries to save the horse, getting a whip lash on his face, and then kisses and fondles the bloody head of the dead animal and rushes with clenched fists upon Mikolka before being caught up and carried away by his father.

The reader had no difficulty in discerning immediately that Raskolnikov the dreamer is playing two roles in the dream: the little boy who empathizes with the suffering beast and tries to protect it and the beast itself, for which he receives a whip lash on the face. Dostoevsky describes Raskolnikov's awakening from his nightmare in words that emphasize his identification with the beaten mare: "Every bone in his body seemed to ache" (p. 78). Later on in the novel, he returns to his apartment after an interview with the police and lies down "trembling like a winded horse" (p. 133). (Usually, however, the figure of a beaten and suffering creature is associated with women, mostly Mrs. Marmeladov.)

The third role played by the dreamer is somewhat less obvious than the first two—it is that of the sadistic Mikolka. This role is suggested both by Raskolnikov's references to an axe upon awakening from his nightmare and by his physical gestures in using this weapon to kill two women. When he awakens, Raskolnikov exclaims, "Good God! Is it possible that I will really take a hatchet, hit her on the head with it, crack her skull, slither about in warm, sticky blood, break the lock, steal and shake with fear, hide myself all covered in blood and with the hatchet—Good God! is it possible?" (p. 78). (The words about blood and breaking the lock and stealing could serve to describe rape as well as murder.) Although Mikolka does not in the nightmare employ an axe on the mare, one of his friends does suggest such a weapon. The identification of Raskolnikov with Mikolka is emphasized by Dostoevsky's description of the murder, which takes place at the end of part one of the novel. Like Mikolka, who beats the horse with a thick wooden shaft, Raskolnikov strikes the old pawnbroker with the butt end of the axe. Like Mikolka, he strikes again and again, and like Mikolka with all his strength "with the back of the hatchet and across the crown of the head" (p. 96). When Raskolnikov murders Lisaveta, however, he does not beat her to death: "She was hit with the blade of the hatchet, which split the top of her forehead open, penetrating almost to the crown of her head." (p. 99).

A further suggestion that Raskolnikov shares some affinities with the sadistic Mikolka is the complicated relationship among the protagonist, the dream figure, and a painter who unexpectedly confesses to the murder of the pawnbroker and her sister. The painter is called first Mikolay, then Nikolay, Demenyev. Raskolnikov starts referring to him by the nickname of Mikolka after the painter's confession, and from then on, police inspector Porfiry also calls him Mikolka. A double for Raskolnikov in that he confesses to a crime committed by the student, Mikolka is an "Old Believer," one who thinks acceptance of suffering in itself, not only suffering for the sake of someone else, is good for the individual. Accordingly, he actively seeks such suffering. One facet of Raskolnikov's psyche as revealed throughout *Crime and Punishment* is religious; he believes literally in the New Jerusalem and the raising of Lazarus, as he admits upon questioning from Porfiry (p. 278). Dostoevsky's linking of the painter, who is a religious fanatic, with Raskolnikov suggests that Raskolnikov's religion too is tinged with the masochism represented by Nicolay. At the same time, Nicolay's nickname of Mikolka suggests an association between the masochism of the painter and the sadism of the dream figure. As we have already seen, the Mikolka of the nightmare and the Raskolnikov of the murder are linked by their performing identical physical actions of repeated striking of a living female creature with a thick wooden shaft. Such an association is again made by Dostoevsky just before Raskolnikov manages to voice his confession to Sonya. When he feels the moment has come, "to his mind that moment was uncannily like the moment when he stood behind the old woman and, disengaging the hatchet from the sling, felt that 'there was not a moment to lose'" (p. 422). As he struck the old woman physically, now he will strike Sonya emotionally; as he struck the old woman physically, so the dream figure Mikolka struck his old mare.

Now that we have seen how Raskolnikov plays three roles in his nightmare, the child who protests against cruelty, the mare that suffers cruelty, and the perpetrator of cruelty, we must consider the roles of father and mother, of man and woman, and of child and adult. The father in Raskolnikov's nightmare is almost totally ineffectual: not only can he do nothing to prevent what is going on, but he rationalizes his lack of power, reiterating that the peasants are drunk and that it is not the business of him and his son. Clearly such position of nonintervention is unacceptable to Raskolnikov, because he runs for help to a father surrogate, an old man with a gray beard, "who was shaking his head and condemning it all" (p. 76). In addition to failing to stop or even to speak out against the torturing to death of the poor old mare, Raskolnikov's dream father is unsuccessful in his effort to take the boy away from the scene (p. 75), managing to catch him up in his arms and to carry him out of the crowd only after the boy has witnessed the whole brutal drama and has rushed at Mikolka with clenched fists. In this second area of ineffectuality, the dream father shows himself to be less powerful than the dream mother, whom the dreamer remembers as having "always used to take him away from the window" when he was upset by witnessing a peasant lashing his overburdened horse.

In contrast to maternal figures is an enigmatic figure of a peasant woman who joins the five companions of Mikolka in the wagon to be pulled by the decrepit mare. This woman is "a fat, red-cheeked peasant. She wore a red cotton dress, the traditional headdress of a married woman, ornamented with beads, and fur-lined boots, and she was cracking nuts and just smiling to herself" (p. 75). Since red is associated with the beefy face of Mikolka and of his brutal companions, and fatness with the kind of easy, sensuous life scorned by the energetic Razumikhin as he recommends it condescendingly to Zosimov in its embodiment in Mrs. Zarnitsyna, it seems that the reader should infer that the most common kind of feminine sexuality is associated in Raskolnikov's mind with tolerance for cruel and bestial behavior, the perpetration of violence. Another kind of femininity, the thin, suffering victim of violence, is suggested by the central figure of the nightmare, the victimized mare. In fact, the only kind of femininity not criticized in this nightmare is that of the mother, who knows how to protect her sensitive child from disturbing sights.

What we learn from Raskolnikov's nightmare, then, is first, that the ideal father should put up a fight against injustice but that Raskolnikov's memory of his father (who died when he was young), does not provide him with such a model. From this we are able to understand one psychological reason for Raskolnikov's mistake in choosing murder as his form of protest against social and moral injustice (poverty and brutality). This is the mistake of someone who in a way is as boyish as the seven-year-old protagonist of Raskolnikov's dream, whose attack on callousness, brutality, and even sadism embodied by the full-grown Mikolka takes a physical form: he rushes at the peasant with his little fists clenched. Later, during his confession to Sonya, Raskolnikov tells her that perhaps he is a man and not a louse, adding, "I may have been in too great a hurry to condemn myself. I'll give them a good run for their money" (p. 434), again indicating that his conception of manliness may be limited to pugnacious self assertion. Not only is such a concept immature in its directness; it is immature in its aiming at instant gratification without consideration of secondary consequences. The refusal to accept responsibility for secondary consequences is what explains the curious amnesia about his crime that puzzles Raskolnikov; he keeps wondering why he continues to forget that he murdered the gentle and exploited Lizaveta as well as her exploitative sister. It also explains why he gets angry when police inspector Porfiry reminds him that his family is now in St. Petersburg, and he "ought to take care of them and look after them properly" (p. 362), instead of frightening them with his surliness. Raskolnikov has behaved like an adult in refusing to let his sister enter a loveless marriage in order to provide for her brother and by appointing Razumikhin to be the deputy protector of his mother and sister, but he is slow to admit that an adult man is not free to take action that must certainly entail suffering upon his family, nor is he free to wallow in self pity or self torment. Porfiry emphasizes the immaturity inherent in masochism by stressing the childishness of the masochistic painter Mikolka, who confesses in place of Raskolnikov to the murder. Raskolnikov comes finally to accept his responsibility for causing pain to his mother and sister just before he confesses to the police: "He felt that he had undeniably made those two women unhappy. Whether right or wrong, he certainly was the cause of their unhappiness" (p. 530). His recognition of his own immaturity in choosing murder as a form of self assertion and social protest is the reason he tells Dunya when bidding her farewell before going to the police, "Don't weep for me. I'll try to be courageous and honest all my life, even if I am a murderer. One day perhaps you'll hear about me. I won't disgrace you, you'll see" (p. 531).

Because the nightmare dramatizes Raskolnikov's feeling that his father was not an adequate model for him, we are not surprised to find Raskolnikov's mother mistaken when she tries to console herself about her son's strange and frightening behavior by deciding, on the strength of one published article, that he is an eccentric genius following in the path of his father, the author of an unpublished poem and novel. In addition to learning from his nightmare that Raskolnikov lacks a model of an effectual father, the second thing we learn is Raskolnikov's strange relation to women, who are fully acceptable to him only in their role as mothers. This enables us to understand the intensity of the relation between Raskolnikov and his mother. When he bids her goodbye before going to confess, they weep together, his mother observing that he is now like a little boy again:

> Yes, yes, he was glad, he was very glad that there was no one there, that he was alone with his mother. It was as though his heart had softened all at once during all that awful time. He fell at her feet and kissed them. And both of them wept in each other's arms. And she was not surprised, and did not question him this time. She had long ago realized that something awful was happening to her son and that now the terrible moment had come for him.
>
> "Roddy, my dear, my firstborn," she said, sobbing, "now you're just as when you were a little boy. You would come and

> hug me and kiss me like that. When your father was living and we had such a bad time you comforted us by just being with us, and after your father's death, how many times, my dear, did we weep at his grave and embrace each other as now. And if I've been crying all this time, it's because my mother's heart felt that you were in trouble, dear." (p. 527)

This passage, combined with a previous admission of Mrs. Raskolnikov that her son has been capricious and cranky at least from the age of fifteen (p. 233), so that she has had difficulty with him for a long time, suggests his unresolved oedipal feelings toward his mother. Her own attachment to him is seen when she disapproves of Raskolnikov's first engagement and is jealous of Sonya, whom she suspects from the first time she sees her of being important to Raskolnikov, even though he himself has never seen Sonya before this meeting. Later Mrs. Raskolnikov blames Sonya for her son's break with her and Dunya. Razumikhin reports to Raskolnikov that his mother has said, "I can see that he has plenty of time for his girl," explaining, "She believes that your girl is Miss Marmeladov, whom she thinks is your fiancée or your mistress, I don't know which" (p. 454). At the last interview between mother and son, she begs to accompany him wherever he is going, along with Dunya and Sonya: "And Miss Marmeladov could come with us too, if you like. You see, I'd gladly take her as my daughter" (p. 526).

Raskolnikov tells Dunya as he bids her adieu that she should not leave their mother alone, for "when I left her she was so upset that I don't think she'll be able to bear it; she will die or go mad" (p. 531). Once in Siberia, he is not sanguine about his mother's illness, which has been reported to him, and he knows she has died before Sonya actually breaks the news to him.

Mrs. Raskolnikov's death occurs after a long period of mental disorder occasioned by the disappearance of her son for reasons she instinctively understands. She becomes convinced that Rodya told her to expect his return in nine months, tires herself out getting the apartment cleaned up and in order, sinks into a fever and delirium and dies two weeks later. The period of nine months is of course the poor woman's delusion about the rebirth of her first born; she envisions the religious rebirth Sonya has read about to Raskolnikov in the form of the Biblical story of the raising of Lazarus, entirely in maternal terms. In a way this is inspired insight, for Raskolnikov is unable to love Sonya wholeheartedly until his mother dies and the "little mother" of the Siberian prisoners replaces Mrs. Raskolnikov.

Just before his confession to Sonya, Raskolnikov complained like an irritable child to her, as she worried about what her crazed stepmother, Mrs. Marmeladov, was doing, "Always the same thing ... All you think of is *them*.

Stay with me" (p. 420). Now that Mrs. Raskolnikov is dead, Raskolnikov's conversion to loving Sonya and treating her affectionately instead of with coldness and anger can take place. Significantly, he engages in the same gesture and action with Sonya as he did when taking leave of his mother: "... suddenly something seemed to seize him and throw him at her feet. He embraced her knees and wept" (p. 577). Sonya quickly understands that the moment has come when Raskolnikov is able to love her: "She understood, and she had no doubts at all about it, that he loved her, loved her infinitely, and that the moment she had waited for so long had come at last" (p. 577).

The Raskolnikov who had admitted to himself that he was cruel to his mother, to his sister, and to Sonya, and who asked himself why they should love him, unworthy of it, so much, has come to attribute his basic motive in murdering the pawnbroker and her sister to his relation with his family: "Oh, if only I were alone and no one loved me and I, too had never loved anyone! *There would have been nothing of all this!*" (p. 532). Dostoevsky never explains what Raskolnikov means by what sounds like his protagonist's final evaluation of the dominating motive within a murky complex. From the foregoing analysis, however, I would summarize by saying that the conflict is only in part the one emphasized by the author: a struggle between mechanistically rational doctrines of social improvement, especially that of utilitarianism, imported from Western Europe and native Russian Orthodox conservative Christianity in the mind of a brilliant, proud, impatient, irascible, charitable, and compassionate young Russian intellectual. An equally central conflict, it seems to me, is the one between sexual perversion and Christian Orthodoxy; in this conflict, Western doctrine is a red herring.

Raskolnikov is a twenty-three-year-old who has not outgrown his attachment to his mother. He asserts his manhood through a violent action with sexual overtones that unleashes elements of sadism and masochism in himself. Having cut himself off from his family by this action, Raskolnikov seeks a substitute for his mother as confessor. Such a substitute must be like a mother, a feminine figure who will not reject her son no matter what he has done, and like a child, too innocent to reproach in a complex way an adult male. At the same time, like a mother, the substitute must offer some form of guidance representing a simple path out of the intellectual and emotional complexities that enmesh Raskolnikov. It is significant in this respect that Sonya's faith gives her the insight to reject Raskolnikov's Napoleonic excuse for the murder: "'You'd better tell me frankly—without any examples,' she begged ... he responds, 'You're right again, Sonya. All this is nonsense—just talk'" (p. 429). The simple path must agree with lessons already absorbed in childhood; in Raskolnikov's case, these lessons are the religion he learned from his parents, especially his mother. Next, the confessor chosen as a substitute for the mother must be desexualized. Yet unresolved sexual attachments to the mother, arousing guilt, enter into the new relationship. Sonya is a prostitute; at the same time, she is an innocent and undereducated young girl who can be made to suffer torment from the self exposure of a young man whose intellectual and emotional torments she is unprepared for. Finally, the confessor, unlike a sister, must lack any impulse of her own to self assertion (like Raskolnikov, Dunya is intelligent, proud, and impatient; characteristically, she comes prepared with a loaded gun to a private interview with the dangerous seducer Svidrigaylov), and must be strong enough from a life of privation and sorrow and a firm religious faith, to survive no matter how much emotional abuse.

Since Raskolnikov's love for women is so convoluted, it is not surprising that Dostoevsky depicts it in a morbidly decorporealized way as the happy conclusion to successful endurance of long torture near the end of *Crime and Punishment*:

> They wanted to speak, but could not; tears stood in their eyes. They were both pale and thin; but in those sick and pale faces the dawn of a new future, of a full resurrection to a new life, was already shining. It was love that brought them back to life: the heart of one held inexhaustible sources of life for the heart of the other. (p. 558)

Notes

1. Letter to A.A. Kraevsky, June 8, 1865. From Dostoevsky's *Letters* in *Crime and Punishment*, Norton Critical Edition, Second ed., ed. George Gibian (New York: W.W. Norton, 1975), p. 476.

2. Fyodor Dostoevsky, *Crime and Punishment*, trans. David Magarshack (Harmondsworth, Middlesex: Penguin Books, 1951). All textual citations are from this edition and translation.

3. Joseph Frank, "The World of Raskolnikov," in *Crime and Punishment*, Norton Critical Edition, p. 567.

4. Edward Wasiolek, "Raskolnikov's Motives: Love and Murder," *American Imago*, 31 (Fall 1974), p. 264.

5. From Dostoevsky's *Notebooks*, III, 108–9, 192 in *Crime and Punishment*, Norton Critical Edition, p. 475.

RICHARD PEACE

Motive and Symbol: 'Crime and Punishment'

Crime and Punishment, in as much as it is built exclusively round one character, has all the appearance of a monolith. This is deceptive; for the fabric itself of the monolith is ordered according to a dualistic structure which informs the whole work. Dualism is both Dostoyevsky's artistic method and his polemical theme. Dualism is the 'stick with two ends' with which he belabours the radicals of the sixties; for, in Raskolnikov, Dostoyevsky has chosen one of their number who, like the heroes of Pomyalovsky's novels, believes that he can conceive a crime rationally, justify it rationally and execute it rationally. It is this emphasis on man's rationality which Dostoyevsky attacks. The underground man had claimed that man's rational faculties constitute a mere twentieth part of his whole being: the error of Raskolnikov is that he mistakes the part for the whole.

Raskolnikov forces himself to subscribe to the monistic view of human nature; he tries to believe that he is self-sufficient and self-contained, that he is capable of acting solely according to the dictates of reason with that wholeness of purpose which distinguishes the positive characters of What is to be done? Dostoyevsky, on the other hand, exposes the dualistic nature of his hero, reveals that there is something else in Raskolnikov's make-up which runs contrary to his rationalism and which gravely undermines it.

Raskolnikov is not the whole man he takes himself to be: he is 'split in two', as his very name suggests (cf. *raskolot'*—to split). His friend Razumikhin points this out when discussing Raskolnikov's behaviour with his mother: 'It is as though two opposing characters inside him succeed one another by turns.' (Pt III, Ch. 2.) The clue to the nature of these 'two opposing characters' may perhaps be found in the ideas on human nature which Raskolnikov propounds in his article on crime. Here humanity is divided into 'ordinary people' and 'extra-ordinary people'; the first category constituting mere human material for the ambitions of the *heroes* of the second category. This is a division of humanity into submissive and aggressive elements, in which submissiveness is equated with stupidity and aggressiveness with intelligence. In inventing this theory, Raskolnikov has merely externalised his own inner conflict between urges to self-assertion (equated with reason) and promptings towards self-effacement (equated with the non-rational). That this theory does indeed reflect an inner struggle can be seen from the fact that Raskolnikov feels compelled to make a choice, and to seek his identity either as 'a Napoleon' or 'a louse'. These two extremes represent symbolically the poles of his own divided character.

Ambivalence permeates the whole novel. On the very first page we see that Raskolnikov, as he leaves his room with thoughts of the murder of one old woman in his mind, is at the same time apprehensive of another such figure—his landlady. This from the very first the reader is made aware of the disharmony in Raskolnikov between a ruthless side and a meek side. This dichotomy is present in scene after scene throughout the novel. The behaviour of Raskolnikov is now self-assertive, now self-effacing; now rational, now irrational; now 'bad', now 'good', and his own ambivalence is both reflected and heightened through the characters and situations he encounters.

Thus, broadly speaking, the first part of the novel may be reduced schematically to the following incidents: Raskolnikov visits the ruthless, self-interested Alyona; he next meets the squirming, self-effacing Marmeladov; in a letter from home he reads that the self-sacrificing Dunya has escaped the clutches of the ruthless Svidrigaylov only to fall prey to the equally ruthless Luzhin; musing on this letter, he sees a libertine ruthlessly pursuing a young girl who is the victim of debauchery: he falls asleep and dreams of a ruthless peasant beating to death his patiently suffering horse; he sees by chance Elizaveta, the self-effacing half-sister of Alyona.

The importance of this interplay of scenes opposing aggression to submission is to be seen in the corresponding shifts of attitude evoked in Raskolnikov himself. Thus his visit to Alyona leaves him feeling that what he contemplates is too terrible ever to be carried out, whereas his encounter with Marmeladov leads him to the conclusion that there is nothing to prevent his doing what he wishes to do. His ambivalent attitude to the suffering of the Marmeladov family is brought out by his instinctive act of self-sacrifice in leaving them money, followed immediately by anger and regret at having done so. The letter from home which throws into relief how closely his own situation parallels that of Marmeladov (i.e. Dunya appears to be about to 'sell herself' in order to support her brother, much as Sonya has become a prostitute in order to support her father) evokes once more an ambivalent response:

> Almost all the time he was reading the letter, from the very beginning, Raskolnikov's face was wet with tears; but when he had finished his face was pale and contorted and a bitter, spiteful, evil smile played on his lips. (Pt I, Ch. 3)

In the next scene, with the young girl and the middle-aged libertine, Raskolnikov's first reaction of selfless solicitude suddenly yields place to ruthless indifference; after insulting the rake and giving a policeman money to call a cab for the girl, there is an abrupt change of mood: Raskolnikov suddenly calls out to the policeman to leave the couple alone, as it is none of his business.

The dream of the peasant beating the old nag to death leaves Raskolnikov feeling that he could never murder the old woman; yet he has only to meet Elizaveta to become once more convinced that the murder will be committed. Symbols of aggression evoke in Raskolnikov feelings of submission; symbols of submission bring out his aggressiveness. The coin of Raskolnikov's inner realm, bearing on one side the head of Napoleon, on the other the effigy of a louse, spins in a constant game of 'heads and tails' with his surroundings.

It is by this juxtaposition of opposites that Dostoyevsky clearly indicates the divided mind of Raskolnikov on the question of the murder itself. As we might expect, this is not carried out entirely in the calculated way in which one half of Raskolnikov would have liked. Thus, though many details such as the sling and the pledge have been planned with thought, other details such as the procuring of the hatchet, the knowledge that Elizaveta would be absent, the failure to lock the door behind him—all these are dictated by pure chance. The author comments: 'In spite of the agony of his inner struggle, he could never during all these weeks believe for a single moment in the practicability of his plans.' (Pt I, Ch. 6.) All these details, then, he had dismissed as trifles worthy of his attention only after he was sure of the main problem. But it is precisely this element of the unplanned, the lapses of the rational mind, which leads Raskolnikov to commit a double murder instead of the single murder he had intended. He forgets to lock the door: Elizaveta comes back.

If we turn once more to the schematic appraisal of events in Part I leading up to the murder, the conclusion may be drawn that the characters encountered can be divided roughly into two categories, and that these categories correspond to those put forward by Raskolnikov himself in his article on crime. Thus in the category of the self-assertive we have Alyona, Luzhin, Svidrigaylov; in the category of the self-effacing—Elizaveta, Marmeladov, Sonya, Dunya. If this is true, it follows that these characters may in a certain sense be taken as symbolising aspects of Raskolnikov himself; for we have already noted the relationship between the categories of Raskolnikov's theory and the poles of his own inner conflict.

This interpretation raises the question of the extent to which *Crime and Punishment* may be regarded as a novel in the realistic tradition; for *Crime and Punishment* is widely so regarded. But realism is a term which needs to be defined. If by realism is meant the exposure of the grim reality of social conditions, then it cannot be denied that *Crime and Punishment* is a great realistic novel. The street and tavern scenes showing the tribulations of the poor of St Petersburg; the two sub-plots, one centred on the Marmeladov family, the other on Dunya—all belong to this realistic theme of 'the insulted and the injured'. But if by realism is meant the depiction of reality purged of all fantastic elements, the claim of *Crime and Punishment* to be a realistic novel is more dubious.

But the Russian realistic tradition is frequently associated with elements of the fantastic. This is particularly true of the writings of Dostoyevsky's great predecessor Nikolay Gogol.[1] It is not that the supernatural enters into *Crime and Punishment* in the way that it does say in Gogol's *Greatcoat*, though two of the characters (Sonya and Svidrigaylov) claim to have seen ghosts; nor is it so much the fact that the novel is permeated by that sense of 'mystic terror' described by Ivan Petrovich in *The Insulted and the Injured*; nevertheless in *Crime and Punishment* dream passes into reality, reality into dream, and the supernatural always seems uncannily present even though it may be explained in terms of the real world.[2]

What is truly fantastic in *Crime and Punishment* is the predominance of coincidence. Characters bump into one another in the street or meet one another by apparent chance in taverns.[3] Not only this; many characters are found to be living alongside one another in the most improbable way. Thus Svidrigaylov lodges next door to Sonya; Luzhin lives with Lebezyatnikov who in turn lives in the same house as the Marmeladov family. Moreover, there is the question of the way various characters appear to be related to one another: Luzhin is related to Svidrigaylov (through his wife) and is the former guardian of Lebezyatnikov; Porfiry is related to Razumikhin. Yet these three devices which, for want of better terms, may be branded as coincidence, co-habitation and collateralization all tend towards the same effect—they draw the characters closer together and in some measure identify them one with another. We are not dealing here so much with the realistic portrayal of character as with its symbolic meaning.

When Raskolnikov exclaims that he has not murdered an old woman: he has murdered himself (Pt V, Ch. 4), he is proclaiming the symbolic truth behind the murder; for his two victims represent the two poles within himself: Alyona—tyrannical, ruthless grasping for herslf; Liza—meek, selflessly doing good for others. It is significant that in Part I, at the end of that sequence of alternating attitudes to the crime, Raskolnikov's determination to commit the murder only becomes finally established when he learns the Elizaveta will not be in the apartment with Alyona. In spite of the strength of his previous doubts, this one overheard piece of information is sufficient to give him the singleness of purpose which he needs. Elizaveta represents the weaker side of himself, and Elizaveta, he now knows, will be absent, therefore nothing can now deter him from his assignation with the stronger side of his nature, represented by Alyona.

But this is of course the mistake of Chernyshevsky and his rationalist followers; man cannot dispose so easily of one side of himself; he cannot exert one side of his nature at the expense of the other, and so Raskolnikov, the would-be rationalist, irrationally *leaves the door unlocked*; *Liza returns and has to be murdered too*. This is why, throughout the initial stages of the murder, Raskolnikov behaves in the zombie-like manner of a man who is 'only half there', whereas after the arrival of Liza he becomes more aware of the reality of the situation: 'He became more and more seized with panic, especially after this second, quite unexpected, murder. He wanted to run away from there as quickly as possible.' (Pt. I, Ch. 7). Symbolically, Dostoyevsky has shown that it is impossible for Raskolnikov to assert one side of his nature without of necessity involving the other: the murder of Alyona inevitably brings in its wake that of Elizaveta.

It is the realisation, at a deep psychological level, of the full horror of this truth which leads to Raskolnikov's breakdown. But what is significant is that Raskolnikov, with one part of himself, again refuses to face this truth; there appears to be an unaccountable blank in his memory once he allows himself to be dominated again by the ruthless, rational side of his character. For the most part, when discussing his theories and defending his actions, it is only the murder of Alyona which is mentioned: Elizaveta is left out of consideration.

Thus he can even defend the murder of Alyona to Dunya just before he goes to make his official deposition to the police, but in this defence no mention is made of Elizaveta. Even in the penal settlement he is still convinced of the validity of his theories and again maintains that it was no crime to kill Alyona: no mention is made of Elizaveta.

Raskolnikov is first reminded that he has also killed Elizaveta by Nastasya, the servant of his landlady. Nastasya was acquainted with Elizaveta, and whereas Alyona exploited Raskolnikov, gave him little money in return for his pledges, Elizaveta, so Nastasya now tells him, rendered him services—she mended his shirts. Shocked at learning this, Raskolnikov turns over in his bed and pretends to study the wallpaper.

As we have seen, Raskolnikov's landlady is linked with Alyona on the very first page of the novel. Moreover it is at her instigation that Raskolnikov is ordered to the police station to pay a debt. This summons, occurring as it does immediately after the murder, appears almost as some sort of retribution from the grave. In the landlady who persecutes him, and the servant who helps him (and is also a friend of Elizaveta) there may be seen a pale reflection of the Alyona/Elizaveta duality.

A much stronger reflection of Elizaveta, however, is to be seen in Sonya. Not only is she too the friend of Elizaveta, but they share many traits of character in common. Both are alike in their self-effacement, their humility, their kindness. Both are 'fallen women'. Sonya is a prostitute; Elizaveta, we learn, has been many times seduced and seems constantly pregnant. More significantly, however, they have exchanged crosses and are thus in some sense spiritual sisters. Moreover, the New Testament from which Sonya reads to Raskolnikov, and which he later keeps under his pillow in Siberia, was given to Sonya originally by Elizaveta. Raskolnikov himself muses on the similarity between these two women and likens them both to 'holy fools'.[4]

All the evidence suggests that Sonya is a restatement of Elizaveta, and it is significant that, when Raskolnikov confesses to Sonya, it is the murder of Elizaveta which for the first time he has in the forefront of his consciousness. Yet not only is there a restatement of Elizaveta; there is too a restatement of Alyona. Towards the end of the novel Sonya's influence on Raskolnikov is very strong, but there is yet another, and contrary influence on him—that of Svidrigaylov. Broadly speaking, Svidrigaylov belongs to that category of the ruthless, self-interested characters to which Alyona also belongs. Unlike Alyona, however, it is not for profit that he exploits 'the insulted and the injured': it is rather for his own pleasure; he satisfies his lust at their expense rather than his avarice.

The connection between these two characters is stated quite clearly in the novel in a scene which deserves to be examined closely, as it not only points to the link between Alyona and Svidrigaylov, but also emphasises the association of Elizaveta with Sonya, and the symbolic relationship of these characters to Raskolnikov himself.

Raskolnikov, having been accused of the murder by an unknown man in the street, returns to his room and begins to turn over in his mind the question of the murder and the problem of his own position

> '*She*[5] must be the same as me,' he added thinking with effort, as though struggling with the delirium which seized him. 'Oh. how I hate the old woman now. I think I would kill her a second time if she came back to life. Poor Lizaveta, why did she turn up then? It is strange, however; why do I scarcely think about her? Almost as though I did not kill her ... Lizaveta! Sonya! Poor and meek, with meek eyes. Dear people; why do they weep? Why do they groan? ... They give all away and look at you meekly and gently... Sonya, Sonya, gentle Sonya.' (Pt III, Ch. 6)

At this point Raskolnikov falls asleep and his threat is acted out in a dream; he attempts to kill the old woman a second time, but she refuses to die. He strikes again and again with his axe, to no avail: the old woman openly mocks him. The bedroom *door comes open*, and the mocking and jeering is carried on by other unknown people. He tries to scream, and wakes up. This is how the scene continues:

> He drew a deep breath, but it was strange, it was as though his dream were still continuing: the door was open and on the threshold stood a man completely unknown to him, who was gazing at him fixedly.

The unknown stranger is Svidrigaylov; he is the continuation of Raskolnikov's dream—the old woman who has come to life again; the old woman who refuses to die.[6] To strengthen the links between the dream and the symbol, Raskolnikov is shown as taking some time to convince himself that the dream is not, in fact, continuing. The same fly that was there in the dream is also present in the room when he wakes up, and the detail of the open door (the significance of which has been noted earlier) is a feature common to both the dream and the ensuing reality. Moreover the beginning of Part IV, in which Svidrigaylov reveals himself more fully, re-emphasises the point once more: '"Is this really the continuation of the dream?", once again this thought came into Raskolnikov's mind.'

Not only does this bridge between dream and reality indicate that

Svidrigaylov is a restatement of Alyona; it also gives an ironical comment on Raskolnikov's failure ultimately to be like them. This time the duality is a verbal one. Svidrigaylov first appears in the doorway, but then he steps over the threshold and enters the room. This act of *stepping over* is here indicated concretely by the very same verb [*perestupit'*][7] which Raskolnikov had used shortly before to describe his figurative act of stepping over; for in his bout of self-questioning before the dream he had said:

> The old woman was only an illness, I wanted to step over as soon as possible ... I did not kill an old woman, I killed a principle. It was a principle I killed, but as to stepping over, I did not succeed in stepping over. (Pt III, Ch. 6)

The musings of Raskolnikov on his ability to step over are vividly illustrated in his dream by his failure to kill the old woman, whereas the ability to do so of the truly ruthless character is emphasised by Svidrigaylov's first action after his intrusion into Raskolnikov's dream: 'Suddenly, but with caution, he stepped over the threshold, and carefully closed the door behind him.'

If, therefore, Alyona and Elizaveta may be taken to represent the two poles of Raskolnikov's own character, this polarisation does not cease on their death; it is restated in the figures of Svidrigaylov and Sonya. Thus it is no accident that Sonya and Svidrigaylov live next door to one another in the same house, just as earlier Elizaveta and Alyona lived in the same apartment.

In the murder of Alyona, Raskolnikov has attempted to assert one side of his character, but has been unable to do so without involving the other side of himself. Elizaveta is murdered too. If murder is the action which expresses his self-assertive side, the other, the self-effacing side, is expressed in action by confession. The scene of Raskolnikov's confession to Sonya is designed to form an exact pendant to the scene of the murder.

The formal arrangement of the two scenes is striking. The murder is preceded by a trial visit to Alyona, during which Raskolnikov promises to come again with a silver cigarette case;[8] the confession is preceded by a trial visit to Sonya during which Raskolnikov promises to come again and tell her who has killed Elizaveta. Both scenes end in a similar way; the murder scene culminates in the ringing of the bell; the confession scene ends with the knocking at the door, which announces the arrival of Lebezyatnikov. Nor is this all; on the subject of the confession Raskolnikov has the same feeling of inevitability that he had experienced over the murder, and there is in both events the same mixture of the premeditated and the unpremeditated: 'He could get nothing out. It was not at all, not at all the way he had intended to confess.'

In fact the whole situation reminds him strongly of the murder

> He felt that this moment was terrifyingly like the moment when he stood behind the old woman and, disengaging the axe from the sling, sensed that there was not a moment to lose.
>
> (Pt V, Ch. 4)

In both scenes Dostoyevsky is making the same point; Raskolnikov, consciously murdering Alyona, unwittingly is forced to kill Elizaveta: Raskolnikov, confessing to Sonya, unwittingly confesses to Svidrigaylov. Just as, in the act of self-assertion, Raskolnikov mistakenly believes that he can involve one side of his personality to the exclusion of the other, so here, in the act of self-effacement, he again tries to involve one side of himself and leave the other out of the reckoning. But the other side cannot be so ignored; *Svidrigaylov is listening to his confession from the other side of the door.*

The fact that Svidrigaylov overhears the confession is again a symbolic statement of the hero's divided psychology. Integration still has to be achieved. Even after the confession, even in the penal settlement itself, one half of Raskolnikov seems still to be convinced of the validity of his theory, convinced that it was no crime to kill Alyona. Yet after the death of Svidrigaylov he does at least round off the confession and make a deposition to the police.

At this point it might be opportune to discuss the role of the police in the novel. Their chief representative is Porfiry, and although it is said that Porfiry represents the new type of investigator resulting from the legal reforms of the sixties, there is nevertheless much in his portrayal which hints at something more than a policeman. Through the insights which the 'two ended stick' of psychology affords him, he appears to know Raskolnikov through and through. Indeed, almost like Providence itself, he appears to know everything. Yet at the same time he is less concerned with apprehending Raskolnikov as a criminal, than with saving him as a human being. There are, in the portrayal of Porfiry, strong elements of some sort of 'secular priest',[9] which can only be explained in terms of the symbolism of the novel. An examination of the significance of the names which the chief characters bear will further clarify this.

The name Porfiry is derived from *porphyra*, the purple cloak which was the attribute of the Byzantine emperors. The full name of Sonya is Sof'ya (Sophia) which evokes the great Orthodox cathedral of Constantinople—Hagia Sophia (The Holy Wisdom of Orthodoxy). Raskolnikov's name comes from *raskol'nik*—a schismatic or heretic. Svidrigaylov evokes Svidrigaylo, a Lithuanian prince who was active during the fifteenth century—so fateful for the Orthodox world. He may be taken as the barbarian *par excellence*, the perpetrator of cynical sacrilege for the goal of self-interest.[10]

Thus on a symbolic level it can be seen that Porfiry is the representative of the temporal power of Orthodoxy, whereas Sonya represents its spiritual power. Both are striving to bring back Raskolnikov, the schismatic, to the true fold, but they are opposed in their efforts by Svidrigaylov, the barbarian who profanes what is holy to achieve selfish ends.

There is yet another character in the novel who serves to reinforce this interpretation of Raskolnikov as the schismatic. Mikolka, the peasant house-painter, is obviously to be taken as a shadowy *double* for Raskolnikov himself. Thus not only is he arrested instead of Raskolnikov on suspicion of the murder, but the psychological evidence which would seem to vindicate him (i.e. his laughter and high-spirits immediately after the murder) is used by Raskolnikov as a means of throwing suspicion away from himself: on the occasion of his first visit to Porfiry Raskolnikov teases Razumikhin so that he may enter Porfiry's apartment laughing and in obvious high spirits.

Porfiry's attempt to play off Mikolka against Raskolnikov ends with Mikolka's false confession; and the explanation which Porfiry gives for this phenomenon is that Mikolka wishes to take on suffering because he is a schismatic—'*On iz raskol'nikov*'. The form in which this is expressed is worthy of note.

But Mikolka does not represent only the 'confessional' side of Raskolnikov. Connected with the name Mikolka is a hint of the same duality which plagues Raskolnikov himself; the peasant who beats the horse to death in Raskolnikov's dream is also called Mikolka. It is perhaps significant too that, just as there had been these painters in the house at the time of the murder, there are also painters present when Raskolnikov returns to the scene of the crime and seems driven to display his guilt.

Religious significance permeates the novel. Some commentators, for example, point to the trinitarian symbolism in the three windows in Sonya's room.[11] Sonya, too, lives with the Kapernaumov family—a name derived from the Capernaum of the New Testament. It is, however, in the theme of Lazarus that the positive religious meaning of the novel resides. Sonya's reading of the story of the resurrection of Lazarus has a great effect on Raskolnikov, and we are told that the New Testament (originally Elizaveta's) which he has with him in the penal settlement, and which is principally responsible for his own 'resurrection', is the same New Testament from which Sonya had read to him the story of the raising of Lazarus. Even before the reading of this story, Porfiry had challenged him on his faith in it, and Raskolnikov had replied that he believed literally in the raising of Lazarus.

However, Dostoyevsky had to sacrifice much of his original intention in the scene where the story is read (Pt IV, Ch. 4), a scene which he himself regarded as the high point of the novel. A prostitute reading holy scripture to a murderer was considered too provocative an incident by his publisher, Katkov, and reluctantly Dostoyevsky had to abandon his original intention. This explains why the theme of the raising of Lazarus is not as fully developed in the novel as its author undoubtedly would have liked.

It may at first sight seem strange that Raskolnikov, who commits a particularly vile murder, should be identified with religious heresy, but the sense in which he is a heretic may be shown by an analysis of the motives which inspired the crime. Here we come up against duality once more. The murder itself, as events turn out, becomes a double murder; but the crime even in its original conception was twofold-murder plus robbery.

More significant still is the fact that Raskolnikov gives two distinct motives for his crime; on the one hand he alleges that his motive was to obtain money for himself and his family: on the other hand, he talks about the crime as an exercise in self-knowledge. For the first explanation to hold, true murder is unnecessary; robbery alone would have sufficed, or even the crime of counterfeiting, which serves in the novel as a commentary theme for Raskolnikov's own crime.

This motive, however, is not quite what it seems: it is not a straightforward question of personal gain. Raskolnikov justifies himself on social grounds; the murder of Alyona, in itself, is seen as the elimination of a social evil; whilst the appropriation of her wealth has the aim of righting social injustices. Although in Raskolnikov's scheme for the righting of social wrongs charity appears to begin at home (he himself and his immediate family are to be the prime beneficiaries of Alyona's wealth) the implications behind such charity are nevertheless much wider; for Raskolnikov believes that by using the money for good deeds he can thereby cancel out the bad deed of murder. The motive is, therefore, in essence a social one, in spite of its personal implications: it is the application of Luzhin's theory of 'enlightened self-interest'.

It is the second motive, however, which is really the personal one; for according to this explanation Raskolnikov is trying to define his own nature, trying to find out whether he is a Napoleon or a louse. This motive, as we have already seen, goes back to Raskolnikov's article on crime; therefore, although it is in essence a personal motive it cannot be divorced entirely from social implications.

The social motivation for the crime links Raskolnikov with the heroes of Pomyalovsky's novels, with the nihilists, among whose ranks Dostoyevsky had already observed a schism. In a social context, Raskolnikov is an extremist and a fanatic, who when faced with a *wall* of accepted social morality *steps over* it, in order to better himself, his immediate family and humanity in general.

The personal motivation for the crime, on the other hand, points to the rebellion of the underground man, to the deification of man's will in his striving towards godhead; for Raskolnikov, in his assault on the wall, is measuring against it the strength of his own will. To this extent he is a rebel in a religious sense; a heretic who believes that the unlimited powers of godhead reside in himself. Indeed, when he is in the penal settlement, Raskolnikov has a dream of a disease sweeping Europe through which men become 'possessed', and each one regards himself as the bearer of truth. The implications behind this dream are those of heresy, and its specific relevance is for Raskolnikov himself.[12]

There are, therefore, in Raskolnikov two types of rebel: a social one and a religious one, and both are linked to schism. There is, of course, no fundamental incompatibility between the two motives he alleges; for it is quite feasible that he could have intended to show himself a Napoleonic man by the same act that benefited others. Yet, despite this, there appears to be a real sense of dichotomy in the mind of Raskolnikov himself. During his confession to Sonya he alleges now one motive, now the other. But there are flaws in both explanations.

If he murdered for money, why was it that he showed so little interest in his acquisitions both at the time of the murder and afterwards? On the other hand, if he were genuinely trying to prove himself a Napoleonic man, can he seriously equate the murder of some pitiable old woman with the grandiose exploits of Napoleon? Even more fundamental is his own recognition that a Napoleon would not have had the doubts about his actions that he himself has had. The mere fact that he had to prove himself shows that he secretly had doubts about his being a Napoleonic man, and this alone shows that he was not entitled to commit the crime.

Once more we return to the idea that the ambivalence of Raskolnikov's character precludes that singleness of purpose which marks out the Napoleonic man from the rest of humanity. Raskolnikov in his confession to Sonya shows himself aware of this. Even before committing the crime he had sensed that the weakness implicit in his self-questioning gave him no right to attempt it, that by asserting one side of his nature at the expense of the other he was dooming himself to failure. The crime, therefore, assumes the nature of an exercise in self-deception masquerading as an act of self-knowledge.

When taxed by Sonya, he is unable in the last analysis to put forward either of these two alleged motives as the real reason for the murder; he falls back on the idea that the murder is in some sense symbolic, claiming that he killed himself (or even, as earlier, a principle) and not an old woman; she was killed, he claims, by the devil. If he is to accept full responsibility for the murder, the only explanation he seems able to offer is that he killed for himself; an explanation which seems to exclude any rational motivation but appears rather to indicate some irrational need to kill for its own sake. In the last analysis Raskolnikov is just as perplexed about his motive for the murder as is the reader.

We have seen that Raskolnikov's failure to achieve his ends is brought about because of the opposing characters within himself. But the process of writing with Dostoyevsky is a process of the splitting and subdividing of idea cells; Svidrigaylov and Sonya, although representing poles of Raskolnikov's character, nevertheless undergo the same sort of polarisation themselves.

At first sight it might appear that Svidrigaylov has no philanthropic side to his nature at all; no other interests but the interests of self. He appears to be a man who can 'step over' with impunity. He has led a life of debauchery; is reputed to have seduced a fourteen-year-old deaf mute, and by this act to be responsible for her suicide; it is also held that he bears some measure of guilt in the death of one of his servants; and he is accused of having poisoned his wife. On all these scores he appears to have a clear conscience.

Yet all these deeds are of a different order from that of the central crime of the novel, in that the reader is given no definite proof of their reality: all Svidrigaylov's crimes belong to a penumbra of hearsay and rumour which surrounds him up to, and even after, his first appearance in the novel. It is the symbolic act of stepping over Raskolnikov's threshold, bringing him out of this shadowy land of imputation into the action of the novel itself, which marks the beginning of Svidrigaylov's growing ambivalence.

Thus, at this very first meeting with Raskolnikov, he shows that he has a human flaw: he is in love with Raskolnikov's sister; and he himself presents us with a possible ambivalent interpretation of his behaviour towards her, by asking whether he is really to be considered a monster or a victim. The philosophy of out-and-out humanism which he expresses in the Latin tag, *nihil humanum*, might seem to permit him everything, but it also makes human weakness possible—Svidrigaylov is in love.

Whatever Dunya's attitude to Svidrigaylov may be (and there are indications that she is not entirely unresponsive to his advances), Svidrigaylov is determined to pursue her by all the means within his power. He attempts bribery, blackmail and in the last resort violence, but Dunya draws out a revolver and fires twice at her would-be seducer. The first bullet grazes his scalp, the second shot misfires, and then, although there is yet a third bullet in the chamber, she throws the revolver away. Svidrigaylov attempts to embrace her, but realising in despair that she does not love him,[13] and that for once in his life he is powerless—powerless to compel her love—he lets her go.

After this scene, Svidrigaylov seems a changed man; he openly acknowledges another side to his character. Thus he calls on Sonya and confirms the arrangements he has made to take care of the remaining members of her family (arrangements which had been first mooted as part of his campaign to win Dunya). He then calls on his sixteen-year-old fiancee and leaves her a present of fifteen thousand roubles (Svidrigaylov's wealth had originally been the lure for this fresh young victim).[14]

He takes a room in a shabby hotel, which in its cramped poverty is reminiscent of Raskolnikov's room, and through a chink in the wall he witnesses a squalid scene of aggression and submission, symbolically recalling the dilemma which haunts Raskolnikov and which now appears to be affecting Svidrigaylov himself. His last action in leaving this room is a futile attempt to catch a fly; the motif of the fly links Svidrigaylov's departure from the pages of the novel with his first appearance in the room of Raskolnikov.

During his brief stay in this room, Svidrigaylov is haunted by dreams which reflect the ambivalence of his relations with women. Thus he thinks of Dunya and falls asleep to dream of a mouse which torments him. His second dream is of the fourteen-year-old girl for whose death his 'love' has been responsible, and his third dream is even more striking; he comforts a five-year-old girl who turns out eventually to be a child prostitute. The central dilemma behind all these dreams is whether the lover is a tyrant or a victim.

The night culminates in his suicide with the revolver loaded with Dunya's one remaining bullet; as Dunya cannot feel sufficiently strongly for him even to kill him, Svidrigaylov is reduced to completing the attempt himself and thus turn murder into suicide. The gun which he uses in this act recalls in the chain of its provenance the New Testament instrumental in resurrecting Raskolnikov; for the revolver is not merely Dunya's, it had come originally from Svidrigaylov's wife, and his relations with her have the same ambiguity as his relations with Dunya (in his marriage and subsequent incarceration in the country was Svidrigaylov his wife's victim, or in the circumstances of her death did he play the role of a monster?). The choice of surroundings for his suicide symbolises the nature of his inner dichotomy. Svidrigaylov shoots himself in front of a tiny Jew in a soldier's greatcoat and an Achilles helmet, and commits an act of self-immolation before a symbol of his own personal tragedy; for in the figure of the Jew wrapped up in the soldier's greatcoat, we have one of the persecuted dressed up as one of the persecutors. This idea is further reinforced by the detail of the Achilles helmet, and by the fact, too, that this incongruous figure is itself referred to as 'Achilles'. Here we have an obvious reference to the hero who is apparently unvanquishable, until his one fatal flaw has been discovered. Svidrigaylov commits suicide because he realises that the question he first put to Raskolnikov has been answered: he is *both* monster and victim, *both* oppressor and oppressed.

If the fate of Svidrigaylov shows that ruthlessness has its weaknesses and its unexpected philanthropy, the way of Sonya, the way of self-effacement, is also seen to have its pitfalls. The dark side of humility is foreshadowed in the person of Marmeladov. He is a weak, submissive character who is responsible for much human suffering; for it is he who must be blamed for the plight of his wife and family. Confession, which for Raskolnikov is the symbolic act of self-effacement, has become for Marmeladov a subtle weapon of aggression. Those who listen to Marmeladov's words of self-denigration feel more uncomfortable than Marmeladov himself; they themselves in some underhand way are being attacked.[15] It may be objected that Marmeladov is not genuinely humble, that he is merely a caricature of humility, but no such criticism could be levelled at his daughter, Sonya, yet the humility of Sonya is shown to have its dark side too.

Raskolnikov does not react uncritically to the influence of Sonya; he points out the flaws in her attitude to life. His objections are that by her very humility, by her very submissiveness, Sonya is vulnerable, and that this does not merely affect herself; for since she is the breadwinner, her family must suffer through her vulnerability, as it had suffered through the shortcomings of her father.

Raskolnikov's point is proved when Luzhin nearly succeeds in having Sonya arrested on a trumped-up charge of theft. Sonya's submissiveness reveals itself as powerless in the face of active evil. She is only saved from prison by the intervention of forceful characters—Lebezyatnikov and Raskolnikov. The fact that Sonya would suffer is not the point. If she were unable to earn money, argues Raskolnikov, the innocent victims of her plight would be her younger brothers and sisters as well as her consumptive step-mother. Although Sonya's submissiveness in the face of Luzhin's active malice does not, in the event, have this effect, the threat is nevertheless there, and it is this incident which comes as the last straw to break her step-mother's long overburdened sanity.

But it is in a second way that the submissiveness of Sonya must be held partly responsible for the death of Katerina Ivanovna and the degradation of her children. Sonya's inability to cope with Luzhin's malice causes her to flee in distress to her room. Raskolnikov follows her there in triumph ('What will you say now, Sof'ya Semyonovna'); for he is seeking to convince himself that his own way of providing for his family, by sacrificing others, is correct;

whereas Sonya's way of doing so, by sacrificing herself, is wrong. He thinks that his criticism of her humility has now been fully vindicated by the plot of Luzhin, but at the same time he also tells her of the effect that this incident has had on Katerina Ivanovna.

On hearing of this, Sonya's first impulse is to go to the aid of her step-mother, but Raskolnikov for motives of his own (the confession), prevails on her to stay. Once again, through her submissiveness, Sonya must be held in some measure responsible for the suffering of others; for had she asserted herself against the arguments of Raskolnikov and gone to take care of her step-mother, the harrowing sequence of events leading up to the death of Katerina Ivanovna could have been avoided. Even if the death itself were inevitable, the degradation imposed on the children before her death could have been prevented by the presence of Sonya, and the greatest crimes for Dostoyevsky are always those committed against children.

It is as though Dostoyevsky is forcing a parallel between Sonya's sin of omission and Raskolnikov's crime of commission, when he makes Raskolnikov put the choice to her of either allowing Luzhin to live and carry on with his underhand deeds or letting Katerina Ivanovna die. Sonya refuses to make the choice, but in reality she has already chosen; the very submissiveness which prevents her from defending herself against Luzhin, also prevents her from denying Raskolnikov's right to keep her from her step-mother's side in time of need. Therefore because she is prepared to allow Luzhin to go on living and commit his vile deeds, she is also prepared to let Katerina Ivanovna die.[16] In the very scene where Raskolnikov yields to the promptings of his own weaker side, Sonya in staying to listen to this confession is also unwittingly culpable herself; active guilt and passive guilt are dovetailed together.

Svidrigaylov, the dark antithesis of Sonya, is the unseen witness both of Raskolnikov's confession of action and also of Sonya's failure to act. By way of stressing Sonya's culpability, Svidrigaylov mysteriously turns up at the death of Katerina Ivanovna, and by quoting back to Raskolnikov his own words on the choice between the life of Luzhin and the death of Katerina Ivanovna, he indicates in one sentence that, not only has he heard the confession, but that he also understands the implications of the death of Katerina Ivanovna for Sonya. Then, as if finally to drive the point home that Sonya's submissiveness has failed to provide a safeguard for her family, it is Svidrigaylov, of all people, who offers to look after them.

These implications behind Sonya's own position during the confession scene would seem to weaken the case for confession itself, and it is only much later that Raskolnikov makes his deposition to the police. Yet neither the confession nor the deposition shows true repentance. Genuine repentance does not come in the novel, not even in the Epilogue; it is a process destined to take seven years after the closing scene of the novel, and could, as Dostoyevsky comments, form the theme for a new novel. It is important to bear these facts in mind; for it is commonly held that the ending of *Crime and Punishment* is unconvincing, that the reader does not really believe in the rehabilitation of Raskolnikov. It is perhaps true that the Epilogue is not written with the same intensity as the rest of the novel, but this should not lead us to assume that the resurrection of Raskolnikov is unconvincing. The Epilogue does not deal with this resurrection: it only marks the beginning of the road.

To regard the hero's rehabilitation as improbable is perhaps to suffer from the same partial blindness that affects Raskolnikov himself: i.e. to disregard the 'Elizaveta' in his make-up. Raskolnikov is not morally corrupt in the normal sense: on the contrary, it is possible to compile an impressive list of his 'good deeds'. Thus, though in a state of penury himself, he gives money away to the needy on various occasions: once to the Marmeladov family; another time to the policeman to whose care he entrusts the drunken girl; yet again to a prostitute in the street. His charity is also stressed by Razumikhin; at the university he had supported a consumptive fellow-student; and later, when the young man had died, he had also taken upon himself to support his father. Nor is his philanthropy lacking in personal valour; even his landlady gives evidence that he had once rescued two small children from a burning apartment, and had himself been burned in the process. Indeed one reason for his crime is, paradoxically enough, his compassion for the 'insulted and injured'.

Yet if the two sides of Raskolnikov's character are ever to be integrated there is a genuine need for contrition. The need to confess, which Raskolnikov feels, may be taken as an urge towards contrition; throughout the course of the novel Raskolnikov has many promptings to confess. Such promptings occur from the very first. Indeed, immediately after the murder he thinks of kneeling down in the police station and blurting out the truth. In his dealings with the police, the idea of confession haunts him more than once; thus to Zametov, the police clerk, he makes a mocking, false confession, and later he even feels prompted to go back to the scene of the crime, and arouse suspicion there by his strange behaviour. Yet most surprising of all is the claim he makes to Sonya, that when he had first heard about her through her father, he had resolved there and then to tell her about the murder. This can only mean that he had thought of telling Sonya about the murder even before it had been committed. The two elements which mark his divided psychology are discernibly associated with one another even prior to their expression in action. Indeed, as might be expected, it even appears that the idea of confession is, in a certain sense, simultaneous in conception with the plan of murder itself; for Raskolnikov claims that he had first discussed the possibility of the crime with another Sonya-like figure, his ailing sweetheart, the landlady's daughter, who has died before the action of the novel begins.

Although this need for confession is fundamental to Raskolnikov's nature, and has resulted in his telling Sonya about the murder and in his ultimate deposition to the police, nevertheless he himself knows full well that confession is not the same as contrition. Even when he has taken on his suffering, and is a convict in the penal settlement, he says how happy he would feel if he could only blame himself for what he has done. That he cannot do so is because, as yet, he has not managed to resolve the conflict within himself; the self-assertive side of Raskolnikov's character, although its position is now undoubtedly weaker, is making its last stand.

The reconciliation of the two opposing elements within Raskolnikov will result in the resurrection that Dostoyevsky prophesies for his hero. The self-assertive side will not be eradicated: its energies will be fused with the gentle, self-effacing qualities of the other side. A new Raskolnikov will emerge to fulfil the exhortation of Porfiry, that he must be a sun for all to see. The beginnings of this integration are discernible in the Epilogue: 'Life had taken the place of dialectics, and something else, completely different, had to work itself out in his consciousness.' The inevitability of this change can be seen by tracing Raskolnikov's development through the Epilogue.

Isolated from the other prisoners through his pride, there is only one person to whom he can turn for help, who represents something other than the hard conditions of the penal settlement; that person is, of course, Sonya. Although all the other prisoners like Sonya, there is still a part of Raskolnikov which struggles against her; but his own intolerable position as an outcast among the outcasts is brought home to him when some of the other convicts attempt to murder him on the grounds that he is an atheist. He falls ill, and in his weakened physical state dreams of a disease sweeping Europe from Asia. This dream is an allegory, which shows Raskolnikov what would happen if everybody were to set himself up as a prophet of some 'new truth'; the relevance of this for Raskolnikov's own theories is obvious.

But Sonya, too, has fallen ill, and is no longer able to see him. First he realises that he misses her; then when next he sees her he realises that he loves her. This sudden love for Sonya is not something unexpected or fortuitous; the foundations have been laid long ago in the novel—it is, if anything, overdue. Raskolnikov's love for Sonya, and the echo she awakens in the humble side of his nature, is the cornerstone on which he may build the edifice of a new Raskolnikov. Through his love for Sonya he comes to the

New Testament, given to him by Sonya and in turn given to her by Elizaveta. Nor is this newfound religious belief entirely unexpected; throughout the course of the novel Raskolnikov gives many indications of his adherence to Christian belief. Thus during his first visit to the Marmeladov family he asks Polechka to pray for him; a request which he repeats to his mother before he goes off to Siberia, and he asserts his faith quite strongly during his first interview with Porfiry.

His love for Sonya, his newfound religious faith, the discipline of the penal settlement—all these are weapons against Raskolnikov's pride and self-assertion. If, however, doubt is still felt on the probability of Raskolnikov's 'resurrection', it should be remembered that at the end of the Epilogue he still has seven long years of suffering ahead of him in which to work out his salvation; and the author himself had direct experience of the way the Russian penal settlement could change a man.

Crime and Punishment is often described as a 'psychological thriller'; this description is quite accurate, but it is a 'thriller' in which suspense is created not through the attempts to detect the culprit, but through the culprit's own wayward efforts to resist detection. Here the reader himself is put in the position of a murderer, and follows with a disturbing degree of self-identification the inner struggles of a psychologically tormented personality.

In this sense *Crime and Punishment* is a 'psychological thriller' at a much deeper level. Behind the story of murder, confession and moral rehabilitation lies an exploration, through symbol and allegory, of the divided nature of the hero; an exploration in which the other characters surround the central figure like mirrors reflecting and distorting aspects of his own dilemma. It is a measure of the greatness of Dostoyevsky that these characters can at the same time stand on their own; for they have individuality in their own right.[17] Moreover symbol and allegory are so skilfully fused into the narrative that their presence, far from exerting a deadening influence, or reducing the novel to a mere mechanical abstraction, enriches and further deepens the significance of the work. *Crime and Punishment* is, above all, an extremely readable novel.

Notes

1. The 'realism' of Pushkin has also particular relevance for *Crime and Punishment*. Dostoevsky was extremely enthusiastic about Pushkin's story, *The Queen of Spades*, valuing it both for the element of the fantastic and for its treatment of the inner struggles and final collapse of the hero. (See M. A. Polivanova, 'Zapis' o poseshchenii Dostoyevskogo 9 Iyunya 1880 goda', in *Vosp.* Vol 2, pp. 361 and 363.)

The story, set in St Petersburg, concerns a ruthless young man with a Napoleonic profile, who plays with people as though they are cards (so the 'realism' of the story is rich in symbol). To gain a gambling secret from an aged countess he poses as the lover of her companion. He unwittingly kills the old woman and is saved by Liza (the companion). The central core of both works is strikingly similar: a tyrannical old woman who bullies a meek Elizaveta Ivanovna is killed by a young man with Napoleonic aspirations. (See also K. Mochul'sky, *Dostoyevsky, Zhizn' tvorchestvo* (Paris, 1947), p. 238.)

Elsewhere in Pushkin we read: 'We all aim at being Napoleons/The millions of two-legged creature/Are merely tools for us.' (*Yevgeniy Onegin*, Ch. 2, stanza xiv.)

2. Thus the 'miracle' of Raskolnikov's unexpected meeting with Svidrigaylov in Pt. VI is explained by the latter as a quirk of memory.

3. B. J. Simmons takes this as a sign of bad writing. See B. J. Simmons, *Dostoevsky. The Making of a Novelist* (Newy York, 1962), pp. 169–70.

4. I.e. *yurodivyy*. The 'holy fool' is a constantly recurring figure in Dostoevsky's novels, and here the comparison is particularly significant in view of the traditional role of the *yurodivyy* as the voice of conscience speaking out against the tyrant (cf. Nikolka in Pushkin's *Boris Godunov*, or the historical figure of Nicholas Salos, who put Ivan the Terrible to shame when he was about the sack the city of Pskov).

5. By this italicized *she* Raskolnikov appears to be referring to Alyona and not his mother (see *D.5*, p. 286), but the apparent continuity of thought between an expression of hatred for his mother and hatred for Alyona is interesting. For a theory on the role played by the mother in the motives for the crime, see Wasiolek's commentary to *The Notebooks for 'Crime and Punishment'*, p. 186. It might also be added that Alyona was the name of the faithful peasant nurse who brought up the Dostoyevsky children. See A. M. Dostoevsky, 'Iz "Vospomiminaniy"', *Vosp.* Vol I, p. 42.

6. It is perhaps significant that during the ensuing conversation with Raskolnikov the reappearance of the dead in the form of ghosts is one of Svidrigaylov's main themes.

7. The full force of *perestupit'* is lost in English: the verb evokes its variant *prestupit'* = 'to commit a crime' (cf. Eng. 'transgress'). The title of the novel itself, *Prestupleniye i nakazaniye*, contains this root.

8. Even this pledge proves to be in two pieces: one of metal, the other of wood (see *D.5*, p. 75).

9. Thus we are told that Porfiry has contemplated becoming a monk (though this is presented as one pole of an enigmantic nature; for on the other hand Porfiry also claims that he intends to marry) (see *D.5*, p. 267).

10. Svidrigaylo spent the eighty-odd years of his life fomenting trouble on Russia's borders. Although nominally a Roman Catholic, he allied himself with Orthodox dissident, Hussites and the Order of the Livonian Knights in his efforts to further his own political aims. In 1434, against the wishes of Muscovy, Svidrigaylo had Gerasim of Smolensk consecrated in Constantinople as Metropolitan of all Russia, only to have him executed the following year. The Dostoyevskys themselves were conscious of being descended from noble Lithuanian stock, and in choosing this name perhaps the author is indulging in a device typical of his writing—self-identification with his worst characters (e.g. the murderer who is the tool of the nihilists in *The Devils* is called "Fedka the convict', and in *The Brothers Karamozov* the murderer Smerdyakov suffers from Dostoyevsky's own affliction—epilepsy).

11. Cf. D. L. Fanger, *Dostoevsky and Romantic Realism: A Study of Dostoevsky in Relation to Balzac, Dicken and Gogol* (Harvard University Press, 1965), p. 23.

12. This idea will be taken up at length in the novel, *The Devils*, where once more it will be interwoven with the theme of heresy (see Ch. 6 of the present work).

The schism [*raskol*] was a term loosely applied to all heretics within the larger Orthodox fold, although the origins of some f the more extreme sects (e.g. the Flagellants [*Khlysty*] and their offshoot the Castrates [*Skopsty*]) appear to be largely pagan and hae little, if anything, to do with the true schism in the Russian Church which took place in the seventeenth century.

Interestingly enough there was even a more recent sect which hailed Napoleon as a new Messiah—the sect of the *Napoleonovy*. See K. K. Grass, *Die russischen Sekten*, (Leipzig, 1907), Vol. I, pp. 562–3; also P. I. Mel'nikov (Andrey Pechersky) 'Pis'ma o raskole', *Sobraniye sochineniy v shesti tomakh* (Moscow, 1963), Vol. 6, p. 238; and F. C. Conybeare, *Russian Dissenters* (Harvard University Press, 1921), p. 370.

13. This realization is brought about, characteristically, through a certain linguistic ambivalence. The Russian *ty* = thou (cf. French 'tu') can convey both great intimacy and great contempt:

'"Leave me alone," Dunya implored.

Svidrigaylov shuddered: this *ty* had not been pronounced as it had been formerly.

"So, you do not love me?" he asked her quietly.' (*D.5*, p. 520.)

14. The name Resslikh occurs in connection with her (*D.5*, p. 526) as it had in Luzhin's account of the supposed seduction by Svidrigaylov of a fourteen-year-old deaf-mute (*D.5*, p. 309). It is with this same Gertruda Karlovna Resslikh that Svidrigaylov claims to be staying, when he hires the apartment next to Sonya (*D.5*, p. 254).

15. Svidrigaylov, for example, has turned self-blame into a fine art, as a weapon to be used for the seduction of women (*D.5*, p. 497).

16. In his argument inducing Sonya to stay, Raskolnikov's final words seem charged with ironic ambiguity: '... for you will remain guilty' [... *ved' vy zhe ostanetes' vinovaty*] (*D.5*, p. 425).

17. Dostoyevsky's distinctive use of language for each character has been remarked on. See, for example, Grossman, *Dostoevsky*, p. 355.

ALBA AMOIA

Crime and Punishment

Probably the most widely known of Dostoevsky's greater novels, *Crime and Punishment* claims priority of notice by reason of its special appeal to our contemporary society as well as its universal qualities. One critic, writing early in the twentieth century, offered this appraisal of the novel's enduring value:

> For the deepest essence of tragedy, though it avoid the final catastrophe—for the evocation, that is to say, of the profoundest feelings of pity and of terror which can purge the reader's heart—there is, I believe, no work of literary fiction that can take its place by the side of Dostoevsky's *Crime and Punishment*.... Who shall describe the multitude of wonderful, heart-searching passages in which [it] abounds? In this book the piteous, the terrible, the human and the sublime seem gathered into a vast compendium.[1]

To readers of our own generation, *Crime and Punishment* offers insight into some of the sources of the antisocial behavior patterns so characteristic of certain predominantly youthful segments of contemporary society. Interwoven with his guiding theme of redemption through suffering, Dostoevsky's reflections on the psychology of crime, punishment, and repentance are as relevant to today's conditions as to those of the 1860s. In its rebellion against established social structures like the family, school, and church, the alienated youth of today unconsciously replicates the attitudes and behavior of such earlier young people as Rodion Raskolnikov, the central figure of *Crime and Punishment*, whose attempt to prove his superiority to established social norms would culminate in the commission of a grisly murder that he would spend the rest of his life in expiating.

Dostoevsky's own situation, in material terms at least, was not dissimilar to that of Raskolnikov at the period in the mid-1860s when the novelist was beginning the composition of *Crime and Punishment*. Like Raskolnikov, cramped "in a square yard of space" and "up to the neck in debt to his landlady [whom he was] afraid of meeting," Dostoevsky was then living in a cheap hotel in Wiesbaden, Germany, deeply in debt and consequently at the mercy of the proprietor and his staff.

Writing in September 1865 to Mikhail Katkov in the hope that his novel could be published in the latter's *Russian Messenger*, the starved and humiliated author described his work as "a psychological study of a crime ... a novel of contemporary life" (*Letters* II, 174.) His synopsis of the book, as he conceived it at that time, still serves as a useful summary of the action:

> A young man, a former student of Petersburg University who is very hard up, becomes obsessed with the "half-baked" ideas that are in the air just now because of his general mental instability. He decides to do something that would save him immediately from his desperate position. He makes up his mind to kill an old woman moneylender. The old woman is stupid, greedy, deaf and ill; she charges exorbitant interest on her loans; she is bad-tempered and she is ruining the life of her younger sister whom she keeps as a drudge. She is absolutely worthless, there seems to be no justification for her existence, etc. All these considerations completely unhinge the mind of the young man. He decides to kill her, rob her of her money, so as to be able to help his mother, who lives in the provinces, and save his sister, who is employed as governess in the house of a landowner who is trying to seduce her, as well as finish his own studies at the university. Then he plans to go abroad, and spend the rest of his life as an honest citizen doing "his duty towards humanity" without swerving from the path of honor and righteousness. This, he is convinced, will atone for his crime, if indeed one can call a crime this murder of a stupid and wicked old woman who serves no useful purpose in life and who, besides, would most probably not live for more than a few months anyhow.

> In spite of the fact that such crimes are as a rule committed in a very clumsy fashion, the murderer usually leaving all sorts of clues behind him since he relies too much on chance which almost invariably lets him down, the young man succeeds in committing the murder quickly and successfully.
>
> Almost a month passes between the crime and the final catastrophe. He is never under suspicion, nor indeed can there be any suspicion against him. But it is here that the whole psychological process of the crime unfolds itself. The murderer is suddenly confronted by insoluble problems, and hitherto undreamed of feelings begin to torment him. Divine truth and justice and the law are triumphant in the end, and the young man finishes by giving himself up against his own will. He feels compelled to go back to the society of men in spite of the danger of spending the rest of his life in a prison in Siberia. The feeling of separation and dissociation from humanity which he experiences at once after he has committed the crime, is something he cannot bear. The laws of justice and truth, of human justice, gain the upper hand. The murderer himself decides to accept his punishment in order to expiate his crime.
>
> ... My novel, besides, contains the hint that the punishment laid down by the law frightens the criminal much less than our legislators think, partly because he himself feels the desire to be punished. I have seen it happening myself with uneducated people, but I should like to show it in the case of a highly educated modern young man.... Our papers are full of stories which show the general feeling of instability which leads young men to commit terrible crimes.... I am quite sure that the subject of my novel is justified ... by the events that are happening in life today. (*Letters* II, 174–75, but translation as it appears in David Magarshack's introduction to *Crime and Punishment*, 12–13.)

Who, then, is this poor St. Petersburg law-school dropout, who suffers from "general mental instability," is addicted to "half-baked ideas," and to whom Dostoevsky gave the unforgettable name of Rodion Romanovich Raskolnikov? (The surname derives from the Russian word *raskol'nik*, signifying a dissident or schismatic.) The author describes him as "quite an extraordinarily handsome young man, with beautiful dark eyes, dark brown hair, over medium height, slim, and well-built." Usually, however, he seems to be sunk in "a sort of deep reverie" or "a kind of coma"; he is given to "indulging in soliloquies"; and if he appears "confused and weak," it is because for days he has had "hardly anything to eat."

Raskolnikov has chosen to set himself apart and be a stranger in his own society. He is a loner and a rebel trapped inside himself. Involved lucubrations and convoluted reasoning have convinced him that he must "cut himself off from everyone and everything." The "half-baked ideas" to which he has fallen a prey grow out of the pseudo-scientific rationalism and revolutionary nihilism of Raskolnikov's generation, described in such books as Turgenev's *Fathers and Sons* and Chernyshevsky's *What Is To Be Done?*, and to which Dostoevsky imputed much of the blame for the violent crimes occasionally committed by educated young people.

To escape from his social and economic limitations and attain a position in which he can exercise the talent he is sure he possesses, Raskolnikov conceives and carries out what has been called a "philosophical crime," the hatchet murder of a "useless, even harmful" old woman who lends money at usurious rates—and whom Raskolnikov has privately condemned to death on what he considers unanswerable intellectual grounds. In addition, he impulsively commits a second murder of a purely expedient character, using his hatchet to split the skull of the woman's half-witted sister when she inadvertently enters the room where her sister has just been murdered. In the wake of this all too vividly described murder, Raskolnikov himself is seized with feelings of "horror and disgust"—a leitmotiv of the novel. For the time being, however, he neither repents nor considers himself a criminal.

As the implications of the deed unfold in his conscience over the following weeks, Raskolnikov at first attempts to justify his action as a "rational" crime, committed in "an act of boldness" by an "exceptional man." "One must have the courage to dare"; "I wanted to become a Napoleon"; "I wanted to find out whether ... I am some trembling vermin or whether I have the *right*"—these are some of the well-known descriptions of his attitude, uttered by himself in the course of his later confession.

Much of the novel is taken up with a process of self-analysis in the course of which Raskolnikov, this nineteenth-century "superman," gradually reveals the nature of his own motivations. Some of these he had already put forward in a published article which he had stressed a supposed distinction between "ordinary" and "exceptional" human beings. A member of the latter group, Raskolnikov contends, has "a right ... to permit conscience to step over certain obstacles ... if it is absolutely necessary for the fulfillment of his ideas on which ... the welfare of all mankind may depend." Such figures as Lycurgus, Solon, Mahomet, and Napoleon, according to Raskolnikov, had been superior benefactors, lawgivers, and arbiters of mankind; and each of them had shed rivers of blood promulgating new laws for a new world order. He, too, Raskolnikov indicated, had determined to commit an act of hubris or moral presumption in order to take his place among humanity's proud exceptions.

Raskolnikov is highly knowledgeable, well-read, and intelligent, as well as courageous; but his almost insane vanity is incompatible with normal social behavior. Ragged, unshaven, and tousled, he is uncommunicative and solitary and wears a fixed expression of haughtiness and arrogant mockery. Mankind fills him with existential nausea—"a sort of infinite, almost physical feeling of disgust with everything he came across—malevolent, obstinate, virulent. He hated the people he met in the street, he hated their faces, the way they walked, the way they moved. If any man had addressed him now, he would have spat on him or perhaps even bitten him" (II, 2).

And yet despite his strange silence—a silence that, in Bernard Shaw's words, is "the most perfect expression of scorn"—Raskolnikov considers himself an idealist who is concerned about the betterment of "all suffering humanity." Deep within his hardened heart he cherishes his family; indeed, one of the original motivations for his crime was the desire to help his mother and sister in their personal predicament. In some ways one is reminded of Dostoevsky himself, who at times preferred to be cruel rather than put his real feelings into words. "I have such a vile, repulsive character," he once wrote Mikhail, "sometimes when my heart is swimming in love you can't get a tender word from me" (*Letters*, I, 150).

Raskolnikov's heart and mind, indeed, seem almost to operate in separate, watertight compartments. His one friend, the warm-hearted Razumikhin—a character most certainly modeled on Mikhail Dostoevsky—observes that Raskolnikov, hiding his real feelings, sometimes becomes cold and inhumanly callous "just as if there were two people of diametrically opposed characters living in him, each taking charge of him in turn" (III, 2). Seeking "the moral solution" for the crime he is about to commit, Dostoevsky tells the reader, Raskolnikov "could no longer find any conscious objections to his plans *in his mind*. But *at heart* he never really took himself seriously, and he went on ... fumbling for some valid objections ... *as though someone were compelling and pushing him to do it*" (I, 6, italics added).

This innate duality defeats Raskolnikov's attempts to rationalize his actions after the murders have been committed. He vacillates between supreme vanity and humble submissiveness, and only later will his conscience enter into the analysis of the sorrow he has brought upon himself. "Whoever has a conscience will no doubt suffer, if he realizes his mistake," he reflects. "That's his punishment—on top of penal servitude.... Let him suffer, if he is sorry for his victim. Suffering and pain are always necessary for men of great sensibility and deep feeling. Really great men, it seems to me, must feel great sorrow on earth." Accused of having turned his face from God, Raskolnikov will readily concede that it was Satan who had tempted him and goaded him into committing the crime: "It was the devil who killed the old hag, not I" (V, 4).

Such traits help to explain why Raskolnikov has been called a "pure" assassin, a seeming contradiction in terms. Rather than a manifestation of innate wickedness, his gratuitous crime seems to be the momentary error of a puppet who has fallen into the hands of Satan. Since he is capable of accepting punishment from within rather than from without, he is not the hardened, unrepentant criminal but rather the sorrowful deviate, sensitive to the voice of conscience, who will freely choose to expiate his crime.

Back in his "cupboard" after committing the two hatchet murders, Raskolnikov feels increasingly confused and shaken as incipient inner torment takes possession of him. "What ... is my punishment already beginning?" he wonders as he feverishly attempts to remove the traces of blood from his clothing. The terror that takes hold of his soul plunges him into that "sickness" that Kierkegaard had described in 1845 as "the natural state of the Christian." It is only after a long illness, marked by fever and delirium, that a haggard and pale Raskolnikov finally resolves to try to undo his crime, "because *he did not want to go on living like that*."

The two options open to him seem to underscore his vacillation between arrogant pride and humble resignation. He can take his own life—a solution he rejects after having witnessed with indifference a woman's attempted suicide by drowning—or he can surrender to the police in an act of final desperation.

One may wonder how far Dostoevsky intended Raskolnikov's two victims to reflect the assassin's own duality. Alyona Ivanovna, the usurer and primary victim, is a loathsome female miser who maltreats her half-crazed sister. She is "a very small, wizened old woman of about sixty, with sharp malevolent eyes, a small sharp nose, and a bare head. Her unattractive, colorless hair ... was smothered in oil. Some sort of flannel rag was wound about her long, thin, neck, which looked like a hen's leg" (I, 1). Raskolnikov knows that Alyona Ivanovna hides her fortune in a securities box whose key is always on her person; he knows, too, that her money is being accumulated for the (to him) senseless purpose of endowing memorial masses for the repose of her own soul. Alyona Ivanovna may be seen as a symbol of the crass venality Raskolnikov so hates that he has no qualms about killing her in the most brutal manner.

The usurer's half-sister, Lisaveta, is another matter. Her presence, it has been noted, seems to hover over the novel even after her death, as though the memory of her personality and tragic fate could never be erased from Raskolnikov's mind. Lisaveta was "a tall, ungainly, shy, and meek woman of almost thirty-five, almost an idiot, who was held in complete subjection by her sister, working for her day and night, bullied and even beaten by her" (I, 5). Although notorious for sexual promiscuity, Lisaveta is good, generous in her poverty, and possessed of a gentle, childlike innocence. Her almost passive stance under Raskolnikov's onslaught—as though she sensed rather than saw the murderer—suggests the blindfolded Fortune against which Raskolnikov turns his rage. When, later in the novel, Lisaveta's name is inadvertently mentioned, Raskolnikov kneels, perhaps in deference to the unpredictable power personified by Fortune.

If Raskolnikov's nature is dual and his emotions are ambivalent, the associates with whom he interacts on a plane of at least nominal equality—his mother and sister, his friend Razumikhin, the prostitute Sonia, and the investigator Porfiry Petrovich—are consistent, integrated personalities. Raskolnikov may be the author of his own punishment, but these are the vessels of his redemption and the mirrors of his soul.

A deep love–hate relationship binds the young man to his mother, Pulcheria, and his sister, Dunya, who have come to St. Petersburg at a crisis of their own affairs. His brooding on their miserable plight had already assumed the "terrifying and unfamiliar guise" of the murder that was taking shape in his mind. So strong and so contradictory are his emotions when he unexpectedly finds them waiting for him in his room, a few days after the crime, that he stands frozen on the spot, face-to-face, as it were, with his own conscience. Prevented from embracing them by a sudden, unbearable awareness of the horror he has perpetrated, Raskolnikov staggers toward them but falls to the floor in a dead faint. When he regains consciousness, his mother glimpses "poignant suffering" and "something unbending and almost insane" in her son's expression (III, 1).

Where Raskolnikov is feverish and agitated, his mother—who, he fears, may either go blind from knitting shawls and weeping, or simply waste away from lack of food—is calm and serene. She looks much younger than her forty-three years—"which," says Dostoevsky, "is almost always the case with women who keep their serenity of mind, the freshness of their impressions, and a pure and sincere warmth of heart to their old age." "We may add in parentheses," Dostoevsky continues, in a curious bit of cosmetic advice to the middle-aged woman, "that to possess all this is the only way a woman can preserve her beauty even in old age" (III, 1).

His sister Dunya, graceful and somewhat haughty in outlook and manner, has just escaped the clutches of the lascivious landowner Svidrigaylov, in whose household she had served as governess. Though anxious to protect his sister from Svidrigaylov's advances, Raskolnikov balks at surrendering her to a wealthy parvenu named Peter Luzhin, a particularly cruel and treacherous representative of bourgeois venality, to whom she has become engaged. "Love yourself before everyone else, for everything in the world is based on self-interest" is Luzhin's philosophy (II, 5).

Dunya's altruistic motive in accepting Luzhin's marriage proposal had been the hope of obtaining funds for her brother's law-school studies and getting him future work in Luzhin's legal office. But while such a marriage would offer escape from the unwelcome attentions of Svidrigaylov, it would clearly place Dunya in an equally unhappy situation. It was her personal helplessness that had first excited Luzhin's interest; he dreamed of her as a submissive wife who would regard him as her savior and look up to him, obey and admire him, humbly and reverently acknowledge him as her lord and master. Such a beautiful and virtuous wife, he had believed, would help immeasurably in furthering his own ambitions.

Raskolnikov, with an instinctive understanding of a woman's feelings, understood perfectly that for Dunya a loveless marriage to such a personage would be no less degrading than outright prostitution—that Dunya, in fact, would "rather live on bread and water than sell her own soul" (I, 4). Refusing to accept his sister's intended sacrifice, Raskolnikov deliberately insults Luzhin, provoking a rupture of the engagement and incidentally paving the way for Dunya's eventual marriage to his friend Razumikhin.

On later visits with his mother and sister, they gently try to engage Raskolnikov in conversation, but he realizes that he "would not ever be able to talk to anyone about anything" (III, 3). On the verge of falling into a deep sleep, in which he will relive the murder and all his subconscious torments, the semidelirious Raskolnikov struggles to confess and at the same time to hide his crime. "Mother, sister—how I loved them! Why do I hate them now?" he asks (III, 6). In a moving farewell scene on the day of his decision to surrender to the police, Raskolnikov kisses his mother's feet and asks for her unqualified love and her prayers.

Throughout the novel, the two women seem to embody Dostoevsky's credo that God is the only source of redemption and that through willingness to face personal suffering, humans may draw close to God. Raskolnikov both loves and hates his family—loving them because they suffer, yet hating them because he is still not prepared to accept suffering himself.

Also consistent through and through, albeit unpolished, is Razumikhin, Raskolnikov's former fellow student and Dunya's admirer and future husband. (His name derives from *razum*, the Russian word for reason.) This frank, cheerful, good-natured, and honest fellow, who "could make himself at home even on a roof," offers a refreshing change from Dunya's other followers. "Razumikhin possessed the gift of revealing his true character all at once, whatever mood he might be in, so that people soon realized who they were dealing with," Dostoevsky writes of this engaging youth.

Razumikhin dreams of establishing a publishing firm in which he and Raskolnikov will be partners—"a business of translating, publishing, and learning all at once" in which he will concern himself with "the business side of the whole thing"—another hint that this faithful friend is modeled on Mikhail Dostoevsky, who had similar qualities of amiability and obligingness. As an epitome of reason and good sense, Razumikhin serves as Dostoevsky's spokesman and commentator on the contemporary state of knowledge and progress: "What are we today?" he sensibly exclaims. "So far as science, general development, thoughts, inventions, ideals, aims, desires, liberalism, intelligence, experience ... [are] concerned, we are all ... still in the preparatory class at school. We've acquired a taste for depending on someone else's brains" (III, 1).

Razumikhin is also Dostoevsky's ideal model of friendship. In a charming and touching scene, we find him nursing the delirious Raskolnikov, putting his arm around him "as clumsily as a bear" and feeding him mouthfuls of soup, first blowing on it to make sure his sick friend does not burn his mouth. But it is in the more serious matter of Raskolnikov's guilt that his friend's unerring sense of pity and affection, as well as his sensitive intuition, are most clearly revealed.

Without the utterance of a single word, Razumikhin is able to interpret the burning, piercing facial expression with which Raskolnikov communicates the ghastly truth of the crime. From that moment, Razumikhin knows that he must assume a decisive role in the affairs of the Raskolnikov family. It will be he who intervenes when Dunya, toward the end of the novel, is again assailed by the lecherous Svidrigaylov and when Raskolnikov himself is exiled to Siberia, leaving his helpless mother and sister behind.

Arkady Ivanovich Svidrigaylov, Dunya's persecutor and one of Dostoevsky's most problematical characters, seems to have somewhat baffled even his creator, who, as though unable fully to grasp his essence, repeatedly used approximative adverbs in describing his features. Smartly dressed, handsome, but "somewhat repulsive" in aspect, Svidrigaylov had "a peculiar kind of face, which looked like a mask: white, with red cheeks, with bright red lips, a light, flaxen beard, and still very thick, fair hair. His eyes were, somehow, a little too blue, and their expression was, somehow, too heavy and motionless" (VI, 3).

Still erotically obsessed with Dunya even after her dismissal from his household by his jealous wife, Svidrigaylov theatrically reappears, in the fourth part of the novel, on the threshold of Raskolnikov's room—a fitting conclusion to the nightmare in which Raskolnikov has just been reenacting his murderous deed. Explaining that he has come to seek the young man's help in a matter concerning his sister, the visitor plunges into a lengthy autobiography from which he emerges as, in his own words, "an idle and immoral man," utterly indifferent to evil. He lives in the depths of a pathological boredom, relieved only by the visitations of persons whose death he has caused. He has strange notions about human psychology ("from time to time women find it very pleasant indeed to be humiliated"), and even stranger ones about the mysteries of life, death, and eternity: "What if ... you suddenly find just a little room there, something like a village bathhouse, grimy, and spiders in every corner, and that's all eternity is" (IV, 1).

Like Raskolnikov, Svidrigaylov neither repents of his misdeeds—he has indirectly caused the death of his wife and a servant—nor does he consider himself a criminal. Before undertaking "a certain journey" he has planned, he has called on Raskolnikov in order to make some "preliminary arrangements," including an offer to Dunya of ten thousand rubles to atone for the embarrassment and worry he has caused her and to enable her to break with Luzhin, her objectionable fiance.

His gesture seems to suggest that though immoral and somewhat mad, Svidrigaylov is no more devoid of altruistic sentiments than is Raskolnikov himself, with whom he claims to have much in common. Svidrigaylov, however, is quite unlike Raskolnikov in his unashamed sexual obsessions. To the younger man, he is nothing but "a low, depraved sensualist ... a dirty villain and voluptuous *roué* and a scoundrel" (VI, 5). Having learned of Raskolnikov's guilt by eavesdropping on a private conversation, Svidrigaylov reveals his true colors in an unsuccessful attempt to use the secret as a means of pressure on Dunya—who, however, summons all her resolution and successfully resists his advances.

The last night of Svidrigaylov's existence, unfolding in macabre hallucinations and reminiscences of past misdeeds, is passed in a grimy hotel where the landowner shares his miserable bed-sheets with a scampering mouse—the animal that has been seen as a reflection of Dostoevsky's obsession with the voluptuousness of evil and the morbid enjoyment of viscid horror. Svidrigaylov's tragic career is ended by the bullet he puts through his head under a high watchtower near the river Neva—the point of embarkation for the "certain journey" he has been planning.

Raskolnikov, in contrast, is more consistent in his invocation of those abstract principles that, he sincerely believes, will lead to the betterment of humankind; but he is waylaid by Satan, who tempts him into the folly of a double murder. Unlike Svidrigaylov, he will reject suicide and find the courage to confess his crime, accept his punishment, and live out his tragic destiny despite what he at first sees as its "absurdity."

Another of the puzzling "preliminary arrangements" made by Svidrigaylov was a guarantee of moral and financial support for the poverty-stricken Marmeladov family, another of the constituent elements of this rich and multilayered novel. Marmeladov, the chronic drunkard of another work of fiction Dostoevsky incorporated into *Crime and Punishment*, had been killed—or perhaps had willfully sought escape—in a street accident in which he had been trampled under horses' hoofs; and Svidrigaylov, before his suicide, not only placed substantial funds in trust for the small Marmeladov orphans but also made provision for rescuing Sonia, the older daughter, from the quagmire of prostitution.

A retired titular counselor long since reduced to penury and alcoholism, Marmeladov had experienced every feeling of degradation in his unequal struggle to preserve his human dignity. Invariably he wore an old tuxedo with only one button, just to "be correct." It was this humiliated individual whom Raskolnikov had encountered in a tavern just after a preliminary visit to the scene of his intended crime. He had found himself unwillingly drawn toward the drunkard, who leaned his elbows on the dirty table, his head in his hands, an anguished look on his face. "It's not joy I thirst for, but sorrow and tears," he had told his reluctant listener.

Confessing all his failures and his sense of guilt, Marmeladov is the first to enunciate an idea that runs through the novel like a leitmotiv: "Poverty is not a crime." "Drunkenness isn't a virtue either," he continues, "but chronic destitution is a crime. When you're poor, you're still able to preserve the innate nobility of your feelings, but when you're destitute you never can. For being destitute a man is not even driven out with a stick, but is swept out with a broom from the society of decent people in the most humiliating way possible.... [W]hen I'm down and out I'm ready to be the first to humiliate myself. Hence the pub!" (I, 2).

A drunkard out of despair, Marmeladov takes voluptuous pleasure in being beaten and humiliated by his wife, Katerina Ivanovna, an "educated woman of high character," who, through misery and illness, has also been reduced to a situation of utter despair. The mother of three small children, she can await nothing but madness and a hideous death from tuberculosis. Roaming the streets of St. Petersburg with her costumed children, forcing them to perform and sing in the hope of earning a few coins, Katerina Ivanovna succumbs to a pitiless fate and leaves her orphans at the mercy of the hostile city.

The poverty of the Marmeladovs, it has been noted, contrasts with that of Raskolnikov by reason of their powerlessness as compared with the latter's relative powerfulness. Whereas the Marmeladov family has been thrust inexorably into drunkenness and prostitution, Raskolnikov can at least enjoy his freedom and detachment from the society he detests. Yet even

Raskolnikov must yield to the overpowering aura of love and affection radiated by the younger Marmeladovs. The ten-year-old Polya, crying softly over the loss of her father, nestles in Raskolnikov's arms, hugging and kissing him hungrily in what becomes a first turning point in the life of the bloodstained criminal. Pressing his unshaven face close to Polya's, he pleads, "Darling Polya ... please say a prayer for me, too, sometimes—'and thy servant Rodion'—and nothing more" (II, 7).

But it is eighteen-year-old Sonia, Marmeladov's attractive, blond, blue-eyed daughter by a previous marriage, who will ultimately bring about Raskolnikov's redemption and salvation. Even before the story opens, Sonia has been goaded by her distraught stepmother to go on the streets to try to earn money for the starving family. And, since their landlady would not tolerate the presence of "a certified woman of the streets," Sonia had been forced to find damp and smoky quarters of her own—a scantily furnished room "rather like a shed"—where her father visited her only to filch money to support his own vice.

Sonia has submitted to her life of sin and shame, passively accepting the terrible consequences her father's drunkenness has settled on the family. Although as a prostitute she is in league with "sinners," she is instinctively guided by an innate generosity and selflessness; she nurtures "*insatiable* compassion" even for the unsympathetic stepmother who has set her on the path of destruction. As a pattern of resignation, love, and forgiveness, Sonia makes no personal claims; love, brotherhood, and human solidarity are instinctive in her. Simple and innocent, she is perhaps the supreme representative of Dostoevsky's "meek" or "gentle" creatures who symbolize all of suffering humanity.[2]

The absence of any reference to Sonia in Dostoevsky's 1865 letter to Katkov suggests that the figure of the redeeming prostitute did not appear significantly in the first version of *Crime and Punishment*. In the extant version, however, Sonia's role is crucial to the explication and ultimate resolution of Raskolnikov's inner turmoil. More than the members of his own family, more than any representative of law and justice, it is Sonia who will redeem Raskolnikov's life, deepen his self-knowledge, and lead the way along the path of repentance. "It was to her, Sonia, that he had gone with his first confession; when he was in need of the companionship of a human being, it was in her that he found the human being; and she would be with him wherever he might be" (VI, 8).

Why did Dostoevsky choose a prostitute as the sole person to whom Raskolnikov can speak freely, to whom he can relate, and with whom he can interact to the exclusion of all others? His choice, reminiscent in some ways of the earlier *Notes from Underground* (see chapter 11), may perhaps find an explanation in what has been hinted at concerning the author's own life. Familiarity with the world of prostitution had represented an important stage in Dostoevsky's spiritual progress and understanding. His contacts with the prostitutes of the Russian capital had changed and enriched his human psychology, impelling him to reflect on suffering, sin, and social misery. To him, they represented important milestones along the path to self-knowledge and ultimate reconciliation with God and humanity. Undeterred by social taboos, Dostoevsky enjoyed his "natural" experiences with prostitutes, who helped him in gaining access to a community of persons well versed in faith and charity. His bitter and tragic "underground man," in contrast, illustrates the inability of an overweening egotist to respond to the genuine love offered him by a woman of that class.

The fateful mystery that culminated in Sonia's decision to go on the street inspires Raskolnikov not only with respect for her personal dignity but also, perhaps at an unconscious level, with curiosity about the parallel mystery culminating in his own decision to commit murder. He sees both himself and Sonia as outcasts, in spite of valuable human qualities, from among those whom society deems worthy of consideration.

The scene in which Sonia puts Raskolnikov's true feelings to their first test is generally accounted the pivotal episode of *Crime and Punishment* (IV, 4). When Raskolnikov visits her a few days after the still unconfessed murder, she bemoans the dire events that have befallen her family; and Raskolnikov gibes at her, grinning callously and painting a black picture of her future and that of her sister Polya in the "nasty, stinking sty" of prostitution. Confronted by Sonia's calm assurance that God is their recourse, the visitor attempts to bring her to doubt the existence of a God who allows so many abominations on earth. Sonia, unable to counter his well-turned arguments, bursts into tears as her tormentor laughs in cruel triumph. But then, moved by the girl's infinite sorrow, his lips trembling convulsively, Raskolnikov bows down and kisses her foot in a Christ-like gesture so out of keeping with his usual behavior that Sonia recoils as from a madman. And, indeed, Raskolnikov at that moment looks like a madman, caught in an insane struggle between the promptings of his mind and heart on the one hand and the devil seeking his soul on the other.

To Sonia's admonition that he must not bow before a dishonorable creature and a "great, great sinner," Raskolnikov replies, "I did not bow down to you. I bowed down to all suffering humanity." "It is quite true that you are a great sinner," he says.

> And do you know why... ? Because you have betrayed and ruined yourself *for nothing*.... It is horrible that you should live in this

> filth which you hate and at the same time know yourself ... that you are not helping anyone by it and that you are not saving anyone from anything.... How can such shame and such disgrace live in you side by side with your other quite different and holy feelings? Would it not have been a thousand times more just and more sensible to throw yourself into the river and finish it all at one blow?

In reality, Raskolnikov knows that Sonia's pure soul lacks the arrogant pride that is needed for a person to take his own life; he knows, too, that he himself had refused that option. In questioning her will to live, Raskolnikov seems to be trying to probe his own heart and his own will to survive.

Noticing a copy of the New Testament—a gift, Sonia tells him, from the murdered Lisaveta—Raskolnikov asks her to find "the place about the raising of Lazarus." Here, it has been observed, is spun an intricate web uniting the murdered victim (Lisaveta), the murderer (analogous to the dead Lazarus), and his resuscitator (Sonia), as all three join in what amounts to a "behold the Lord" happening. Sonia reads aloud the eleventh chapter of St. John's Gospel, slowly and distinctly, the value and power of her voice and body uniting to act out the supernatural event. Raskolnikov is struck with amazement at her exaltation and joyous anticipation of the miracle.

In these pages, Dostoevsky brings out the innate skill of the unschooled, uneducated, and unsophisticated Sonia in arousing the sensitivity of the educated man to the wonders of speech. The *Word* as Logos—a divine gift to humans—is frequently stressed throughout the novel: the illusion of *words* versus reality; the *new word* as synonymous with a new order; the *word* as revelatory of true inner feelings, etc. Mediated through Sonia's evangelical spirit, the Gospel—the expressed mind and will of God—turns Raskolnikov toward Christ. Ultimately, he too will be resuscitated, like Lazarus, and reintegrated into the Russian national community through the miracle of the *word*. Such is the essence of this crucial scene, in a dingy room bathed in a poetic atmosphere where "the murderer and the harlot ... met so strangely over the reading of the eternal book."

Revealing to Sonia that he has now broken definitively with his family, Raskolnikov attempts to link himself to the young girl: "I have only you now ... Let's go together.... We're both damned.... All I know is that we must go the same way.... We've one goal before us!" Yet he remains ambiguous, underlining on the one hand his Christlike attitudes ("We have to break with what must be broken with once and for all ... and we have to take the suffering upon ourselves"), while on the other he is still obsessed with "freedom and power—power above all. Power over all the trembling vermin and over all the anthill. That's our goal."

Thoroughly dazed by his strange words, Sonia is even more confounded and horrified when Raskolnikov tells her that if he returns on the morrow, he will reveal the name of Lisaveta's murderer. And he does return, with the double purpose of tormenting her afresh and of asking her forgiveness for his cruelty. A prey to constant ambivalence and extreme emotion, Raskolnikov at one moment is overcome by a sensation of bitter hatred for Sonia; yet, in looking intently at her anxious expression, he finally realizes that "there was love in that look"; whereupon "his hatred vanished like a phantom. It was not hatred at all: he had mistaken one feeling for another. It merely meant that *the* moment had come."

As the two confront each other face-to-face, just as Razumikhin had learned of his friend's guilt without a single word being spoken, Sonia now divines that Raskolnikov, the man she loves, is himself the murderer of the usurer and her sister. "Her feeling of horror suddenly communicated itself to him; exactly the same expression of terror appeared on his face; he, too, stared at her in the same way" (V, 4). The two sinners are one person reflected in a single image.

Embracing and kissing him, sobbing hysterically, Sonia understands that Raskolnikov is truly the unhappiest man in the world. She drops to her knees before this suffering man who has hopelessly lost his battle for separation from others. "A feeling he had not known for a long time overwhelmed him entirely, and at once softened his heart. He did not resist it: tears started in his eyes and hung on his eyelashes" (V, 4). He begs her not to leave him; she pledges to remain forever at his side—even to follow him to prison in Siberia.

But now Sonia seeks to probe the reasons for the suffering man's crime. His varied explanations, ranging from a banal need for money to an altruistic desire to help his hungry mother, culminate in what he describes as a misguided attempt at self-validation: "I wanted to *dare* and—and I committed a murder. I only wanted to dare, Sonia, that was my only motive! ... I wanted to murder, Sonia, to murder without casuistry, to murder for my own satisfaction, for myself alone.... I had to find out ... whether I was a louse like the rest or a man."

In gloomy exaltation, Raskolnikov tries to analyze the growing bitterness and spleen that had led him to set himself apart, skulking "like a spider" in his low-ceilinged hovel. Instead of studying, he confesses, he had sold his books; instead of seeking employment, he had preferred to lie on his couch and think about "the people"—fools who never change—and nurture his own need to commit an act of daring. "He who is firm and strong in mind and spirit will be [the] master [of the people]," he tells Sonia. "He who dares much is right.... He who dismisses with contempt what men regard as sacred becomes their lawgiver, and he who dares more than anyone is more right than anyone." How sadly does Sonia realize that "this gloomy expression of faith was Raskolnikov's religion and his law" (V, 4).

At the end of his long tirade, his face hideously contorted with despair, Raskolnikov turns to Sonia to seek an answer. What should he do now? Her eyes flashing fire, Sonia proclaims the Christian message. He must immediately go to stand at the crossroads, prostrate himself, kiss the earth he has defiled, and bow down to all four corners of the world, saying to all men aloud, "I am a murderer!" This is the only way, Sonia maintains, that he can relieve his soul. "Then God will send you life again.... Accept suffering and be redeemed by it—that's what you must do."

Sonia nourishes a genuine belief in God's goodness; she believes that humans have an urgent need to confess, ask pardon of others, put themselves in a position of inferiority. Raskolnikov, for the second time, is struck with amazement at Sonia's exaltation and the power of her *words*. It is as though Christ had whispered his secret to her, investing her with authority to demand Raskolnikov's self-denunciation. Sonia seems in league with Christ himself, the source of her convictions and her fortitude.

After the all-important confession scene, Raskolnikov wanders aimlessly through the streets, possessed by a feeling of dreary desolation and discerning only a dismal future—"a sort of 'eternity on a square yard of space'" (V, 5). The reader glimpses Raskolnikov's existential anguish in the oppressive feeling of "an idiotic and purely physical malady, caused by a sunset." Returning to his "cupboard," he receives a visit from Porfiry Petrovich, the fat, round little police investigator, small of stature but of great astuteness, with whom he deliberately enters into a game of thrust and parry, flirting with danger in a cat-and-mouse duel that will unfold through chapter after chapter.

Porfiry, like Svidrigaylov, is a figure hard to define. As representative of law and justice, he seems a genuine believer in God and appears truly concerned about Raskolnikov, who, however, regards his examiner with "disgust and undisguised hatred." Dostoevsky seems not without sympathy for his personified rubber ball, "rolling in different directions and rebounding all at once from every wall and corner." Allowing Porfiry to describe himself as "a figure that arouses nothing but comic ideas in people. A buffoon" (V, 5), the novelist does not lack respect for the "profound psychological methods" by which the investigator keeps his suspect in a "state of continual terror and suspense" until he eventually turns himself in.

"You see," Porfiry explains,

> he [the criminal] won't run away from me because there's no place to run to. He won't run away from me psychologically ... even if he had some place to run to, because of a law of nature. Ever watched a moth before a lighted candle? Well, he, too, will be circling round and round me like a moth round a candle. He'll get sick of his freedom. He'll start brooding. He'll get himself so thoroughly entangled that he won't be able to get out. He'll worry himself to death. And what's more ... he'll keep on describing circles around me, smaller and smaller circles, till—bang! he'll fly straight into my mouth and I'll swallow him! (IV, 5)

Porfiry understands how to play upon Raskolnikov's most sensitive trait, his obsession with the "exceptional" man. Shrewdly referring back to Raskolnikov's published article, the investigator undertakes to demonstrate the weakness of "the man who is an *exceptional* case." "[He will] tell his lie wonderfully well, most cunningly, in fact," Porfiry says,

> so that it would seem that he had scored a real triumph and could henceforth enjoy the fruits of his wit—but, bang! off he goes in a faint at the most interesting and most inappropriate moment.... He'll turn pale ... as though in mere play; but, unfortunately, he'll turn pale *too naturally* ... and again he arouses suspicion.... Comes [to] himself and starts demanding why he has not been arrested long ago.... Human nature is a mirror, sir. A mirror, clear and smooth. Look into it and marvel.... But why have you gone so pale, my dear fellow?

Overcome with emotion and involuntarily following Porfiry's own script, Raskolnikov protests:

> Porfiry Petrovich, I ... I can see very clearly ... that you really suspect me of the murder of that old woman and her sister Lisaveta.... If you think that you have a legal right to charge me with the murder, then charge me with it. If you want to arrest me, then arrest me. But I shall not permit you to laugh in my face and torment me.

Some writers have seen a good deal of Dostoevsky himself in Porfiry's subtle psychologizing, especially in his judgment of Raskolnikov's crime and of his moral need for atonement. But there is an alternative view that holds that Porfiry's devious inquisitorial methods make a travesty of real justice—

that, in fact, the villainous Porfiry sadistically abuses his power, indecently enjoys Raskolnikov's agony and, incidentally, drives to *his* breaking point a young workman who, after having been wrongly accused of the same crime, makes a false confession out of mere terror.[3]

But where Porfiry's tactics and methods fail, Sonia's succeed. For it is only after making his confession to the prostitute and doing his public penance, to the jeers of the passersby, that Raskolnikov will surrender himself to the investigator. Porfiry will maintain to the end that the criminal "*can't do without us*" (VI, 2); but this is true only in the sense that Raskolnikov, like a Prometheus or a Sisyphus seeking punishment from the gods, cannot "do without" the expiation of his crime. The epilogue to *Crime and Punishment* offers a glimpse of the eagle gnawing at the vitals of this Prometheus, of the stone this Sisyphus must incessantly roll to the summit, until his tragic plight is ultimately resolved through the sovereign power of love. Like much else in Dostoevsky's literary output, this epilogue has been the subject of diametrically opposed evaluations. Some see it as a mere appendage, lacking congruity with the rest of the novel and hastily written to satisfy an editorial requirement. Others consider it the very key to the author's intentions and the culmination of the novel's entire movement.[4] In its pages, based in large part on Dostoevsky's own prison experience, the novelist accompanies Raskolnikov toward the recognition and avowal of his guilt, foreshadowing the spiritual change occurring in his mind and heart under the influence of Sonia's calm, courageous love.

In the opening paragraph of the epilogue, the reader's eye is guided from the vast to the particular. "Siberia" telescopes into "the banks of a broad, deserted river," where "there stands a town"; in the town, "there is a fortress"; in the fortress, a prison, and in the prison, Rodion Romanovich Raskolnikov. There, Raskolnikov falls "ill from wounded pride." The true source of his illness, it appears, is his inability to understand why he should be a helpless plaything of the gods, why all his efforts to escape the situation should have been in vain. "What he was ashamed of was that he, Raskolnikov, should have perished so utterly, so hopelessly, and so stupidly because of some blind decision of fate, and that he should have to humble himself and admit to the *absurdity* of that sort of decision."

Contemplating the desolate steppe in this mood of frustration, Raskolnikov notes the approach of a thin, pale, shabbily dressed figure who turns out to be an evanescent, almost unreal Sonia. She has followed him to Siberia, and though her physical strength is being sapped by hardship, she seems to possess unlimited spiritual resources and all the fortitude that is needed to give Raskolnikov the courage to face his tragedy. Sonia releases the man she loves from his morbid oppression; she lightens his burden by making her own heavier; she dispels his frightening nightmares by appearing at his side, overflowing with gentleness and love.

Raskolnikov's long-awaited redemption, the final integration of his heart, mind, and soul, takes place during Sonia's visit. When the guard's back is turned, Raskolnikov lowers his eyes, throws himself at Sonia's feet, and weeps as he embraces her knees. Sonia understands that the moment she has waited for has finally arrived. Tears well in the eyes of the criminal and of the harlot. Pale and thin, with ravaged faces, they turn together toward "the dawn of a new future, of a full resurrection to a new life.... It was love that brought them back to life: the heart of one held inexhaustible sources of life for the heart of the other." Having accomplished his pilgrimage in the company of Sonia, "the sinner," Raskolnikov is restored to a better, higher, more worthy state and has earned the right to return to the human fold. Love, the miracle of reciprocal love, allows him to be reborn.

Notes

1. Irving, ibid., vii, xi.
2. Romano Guardini elaborates a portrait of Sonia as a child of God in *L'Univers religieux de Dostoïevski* (Paris: Editions du Seuil, 1963), 50–63.
3. Cf. "The Case Against Porfiry," in Leslie A. Johnson, *The Experience of Time in "Crime and Punishment"* (Columbus, OH: Slavica Publishers, Inc., 1985), 76–95.
4. Cf. Jacques Rolland, *Dostoievski. La question de l'Autre* (Lagrasse: Editions Verdier, 1983), 131–39.

NINA PELIKAN STRAUS

"Why Did I Say 'Women!'?": Raskolnikov Reimagined

Although feminist approaches to Dostoevsky's *Crime and Punishment* are long overdue, they will no doubt meet with some resistance. Dostoevsky's repudiation of a socialism concerned with woman's oppression and his involvement in the philosophy of the soil (*pochvennichestvo*) might indicate that feminist ideas play no part in his thinking. The recasting of Sonya in his notebooks to embody that philosophy in the novel is evidence of his conservatism. Yet Bakhtin's description of Dostoevsky's multivoiced discourse invites feminist speculation, particularly in terms of his emphasis on the idea of the *other* in the project to revise *Problems of Dostoevsky's Poetics*. In his notes, Bakhtin offers an image of consciousness that might serve as the germ of a feminist hermeneutics: "Just as the body is initially formed in the womb of the mother (in her body), so human consciousness awakens surrounded by the consciousness of others" [qtd. in Todorov 96].

Several recent studies explore this germ in their shift away from a focus on Dostoevsky's "hero" imagined as a self-sufficient entity toward an analysis of the male character as an "unaccomplished, incomplete, heterogeneous being" [Todorov 103] formed by relations to others, especially women. Malcolm V. Jones notes the "transvocalization" of men's and women's voices in the Olya story *A Raw Youth*, and Elizabeth Dalton describes the incorporation of feminine traits into Myshkin's character in *The Idiot*. Louis

From *Diacritics* 23, no. 1 (Spring 1993). © 1993 by The Johns Hopkins University Press.

Breger's claim, that in *Crime and Punishment* Raskolnikov's "split images of women have been bridged through Sonya's love," further emphasizes the effect of women upon the hero's life. Each of these approaches nevertheless stops short of a specifically feminist orientation. Breger's replacement of the older stereotype of Sonya as a "saint" by the idea that she is the novelist's "fantasy of the perfect therapist" [53] does little to undermine critiques of Dostoevsky's male chauvinism and his "melodramatic tradition" regarding women [Heldt 37]. A Bakhtinian feminism leads in another direction, focusing on Dostoevsky's "new model of the internally dialogized world" [*Problems* 291] by exploring the novel's female imagery in relation to Raskolnikov's self-knowledge.

While feminist approaches to Dostoevsky's other novels may be promising, the murder-of-women and salvation plot of *Crime and Punishment* offers the most concentrated exposure of a young man's experience of violence toward women in relation to the construction of his masculine self. Other Dostoevskian narratives offer the building (or destruction) of the hero's character in relation to women, yet none explores so relentlessly the identity confusions such relations generate. In *Crime and Punishment* Dostoevsky renames men's experience in response to "the feminine" and points to the possibility of Raskolnikov's becoming a representative "life poised on the threshold" [Bakhtin 63] of reinvented forms of the "masculine." The following pages indicate how stereotypes about gender have structured previous readings of the heroic in the novel, and how it is precisely these stereotypes that are challenged by Dostoevsky's polyphonic language.

The question is no longer whether "the emotional core of *Crime and Punishment* is ambivalence towards mother figures and women," as Breger persuasively argues [16], but whether Dostoevsky creates a one-way bridge from Sonya to Raskolnikov which merely consolidates traditional gender roles. Although feminist issues like the "woman question" [*CP* 380] and "the society of the future" [*CP* 384] are presented satirically throughout the novel, they appear to be increasingly central to it. Despite critical interest in the "rationality which Dostoevsky attacks" and the puzzle of the "something else in Raskolnikov's make-up which runs contrary to his rationalism" [Peace 34], scant attention has been paid to the problematic of the male role linked to the image of rationality and power with which Raskolnikov, and by implication Dostoevsky, struggles. Critics have described the novel's immersion in social problems, particularly of "fallen women," sparked by M. Rodevich's article of 1862 [Fanger 185–86], and the "utilitarian calculus" to which such women were subjected [Frank, "World" 32]. But none has yet suggested that Dostoevsky's attack on masculine notions of autonomy, power, and rationality accords with some feminist insights; nor have feminists yet explored the implications of women's historically changing roles as they resonate through Dostoevsky's novels. Such resonances suggest feminism's further dimensions: the struggle with masculinity by the masculine; the testing of the masculinist *idea* within the male-authored novel [see Bakhtin 114–15]. Dostoevsky's obvious mockery of crude feminism of the socialist-utilitarian (Chernyshevskian) type does not resolve the more interesting question of Raskolnikov's relation to ideas about "the masculine" or "the feminine," but rather opens that question for reconsideration.[1]

A reimagining of *Crime and Punishment* begins with the reader's capacity for "self-reflection on [his or her] complicity with inherited systems of representation" [Jardine 64], as exemplified by assumptions about "the self" that inform, for example, Breger's psychoanalytic approach or Wasiolek's conception of Dostoevsky's "metaphysic." "Raskolnikov killed the money lender for himself, and himself alone," Wasiolek writes. "In the context of Dostoevsky's metaphysic, 'for himself alone' is a profound statement, pointing to the self's capacity to exercise its freedom without limit" [77]. Whether Raskolnikov's capacity is a freedom or a pathological fantasy, whether this notion of the self extends both to men and women, remains a puzzle deepened by Bakhtin's metaphor of womb-like otherness surrounding consciousness. A Bakhtinian feminism reengages the question of Raskolnikov's motives by suggesting that his "self" is not a self-sufficient entity, but is constituted by the variously assimilated voices of others: his mother's and Dunya's voice, the intellectual's voice associated with "Napoleon," and Sonya's voice, to name just a few. A focus on the meaning of the "deep reverie" (*zabytiye*, literally, *oblivion*) into which Raskolnikov has sunk when we first meet him is associated less with freedom than with his immersion in female voices and images returning from oblivion or repression [*CP* 20].

For feminists, "the feminine" may be socially constructed, but for Raskolnikov its polarity to "the masculine" is initially experienced as essentialist. Raskolnikov is obsessed with guilt about his landlady and her daughter and with responsibility for his mother and sister, whose female dependencies "stifle[ ] and cramp[ ]" him [57]. He is immersed in the dream of the beaten nag and in revolting visions of the female pawnbroker, whom he perceives, in contrast to himself, as "vermin." Female images (nag, pawnbroker, landlady, sister, mother) are sources of uncontrollable misery which he longs to transcend through the "fascinating audacity" of a violent, manly act. This act, associated with the fantasy of man's unlimitable freedom and the "uttering [of] a new word" [20], receives its charge from the contrasting idea of woman's bondage: from Dunya's potential bondage to

Luzhin in marriage, from his mother's bondage to himself as her "guardian angel" [213], and from Sonya's bondage to prostitution. Raskolnikov's encounters with women continually test whether "everything is in a man's own hands" [20], whether he can conceive of his identity as (metaphysically) bound or unlimited, as (socially) victimized or heroic, as (dialogically) related to women or severed from them in sublime masculinist autonomy. He links females with ideas of cowardice, limitation, and victimization, and masculinity with power, money, courage, and the capacity to create victims. The pawnbroker and Lizaveta are Raskolnikov's victims; his mother and sister are Luzhin's and Svidrigaylov's; and "Mother Russia" is Napoleon's. He murders the pawnbroker as the cab driver of his dream murders the nag, as Napoleon murders "vermin," and as Svidrigaylov may have murdered his wife. Patterned so that Raskolnikov's gendered associations are gradually contradicted, the novel moves toward pandemonium: the "terrible uproar" of the funeral scene in which women scream, Luzhin is unmasked, and Dunya resists and defeats Svidrigaylov [404]. Only through the experience of gender roles reversed or conflated can Raskolnikov glimpse the transformed image of manhood Dostoevsky seeks for him.

Dostoevsky's diffusion of sex-stereotyped images is nevertheless at odds with Raskolnikov's initial gender essentialism. The novel begins with Raskolnikov's dream of a (male) cart driver beating a (female) nag and continues with Raskolnikov hacking the female pawnbroker to death, but the image of men beating females is inverted, finally. Duplicated images of beating, several of them reversing the gender relations of the others, show how Raskolnikov discovers that what he beats *beats him*. An early image of Katerina pulling her husband "by the hair" [32] is followed by the image of Raskolnikov bringing a hatchet across the "crown" of the female pawnbroker's head [96]. Raskolnikov then dreams of "hitting the old woman on the head with all his strength, but at every blow of the hatchet ... [she] simply rocked with laughter" [194]. Raskolnikov's fall into a "fathomless chasm" and into a simultaneously "higher" realm where his dialectic "vanishes" [132–33] is also dramatized by Marmeladov's being crushed to death by a horse, implying the retaliation of the beaten mare in Raskolnikov's dream upon her male persecutor [195]. The idea of "the feminine" in *Crime and Punishment* is the symbolic hatchet that breaks open men's heads by destroying the distinctions between "low" and "high," "docile" and "powerful," victim and master, the coward and the hero. The hierarchy of Raskolnikov's sexist imagery decomposes as he discovers that he is "a louse ... nastier than the louse [he] killed" [292] and that his Napoleon fantasy is a "frightful muddle" [470]. By exploring the ways in which the masculine–feminine polarities reflected in Raskolnikov's consciousness are undermined, we come to read *Crime and Punishment* as a text in which Dostoevsky discovers the politics of gender, a text in which Raskolnikov's crime and punishment are engendered.

*Raskol*nikov, whose name means *schism*, soon discovers himself as a "self created within a split—a being that can only conceptualise itself when it is mirrored back to itself from the position of another's desire" [Lacan 5], namely women's. His problem with socially constructed femininity is dramatized early in the novel through the characters' ironic discussion of "whether a woman is a human being or not." Razumikhin offers Raskolnikov three rubles for a translation of a German text on this subject that will "sell like hotcakes!" For Raskolnikov the subject hits a nerve. He takes the text and three rubles, walks out of the room, and then returns both text and money. Raskolnikov acts as if he has "the d.t.'s" (*belaya goryachka*: literally, white-hot fever). He explains his "confused" action by murmuring, significantly, "'I don't want translations'" [130–31]. Instead, he wants the real thing, horrific or blissful experience with women. But his experience is not limited to Sonya. As part of a cluster of female images which gradually transforms Raskolnikov by disrupting his compulsive need to divide "man" into "hero" and "vermin," Sonya is only part of Raskolnikov's masculinist crisis. She is Raskolnikov's savior-therapist on a religious or therapeutic level, but his puzzle and poison in feminist terms. Her demand that he confess his crime and "kiss the earth you have defiled" [433] links Raskolnikov's defilement of Mother Russia not only with the feminine essence Sonya symbolizes but also with the degraded femininity of the old pawnbroker. Although the novel initially seems structured as a regression to fantasies of destroying symbolic maternity [Barker 123], it moves quickly from the murder of Alyona towards images of youthful female sexuality embodied by Sonya, Dunya, and Svidrigaylov's raped girls. This is not to say that Raskolnikov's experience radiates less from the act of murdering the pawnbroker, but that this act does not completely account for what else happens in the novel. The relation of Raskolnikov's nonsexual but violent crime against two women and Svidrigaylov's sexual crimes against women can be understood in terms of a vague analogy between the two; that is, they are "doubles" in psychoanalytic terms. But something like "the failure of the [double] metaphor to attain and name its proper meaning" [Felman 128] is also at work in the novel when it shifts in part 6 from a focus on Raskolnikov to a focus on Svidrigaylov and his experiences with Dunya. The woman question enters the text not through any "objectified words in Dostoevsky, since the speech of his characters is constructed in a way that deprives it of all objectification" [Bakhtin 203], but through characterological links between brother and sister (both reformers capable of martyrdom [487–89]), and through the gap that exists between the sexually saturated subplots and the central crime-and-punishment plot.

It is precisely the relations between the later Dunya–Luzhin–Sonya/Svidrigaylov–Dunya subplots, involving attempted or actual sexual violation, and the earlier Raskolnikov–Alyona–Lizaveta murder plot, in which sex seems absent, that mark Dostoevsky's novel as bearing a feminist problematic. This problematic is carried by the surprising upstaging of Raskolnikov by Svidrigaylov, the interrupted focus on Raskolnikov by the Dunya/Svidrigaylov scene, and by Svidrigaylov's dream of the child whore which bears something like a "sidelong glance" at Raskolnikov's dream of the beaten mare. What is missing from Raskolnikov's discourse and experience is present in the resonating relations among the two men, Dunya, and other women: in their "hidden polemic, polemically colored confession, hidden dialogue" [Bakhtin 203], which defines "man" as he who violates women, which defines masculinity at femininity's expense, and which defines a "new" kind of woman as a resisting heroine or martyr [*CP* 487]. This hidden polemic about men and women is not disclosed by Raskolnikov's murdering of the pawnbroker. Instead that crime serves as an opening for Raskolnikov to come in contact with Svidrigaylov, who in turn comes in contact with Dunya, the experience of which enables both men to admit their sense of "insect" suffering and hopelessness [*CP* 305].

Dostoevsky's deliberate convergence of the crime and sex-crime issues in the novel's second half thus forces the woman question and the Napoleonic question (whether Raskolnikov is a "man" or a "vermin") to enter into a dialogic relation with each other. The two men's words about Dunya and Sonya, suggesting obsessions with female sexuality, are dialogically informed by Raskolnikov's words about the beaten mare in his dreams. The nonsexual words that inform Raskolnikov's beaten-mare dream reveal the *contexts* of Russian women's lives [see Bakhtin 293]. In axing the pawnbroker, the symbolic master Raskolnikov will "whip the little grey-brown mare." Taking things into "a man's own hands," he is compelled not to "spare her"; she must be "showered with blows"; she must drown in blood because she is a man's "property" [*CP* 74–76]. Or, in a dreamlike reversal of meanings, he must kill "her" because she has taken his property (as Alyona takes Raskolnikov's property in pawn) or because he is not psychologically his own property. All these words reveal the contexts to which *Crime and Punishment*'s women are subjected in varying degrees and the pattern through which Raskolnikov becomes more and more identified with women and their contexts. Katerina carries the load of her family upon her sickly, tortured back, crying out on her deathbed that "they've beaten the mare to death" [448]; Sonya can be bought or sold as sexual property; Svidrigaylov beats his wife until she dies; Dunya's virgin blood will flow if she cannot convert the master or persuade him to spare her.

Not only Sonya's situation but Dunya's discloses the masculinist desire (as dramatized by Luzhin and Svidrigaylov) to purchase woman as a thing, to violate her morally or physically as the instantiation of man's superior power. Raskolnikov's resistance to Sonya shares with his hatred of the female pawnbroker a terror of the sex–violence complex he associates with men and fears in himself, an association verified by Svidrigaylov's attempted rape of his own sister. The question of what men do *to*, *for*, or *with* women drives Raskolnikov toward *others* besides Sonya, thus enlarging the dialogue between masculinist identity and crimes against women. His emotional turmoil unravels in relation to Sonya or what Peace calls "the 'Elizaveta' in (Raskolnikov's] make-up" [54]; through conversations with Porfiry that trivialize his Napoleonism; but also in terms of the "Dunya" who evolves within him and through the "Svidrigaylov" he confronts.

The pattern that relates Raskolnikov's Napoleon ideology to both his and Svidrigaylov's crimes involves images of violence done to females, even though Raskolnikov's discourse with Porfiry attempts to suppress the connection that other discourses in the novel make clear. The novel is saturated with writings about crime (Raskolnikov's article), arguments about crimes redeemed by penitence (with Sonya), conversations about criminal motivation (with Porfiry), and disclosures of the pleasures of sex crimes (with Svidrigaylov). Yet nowhere do Dostoevsky's words objectify the connections between Raskolnikov's notion that there are "two categories" of human being—the "inferior" and the "talent[ed]" capable of both crime and of saying a "new word" [*CP* 279]—and his ideas about femininity and masculinity. These connections are made because Raskolnikov cannot impede the dialogic flow of the novel's language (of which his own is only a part) by suppressing the reader's awareness of the relation between his Napoleonic theory and the murder which he, a possibly *talented* young man, has perpetrated against a distinctly *inferior* and nearly *wordless* old woman. Nor can Raskolnikov's words stop the "agitated, verbal surface" of a work in which "everything is on the borderline ... everything is prepared ... to pass over into its opposite" [Bakhtin 167], so that the parallel between Raskolnikov and Svidrigaylov becomes increasingly close. Although Raskolnikov commits crimes "on principle" and Svidrigaylov is compelled by sensuality, each man's experience with females mirrors the genderized structure of an action imagined as necessary for male transcendence in the Napoleon fantasy. The two worst crimes, murder and attempted rape, are positioned at opposite ends of the novel: bookends that symbolize the two "supreme effort[s]" of a perverted masculinist script [*CP* 279]. While the article "On Crime" articulates the supreme fantasy, the novel reveals that fantasy's consequence: violence toward "vermin" who turn out to be female. What the novel articulates as a rethinking of male roles, Raskolnikov's article perverts; yet each reveals that male criminality is never disassociated from fantasies about women and sex. If "it takes a strong soul to endure [Dostoevsky's] works" [Catteau 455], this is because the novel and its "intellectual" discussions are haunted by images of battered, violated, and murdered females. Raskolnikov's vision of the "masses" as "cows" [*CP* 279] points to "Napoleon" as a bull or phallic signifier. Only a "Napoleon" is capable of violating "Mother Russia." Thus Raskolnikov's question to himself suggests the nature of Dostoevsky's "borderline" feminist inquisition: "Why did I say 'Women!'?" [*CP* 268].

Raskolnikov's Napoleonism, like his relation to women, is in Bakhtin's terms a "*live* event" [88], a masculinist "idea-prototype" whose "resonance" must be played out and exposed [168, 92]. Overtly expressed in Raskolnikov's writings and his conversations with Porfiry, the little-Napoleon conducts of other male characters in the novel express this idea-prototype in nearly parodic form. Initially experienced through Raskolnikov's murder of the female pawnbroker, whose life "amounts to no more than the life of a louse" [*CP* 84-85], the idea is later played out through Luzhin's and Svidrigaylov's relations with Sonya and Dunya. Treated as inferiors, each female figure enters Raskolnikov's "thoroughly dialogized interior monologue ... a dialogue of ultimate questions and ultimate life decisions" [Bakhtin 74]. These ultimate decisions are related to problems involving women's bodies, women's socioeconomic role, and the religious and mythic symbolisms that entrap both sexes. Sonya, Dunya, her mother, Katerina, Lizaveta, and the pawnbroker each represent a familiar feminine situation. All of them indicate how *woman* is a dominant fetish of Raskolnikov's culture, constituted by a *lack*.[2]

Sonya's woman problem is that she lacks money and must sell her body to men. Dunya's deprivation and sacrificial impulse for her brother's sake tempts her to sell herself in marriage to Luzhin. If Alyona brokers jewelry, Sonya and Dunya broker youth and sexuality. The pawnbroker's suspiciousness, the way she jumps back "in panic" when a man "advance[s] straight on" [*CP* 94], dramatizes the elderly female's experiences of male brutality even before her encounter with Raskolnikov. Lizaveta is not just any docile woman, but a pregnant woman, perhaps the victim of rape. Along with Katerina and Alyona, she represents the socially degraded female whom Raskolnikov must kill in himself in his attempt to establish a sense of male superiority. Like Svidrigaylov, Raskolnikov must initially mock, penetrate, or hack at a woman to assert a masculine identity which would otherwise be indistinguishable from her docile "vermin" status.

Exploring masculinist fantasies, which feminism also critiques, Dostoevsky represents Raskolnikov as magnetized toward two symbolically gendered extremities, each of which is psychologically imprisoning. Whereas the Napoleonic idea embodies masculine fantasies of freedom and modernity, the reaction to cruelty by embodying it, the idea of Sonya embodies docility and Christianity, the reaction to cruelty by bearing it. In acting out both these roles, Raskolnikov reveals the socially constructed sexual polarities within himself. Not only the novel's women, but its central male figures are represented as oppressed by patriarchal hierarchies and by myths about masculine freedom. Svidrigaylov's question, "am I a monster or am I myself the victim?" [*CP* 297], is also Raskolnikov's. The consequence of the "self's capacity to exercise its freedom without limit" is a suffering that Raskolnikov shares with men who make women suffer.

In one such scene of mutual suffering, Sonya attempts to undermine Raskolnikov's masculinist fantasy of some new "law ... unknown at present" that will bring "into the world by some ... mysterious process ... one man out of a thousand" [*CP* 280]. Reading the Lazarus story to Raskolnikov, Sonya is convinced that such men have already appeared in the form of Jesus and Lazarus. Reacting in the name of the "rational" against Sonya's "feeble-minded" faith [*CP* 341], Raskolnikov expresses anxiety concerning a transformed form of masculinity suffered by sons who "appropriate those specific components of the masculinity of their father that they fear will be otherwise used against them" [Chodorow 176]. Raskolnikov must reconceive himself not through Sonya's "relentless condemnation" of his "supreme effort" [*CP* 385], but in terms of a manhood fearless enough to withstand what men like Napoleon, Luzhin, and Svidrigaylov will use against him. This new version of courage finds its image less in Sonya than in Dunya, who outwits the male forces Raskolnikov confronts. Until the last pages of the novel, however, Raskolnikov resists the incorporation of this *other* so close to him. Instead, he imagines that he "alone" must face a "test" that will drive him to "senile impotence" [*CP* 531]. What is his fantasy? Raskolnikov fears becoming "vermin," a crawling female or cowlike form of life easily squashed by men in power.

At the core of his attraction for and terror of Sonya, at the core of his growing knowledge of Dunya, is the image of himself as a maimed female. He runs from this image of himself but also pursues it. As Wasiolek notes, he is "terrified and crushed by the thought of not being pursued" and "breathes life into the pursuit, providing it with clues" [71]. Images of being pursued, of falling to his knees, and fainting mark Raskolnikov's journey toward an identification with women but also toward a difficult new version of masculinity. Marmeladov's description of the way Katerina goes "down on her knees, and kiss[es] Sonya's feet" [*CP* 35] inspires Raskolnikov to mimic the gesture in the Lazarus scene, perhaps ironically. Fainting and falling when he first encounters his mother and sister, he is reminded of another pair, the murdered pawnbroker and Lizaveta [212]. His falling replicates the way Alyona "dropped to the floor" at his feet [96]. It recalls the meaning of Sonya as a *fallen woman*, and the meaning of Dunya's engagement to Luzhin—"which means you're selling yourself," he tells her [249]. Female figures, moreover, reflect the beaten mare in his dream who "collapsed on the ground" and is "whipped across the eyes" [76–77]. Wounded female eyes, associated with the "meek and gentle eyes" of Lizaveta and Sonya [292], represent a challenge to Raskolnikov's masculinist supremacy associated with his Napoleonic theory. As the mirror of Napoleonic masculinity begins to crack, all the females gazing back at Raskolnikov begin to appear in it. As they do, his fainting body speaks against him from within him.

Raskolnikov's self-knowledge grows in proportion to his developing sense of Katerina's, Sonya's, and Dunya's female situations in relation to husband, father, fiance, and brother. Raskolnikov's fear of his "landlady's ... demands for payment" [19] and his disclosure in the police station that "from the very first I promised to marry [the landlady's] daughter" [120] compose elements of a script in which his masculine role is embedded. Like Marmeladov's, Luzhin's, and Svidrigaylov's, Raskolnikov's script involves continual complicity in the debasement of women. Luzhin's ability to tempt Dunya in marriage and "debase her spirit and her moral feelings" [61] is the consequence of Raskolnikov's inability to care for her; a consequence which in the parallel case of Marmeladov drives Sonya to prostitution. Like Svidrigaylov, who locks Dunya in his room with a key, like Marmeladov who "stole by a cunning trick the key from [his] wife's trunk" [38], Raskolnikov steals into the pawnbroker's room and finds the "notched key" which opens her "biggish box" [98]. If fainting before women distinguishes Raskolnikov from the men around him, stealing from women or penetrating into women's boxes or bodies is the metaphor through which Dostoevsky connects Raskolnikov to them. Raskolnikov's dream of obtaining heroism by "step[ping] over a corpse" [277–78] and stealing Alyona's money finally cannot be severed from Luzhin's and Svidrigaylov's base heroics using "dirty trick[s]" and "bluff[s]" to seduce women [415–17]. Watching Luzhin and Svidrigaylov in predatory action coupled with cash offerings, Raskolnikov glimpses the sexual-symbolic order in which his image of Napoleonic heroism is grounded. Through the action of other men with women he becomes "dimly aware of the great lie in himself and his convictions" [553].

No doubt for Dostoevsky the great lie has an ultimate religious significance. But for Raskolnikov the rupture with lies is apprehended through concrete experience with women, who appear as the symbolic vermin of a patriarchal society he has incorporated but from which he seeks escape. The escape from the masculinist prison of false heroics and lies begins with Marmeladov's death [206] and gathers momentum with the knowledge that Svidrigaylov is accused of beating his wife to death and of causing the suicide of a fifteen-year-old because he had "cruelly interfered with her" [314]. Luzhin's false accusations against Sonya [405] soon follow, with the consequence that Raskolnikov is able to see *himself* in the sexist mirror of Luzhin. If Raskolnikov's "inner speech is constructed like a succession of living and impassioned replies to all the words of others he has heard or has been touched by" [Bakhtin 238], his statement that he "knew perfectly well [he] was not a Napoleon" [*CP* 432] is a concession not to failure but to the possibility of altering his image of the masculine self. Porfiry's words, "a great act of fulfillment [is] before you" [*CP* 472], further stimulate the possibility of an alternate future that evolves from Raskolnikov's recognition of the connections between Napoleon's victims, the beaten female horse of his dream, the pawnbroker whom he axed, the tortured Katerina, the prostituted Sonya, and Svidrigaylov's rape victims, who might include Dunya. What Porfiry increasingly exploits as he drives Raskolnikov toward confession is the emotional borderline the young murderer crosses when he is no longer able to distinguish between identification with masculine experience and identification with feminine experience.

Running between Sonya and Porfiry, both of whose asexual bodily attributes signify gender confusions, Raskolnikov is led towards the undermining of his masculine role. Victimized by Porfiry's inquisition, Raskolnikov's sickness appears as a defense against the cruelties of a misogynist society that perpetuates the beatings it punishes as crimes and that treats men without power like women. His transformation thus has multiple sources, reinforced by Porfiry's appearance in the novel as a peculiar feminine–masculine compound. "The expression of [Porfiry's] eyes was strangely out of keeping with his whole figure, which reminded one somehow of the figure of an old peasant woman" [267]. Raskolnikov is provoked to partial confession through Porfiry's maternal image and through his strangely castrating discourse: "he'll fly straight into my mouth, and I'll swallow him!" [355]. Attempting to liberate him from the world of dead men's voices, Porfiry insists that Raskolnikov's crime bears "no resemblance whatever to any previous case" [354]. Yet the reader may remember that "exactly the same ideas" about murdering the pawnbroker "just beginning to stir in [Raskolnikov's] own mind" were articulated by ordinary young officers in a Petersburg restaurant a short time before Raskolnikov committed the crime [84–85]. Porfiry's discourse exists alongside other words and images that overlap to form a pattern revealed to the reader: the notion of Raskolnikov's crime as a disease [*CP* 90], the resonance between Raskolnikov's Napoleonic theory and other misogynist worldviews shared by men of his generation. Because Porfiry has not heard the young officers' words about murdering the old woman, because he has no knowledge of Svidrigaylov's sexual violence toward young women, his solutions for Raskolnikov, like Sonya's, remain partial. Porfiry intuits Raskolnikov's suicidal impulses, but he is not privy to the female-imaged crisis that Raskolnikov's confession to Sonya suggests: "Was it the old hag I killed? No, I killed myself, and not the old hag. I did away with myself at one blow and for good" [433].

Related to his growing identification with women, Raskolnikov's suicidal impulses foreshadow the motive behind Svidrigaylov's suicide. Raskolnikov's self-knowledge emerges partially from his ambiguous struggles with Sonya's Christianity and partially through Porfiry's mockery of his Napoleonism. But knowledge also comes to him by way of Dunya's resistance to Svidrigaylov and Raskolnikov's identification with both of them. A series of events connected with women leads to the confession of his crime. Svidrigaylov confesses his "disgusting stories" of lust and violence to Raskolnikov [494]; he attempts the rape of Dunya and she shoots at him [507]. In what appears as a *non sequitur* in the police station, Raskolnikov listens to the assistant superintendent discuss "short-haired young females," who "have a most immoderate desire for enlightenment," and the issue of "what more do [women] want" [540–41]. This textual glancing at feminist questions and Dunya is followed by the announcement that Svidrigaylov has shot himself and by Sonya's appearance at the police station. Only then does Raskolnikov admit "It was I who killed the old woman" [541–42]. Although Dostoevsky has sought to keep Raskolnikov's crime clean of sexual implications, he is finally unable to forestall the convergence of sex with violence, of Raskolnikov's "disease" with Svidrigaylov's, and of feminist with religious and ethical issues.

The Dunya–Svidrigaylov chapter therefore occupies a peculiar position in the novel because it is explicitly about sexual relations and the masculine problematic. Melodramatic as the Lazarus scene between Raskolnikov and Sonya, the scene is a reversal, with the man rather than the woman humiliated by the struggle. Dostoevsky's intention to transform *man* through *woman's* religious faith, to "settle[ ] the issue by nudging Raskolnikov into God's camp" [Wasiolek 84], is complicated in the second scene by the intrusion of the psychology of a *new* woman and a transformed man whose life framework is power and sexuality rather than religion and theory. Although Dunya's experience with Svidrigaylov is not mentioned in the police station when her brother makes his confession, the assistant superintendent's words about "short-haired" (feminist) women and "educated" men [*CP* 540–41] forge dialogic connections between the Svidrigaylov–Dunya scene and the scene of Raskolnikov's confession in the police station with Sonya present. While Raskolnikov's fantasy is to reform the world of heroes through his Napoleon theory (which Sonya resists), Dunya's "passion for reform" moves in a feminist direction towards advocacy for other women [*CP* 489] to which Svidrigaylov submits. This glance in a feminist direction through Dunya on Dostoevsky's part is not a fully developed or integrated part of the novel's surface. In fact, the image of Dunya and Svidrigaylov interrupts that surface somewhat the way the central clue to a dream's meaning appears extraneous to the dream's manifest content. It shifts the notion of transformation away from religious conversion to what looks like the feminist conversion of a male chauvinist. Dunya, a much less fully realized character than Svidrigaylov, remains part of what Bakhtin calls the novel's "hidden interior," perhaps its most hidden part, justifying the impression that the novel's "narrative practices and psychology [are] violently at odds with [its] ideological intentions" [Bernstein 365]. It is the religiously pure and simple Sonya, and not the complex Dunya, who must *appear* to be the source of Raskolnikov's conversion, even if the novel's imagery, its self-interception, and its hidden dialogue suggest the contrary. Slipping from Dostoevsky's anti-feminist/socialist stance, Dostoevsky's "encounter" with Dunya, once set in verbal motion, forms "new aspects and new functions of the word" for the novel and for the reader [Bakhtin 266]. It is only *through* Dunya's effect on Svidrigaylov that Raskolnikov's confession and self-transformation can be achieved; it is only through the connections between religious and feminist ideologies of conversion that "the woman question" can be contextualized. Dunya's visit to Svidrigaylov's rooms explores the question that Dostoevsky has treated satirically through Lebezyatnikov—whether "in the future men and women can have access to each other's rooms" [*CP* 384]. Now this question must be taken seriously.

Dunya's capacity for a violent act against Svidrigaylov undermines the gendered contraries at the heart of Raskolnikov's fantasy of male freedom and female bondage. Locked in Svidrigaylov's room, threatened with the fact that "rape is very difficult to prove," Dunya shoots at her violator with his own gun, first grazing his hair with the bullet.

> Now she would kill him—at only two feet away! Suddenly she threw away the gun. A heavy weight seemed to have lifted

> suddenly from his heart, but possibly it was not only the weight of the fear of death.... It was a release from another more forlorn and sombre feeling which he himself could scarcely have defined in all its strength. [506–08]

Dunya's response to Svidrigaylov combines (stereotypically male) self-defense with (stereotypically female) compassion for the other, dramatizing a cross-gendered role that Raskolnikov can "grasp" only "to a certain extent" [*CP* 540] and that Svidrigaylov can "scarcely define." Release from Svidrigaylov's masculinist monologue turns upon Dunya's final refusal to use the man's own methods against him, leading to his being "seized by the other's discourse, which has made its home in it" [Bakhtin 219]. Dunya's image and voice thus invade Svidrigaylov just as the images of beaten mare, axed pawnbroker, and prostituted Sonya invade Raskolnikov's narcissistic solitude. Her interception in the genderized nightmare destroys stereotypes as it exposes the masculinist disease and "something in common" [*CP* 302] which Svidrigaylov and Raskolnikov share.

The feminist reader has nowhere to flee from the implications of Dostoevsky's connection of Raskolnikov with Svidrigaylov. In *Crime and Punishment* the rapist is the murderer's double, and each symbolizes the degenerate form to which the secular Westernized "metaphysic" of free male individuality and genderized oppositions have driven him. Dostoevsky's critique of freedom suggests the woman-violating form to which socially constructed masculinity is sometimes addicted. The novel makes clear that just as the peasant Mikolka beats the mare because she is his "property" [77], just as Napoleon is the conquerer of territories, so Svidrigaylov imagines himself the "conquerer of women's hearts" [488], and Raskolnikov temporarily imagines he can become "one man out of a thousand" by killing a greedy old woman. Svidrigaylov's question to Dunya, "so you don't love me?" [508] coexists with Raskolnikov's question, "why did I say 'women!'?" and with the assistant superintendent's question, "what more do [women] want?" For both Raskolnikov and Svidrigaylov, disease has its origins in male fantasies that construct women as barriers men must penetrate to achieve masculinity—fantasies symbolized in the novel's last section by Svidrigaylov's dream.

The dream which Bakhtin characterizes as *menippea* [155] marks the alpha and omega of masculine images of women as it assimilates the temptress to the victim, the Orthodox Madonna to Magdalene, the girl to the woman, and both to the whore who is man's desire and debasement. As Svidrigaylov lifts the covers from the sleeping girl-child, Dostoevsky uncovers the fantastic core of his female image repertoire: "But how strange!

The colour of the little girl's cheeks seemed brighter ... her eyelids were opening slowly, as though a pair of sly, sharp little eyes were winking at him not at all in a childish way, and as though the little girl was only pretending to be asleep."

Svidrigaylov's dream suggests "the universal genre of ultimate questions" [Bakhtin 146] involving masculine relations to power and female sexuality. The dream asks whether women are human, whether females mean what they say, whether females desire rape:

> Yes, yes, that was so: her lips parted in a smile; the corners of her mouth twitched.... She was laughing! ... There was something shameless and provocative in that no longer childish face. It was lust, it was the face of a whore, the shameless face of a French whore.... But at that moment he woke up. [520–21]

Replicating fragments of Raskolnikov's experience, the dream echoes the "winking" of the "peasant woman" Porfiry and the laughing of the pawnbroker in his dream, as well as her "sharp, sly" eyes. The child's face mirrors the childish face of Sonya, the fact that Sonya is a "whore," and that whores like Napoleon are "French." Like Sonya, Dunya is tempted to sell herself to men such as Luzhin, but in Svidrigaylov's dream men are also sold an identity that drives them to despair and suicide. Dostoevsky's religious intentions for Raskolnikov do not disguise what his society has projected upon women.

Learning that Svidrigaylov has shot himself, Raskolnikov "felt as if some heavy weight had descended on him and pinned him to the ground" [541]. His feeling inverts Svidrigaylov's sense that "a heavy weight seemed to have lifted suddenly from his heart." The weight of sexual crisis, no longer sublimated into abstract questions of freedom or power, shifts to Raskolnikov. He is weighed down by Dunya's and Sonya's meanings, by the "key" that Svidrigaylov has literally thrown to his sister and, by symbolic implication, to him [509]. If he does not fully incorporate Sonya's Christianity, he nevertheless falls into the new world Sonya and Dunya occupy. In this world, where women affect men intensely, the dialectic between masculinity and femininity, hero and vermin, oppressor and oppressed begins to close. For Raskolnikov, "Life had taken the place of dialectics, and something quite different had to work itself out in his mind" [580].

This difference discloses Dostoevsky's new version of a masculinity that will escape violence but resist impotence. Raskolnikov attempts but ultimately fails to live out the most heroic version of male courage available to him (Napoleonism), yet Dostoevsky represents his failure as a triumph. Each defeat of an unwanted sexual advance on the part of other men in the novel can also be read as Dostoevsky's undermining of a false conception of masculinity that must be extinguished in Raskolnikov. Against these masculinist fantasies, Dostoevsky empowers Sonya with a hardly believable compassion and Dunya with a virtue, understanding, and strength that can be read as Dostoevsky's alternative to traditional notions of masculine heroism. As matured variants of the raped girl-child figure which haunted Dostoevsky all his life,[3] Dunya and Sonya perform a partial revenge against their male violators. If for Dostoevsky child rape ending in murder was the worst crime, then a young woman's resistance to rape, leading to the self-conscious transformation of the rapist, would constitute a new type of male transcendence and consciousness. More important, it would acknowledge female power in an alternate form to Sonya's. If Svidrigaylov is Raskolnikov's double in the deepest sense, Svidrigaylov's conversion from pathological sexuality to a momentary dialogic relation with Dunya is the feminist parallel to Raskolnikov's religious conversion through Sonya.

Originating in Raskolnikov's experience with women, Dostoevsky's challenge to himself ends the novel: "He would have to pay a great price for it ... he would have to pay for it by a great act of heroism in the future" [559]. This heroic act is Dostoevsky's creation of male figures, particularly Prince Myshkin and Alyosha Karamazov, who incorporate socially constructed "feminine" traits and are intensely sensitive to the problem of man's violence against women.[4] Yet Myshkin and Alyosha cannot be imagined without their most important predecessor—Raskolnikov. *Crime and Punishment* presents scenes in which no authentic male heroism exists without a man's willing entry into dialogic relations and identifications with women, substantiating certain feminist hopes for the future of both sexes.

Notes

1. If Dostoevsky thought little of Chernyshevskian feminism, his affair with the feminist Apollonaria Suslova, which ended in 1865 (the year he began work on *Crime and Punishment*), nevertheless suggests that his attitude towards the woman question was ambiguous and complex. Although negative and satiric comments about that question can be found in his novels (particularly *A Raw Youth* and *The Brothers Karamazov*), these are also undermined by his imagery and by his presentations of strong, ethical women like Dunya. In this regard, a letter from 1865 indicates that Suslova's fiery criticisms of him, related to her disappointment in him, turned his thoughts toward the masculine–feminine problematic that tortures Raskolnikov (see *Selected Letters*, 212–131).

2. I use the word lack in the sense of Lacan's interpretation of Freud's notion of the female as "castrated, "that is, stressing its linguistic rather than psychosexual sense. Raskolnikov's Napoleonism can be understood as a symptom of phallocentric narcissism (subject to Dostoevsky's deconstruction) in the sense that "the human social order ...

refracted through the individual human subject is patrocentric, "reflecting not biological but cultural-symbolic *language* conditions" [Lacan 23 f].

3. In his biography of Dostoevsky, Geir Kjetsaa describes the following incident: in 1870 Dostoevsky and his "guests were discussing what ought to be considered the greatest crime.... 'The most fearful crime is to rape a child,' the writer said quickly and nervously. 'To take life—that is dreadful, but to destroy faith in love's beauty is an even more dreadful crime.' And he related the [childhood] episode at the hospital for the poor [when he learned that a girl who was his friend had been raped and murdered].... 'All my life I have been haunted by that memory [Dostoevsky continued], which was the most dreadful crime, the most fearful sin.... It was with that crime that I punished Stavrogin'" [327 f.]. It is also the crime for which he punishes Raskolnikov's "double"—Svidrigaylov.

4. Dostoevsky's challenge to create a "heroism in the future" is attempted through the character of Myshkin, but is most successfully accomplished in the figure of Alyosha. In *The Brothers Karamazov*, Alyosha is haunted and motivated by his mother's miserable life. He faints when his father describes how he tortured Alyosha's mother, "the shrieker" [bk. 3, ch. 8]. Alyosha's last speech to the boys sanctifies memories of childhood which refer to the memory of his mother's face, connected not only to his longing for man's self-transformation through Christian belief, but also to his identification with women.

Works Cited

Bakhtin, Mikhail. *Problems of Dostoevsky's Poetics*. Trans. Caryl Emerson. Minneapolis: U of Minnesota P, 1984.

Barker, Adele. *The Mother Syndrome in Russian Folk Imagination*. Slavica, 1985.

Bernstein, Michael Andre. "'These Children that Come at You with Knives': *Ressentiment*, Mass Culture, and the Saturnalia." *Critical Inquiry* 17 (1991): 358–72.

Breger, Louis. *Dostoevsky: The Author As Psychoanalyst*. New York: New York UP, 1989.

Chernyshevsky, Nikolai. *What Is to Be Done?* Trans. Michael R. Katz. Ithaca: Cornell UP, 1989.

Chodorow, Nancy. *The Reproduction of Mothering: Psychoanalysis and the Sociology of Gender*. Berkeley: U of California P, 1978.

Catteau, Jacques. *Dostoevsky and the Process of Literary Creation*. Trans. Audrey Littlewood. New York: Cambridge UP, 1989.

Dalton, Elizabeth. *Unconscious Structure in* The Idiot. Princeton: Princeton UP, 1979.

Dostoevsky, Fyodor. *The Brothers Karamazov*. Trans. Richard Pevear and Larissa Volokhonsky. San Francisco: Northpoint, 1990.

———. *Crime and Punishment*. Trans. David Magarshack. London: Penguin, 1951. [*CP*]

———. *The Notebooks for Crime and Punishment*. Trans. and ed. Edward Wasiolek. Chicago: U of Chicago P, 1967.

———. *Prestuplenie i nakazanie* [*Crime and Punishment*]. Moskva: Ruskaya Yazik, 1984.

———. *Selected Letters of Fyodor Dostoevsky*. Ed. Joseph Frank and David I. Goldstein. Trans. Andrew R. MacAndrew. New Brunswick: Rutgers UP, 1987.

Fanger, Donald. *Dostoevsky and Romantic Realism*. Cambridge: Harvard UP, 1967.

Felman, Shoshana. *Writing and Madness*. Trans. Martha Noel Evans. Ithaca: Cornell UP, 1978.

Frank, Joseph. *Dostoevsky: The Stir of Liberation: 1860–1865*. Princeton: Princeton UP, 1986.

———. "The World of Raskolnikov." *Encounter* 26.6 (1966): 30–35.

Heldt, Barbara. *Terrible Perfection: Women in Russian Literature*. Bloomington: Indiana UP, 1987.

Jardine, Alice. *Gynesis*. Ithaca: Cornell UP, 1985.

Jones, Malcolm V. *Dostoevsky after Bakhtin: Readings in Dostoevsky's Fantastic Realism*. New York: Cambridge UP, 1990.

Kjetsaa, Geir. *Fyodor Dostoevsky: A Writer's Life*. Trans. Siri Hustvedt and David McDuff. New York: Viking, 1987.

Lacan, Jacques. *Feminine Sexuality: Jacques Lacan and the école freudienne*. Ed. Juliet Mitchell and Jacqueline Rose. Trans. Jacqueline Rose. New York: Norton and Pantheon, 1985.

Peace, Richard. *Dostoevsky: An Examination of His Major Novels*. Cambridge: Cambridge UP, 1971.

Todorov, Tzvetan. *Mikhail Bakhtin: The Dialogical Principle*. Trans. Wlad Godzich. Minneapolis: U of Minnesota P, 1984.

Wasiolek, Edward. *Dostoevsky: The Major Fiction*. Cambridge: MIT P, 1964.

Character Profiles

RODION ROMANOVICH RASKOLNIKOV

Is the protagonist of *Crime and Punishment* a criminal who should be punished, or a tortured young man who makes a terrible mistake? Dostoevsky depicts a complicated psychological portrait of the main character, Rodion Raskolnikov, also known by "Rodya," "Rodenka," and "Rodka." A brilliant, impoverished former law student, Raskolnikov lives in the slums of "airless" St. Petersburg. Although he has no money, he does not look for a job. He cannot seem to find the motivation to break out of this poverty, and "completely absorbed in himself," he often dreads social contact. Highly knowledgeable, well read, and a loner, Raskolnikov has "cut himself off from everyone and everything." When the novel begins he is "badly dressed," and his appearance only becomes more disheveled as the novel continues.

The first part of Raskolnikov's name, "raskol," literally means "split," and this dualism is key to his character—cold intellect versus natural compassion. His friend Razumikhin describes him as morose, gloomy, and proud, but admits Raskolnikov also has a kind heart: "[I]n truth, it is exactly as though he were alternating between two opposing characters." Raskolnikov commits a brutal crime; he's self-centered and often repugnant. However, he also wants to do good and at times seems stunned by his own thoughts: "How could such a horrible idea enter my mind? What vileness my heart seems capable of!" This ambivalence plagues him from the beginning to the end of the novel, both in committing the crime and confessing to it.

Although he would like to merely be an objective onlooker, Raskolnikov feels sympathy toward other people's problems, such as the plight of the Marvmeladov family. Appalled by their poverty, he pays for the funeral of Semyon Marvmeladov, the drunkard father killed in an accident. He also wants to save his own sister from an unhappy marriage, and stop his mother from sacrificing herself for him. The nihilistic Svidrigailov says to him, "You are an *idealist*!"

In other moments throughout the novel, however, Raskolnikov despises everyone, including his family. While Raskolnikov believes in the betterment of humanity, he is simultaneously nauseated by people, feeling "a sort of infinite, almost physical feeling of disgust with everything he c[omes] across." He is perpetually scornful toward others, and is absorbed in himself; this hubris eventually leads him to take another's life.

Intellectually and emotionally isolated, he divides humanity into the "ordinary" who must live in submission and are obligated to obey law, and the "extraordinary," "supermen" who are above the law. Under the influence of his own pride and vanity, he tests his conviction that he is a superman by murdering the greedy pawnbroker, Alyona Ivanovna, an old woman he believes no one will mourn. He defines this murder as a crime of principle, and claims that certain superior people in a society stand above the ordinary human and moral laws. However, the plan misfires; he kills not only the pawnbroker but also her "simple" half-sister, Lizaveta.

After the murder, Raskolnikov feels "a boundlessly full and powerful life welling up in him." However, exhilaration soon mixes with fear and confusion as he tries unsuccessfully to free himself of the evidence: "What ... is my punishment already beginning?" Although he tries to justify the murder, he is haunted by a nightmarish guilt that conflicts with his cold reasoning. He alternates between trying to outwit the police and suffering moments of severe guilt. The reader follows this study of a criminal's conscience, witnessing his paradoxical emotions and his struggle with justification as he aimlessly wanders the city's hot, crowded streets.

Raskolnikov calls attention to himself as a suspect, as he is obsessed with details of the crime, and once passes out at police station as the crime is being discussed. His bizarre behavior leads some, including his mother and sister, to question his sanity. His mother, for example, notices in her son "something unbending and almost insane." Raskolnikov also is tormented by his contradictory feelings, as well as numerous hallucinations, and he questions his own state of being. Torn by guilt and struggling with self-doubt, but still clinging to the idea that he is above the law, he repeatedly talks himself into, then out of, confessing. He becomes physically ill. He suffers from fevered hallucinations, lethargy, and lapses of memory, and his dreams are difficult to distinguish from reality. When he emerges from the illness, nursed by the kind-hearted Sofia "Sonia" Marmeladev, he is pale and haggard, agitated and feverish.

The other characters in the novel can be considered in relation to him as reflecting different aspects of his personality. For example, he is attracted to both Sonia and Svidrigailov, who are polar opposites. He admires Sonia's selflessness, and Svidrigailov's intellect, willfulness, and disdain for society. Yet, it is Sonia he finally confesses to, going to her "when he was in need of the companionship." Eventually, she brings about his salvation by convincing him to admit to his crime. Sentenced to seven years in Siberia, Raskolnikov at first is as arrogant and self-involved as ever. However, in the epilogue, he apparently sheds his egotism, realizing his love for Sonia, as Dostoevsky attempts to show how a tragic hero finds redemption and rehabilitation.

ARKADY IVANOVICH SVIDRIGAILOV

Acting as foil to the protagonist, Svidrigailov exhibits both similarities to and differences from the main character. Like Raskolnikov, Svidrigailov is a criminal. He too suffers from vivid, terrifying dreams and is haunted by the dead. He is generous with his money, becoming a benefactor for the Marvmeladovs. Like Raskolnikov, Svidrigailov possesses conflicting personality traits, both depraved and altruistic. Their major difference comes from his world view: in contrast to Raskolnikov's theory of the "superman," Svidrigailov is a nihilist, believing that he owes allegiance to no person or system, that there is no meaning to be found in the world.

Tortured by boredom, and overcome by nihilism, Svidrigailov is often described as representing the baser side of Raskolnikov's dual personality. Yet at the same time, Svidrigailov himself is a complex, paradoxical figure, and many see him as the most memorable in the novel. Even his physical description is perplexing. He looks younger than his actual age, around 50, and he dresses quite elegantly, carrying a cane and wearing gloves. Tall, with wide shoulders, he has thick hair and blue eyes, "too blue," and on first glance, he "ha[s] an air of a gentleman." Raskolnikov, however, notices that he also possesses "a rather strange face, almost like a mask."

A wealthy, unscrupulous landowner, Svidrigailov makes inappropriate advances toward Dunya, Raskolnikov's sister, and becomes obsessed with her, arguing that he needs her as a salvation from evil and boredom. Although he does not actually appear until halfway through the novel, his character has been developed through insinuations and accusations. The reader learns of him through the accounts of the others. He is rumored to have murdered a serf, and then is implicated by gossip in the death of his wife. He may also be responsible for causing a young girl's suicide.

However, when Svidrigailov first appears, Raskolnikov finds him "almost excessively amiable," despite his sister's description: "He's a horrible man! I can't imagine a worse." Svidrigailov's excessive sexuality and perpetual boredom dominate his personality. Early on, he tells Raskolnikov, "You know, I take no particular interest in anything.... especially now, I have nothing to occupy me." In the several conversations he has with Raskolnikov, Svidrigailov is cheerful, cynical, and frank about his personal life. He explains that his dead wife was a considerably older woman who bailed him out of debtor's prison, and now he is haunted by the visions of her, even as he continues to pursue Dunya. He denies killing his wife, but admits to degrading young women, considering debauchery "an occupation of the sort." He displays exaggerated bravado and voices his strong opinions, making no excuses for his lechery. He accepts his own description of himself as an "idle and immoral man." He freely talks of his engagement to a sixteen-year-old whose youth and attractiveness, like that of other virginal girls he has preyed on, excite him; she is an "unopened bud."

Svidrigailov believes that debauchery saves him from being "bored to death": "If it were not for it, one might have to shoot oneself without more ado." Like Raskolnikov, Svidrigailov does not repent. Raskolnikov's feelings toward him are mixed; he calls him a "vile, disgusting, salacious creature" yet is also attracted to Svidrigailov's power, recognizing "something about Svidrigailov that was at least out of the ordinary, if not mysterious."

Svidrigailov once asks, "[A]m I a monster or myself the victim?" a resonating question which also addresses the duality of Raskolnikov's character. However, unlike Raskolnikov, Svidrigailov loses the desire to continue living. He tries again to seduce Dunya, this time blackmailing her with the information he possesses that would implicate her brother in the murder. Dunya wields a gun when he becomes aggressive, and although he truly believes he loves Dunya "infinitely," Svidrigailov finally realizes she will never love him. Perhaps he himself is incapable of true love. After Dunya rejects him, he does something again unexpectedly altruistic, leaving 15,000 rubles to his young fiancée. Then, in a symbolic gesture of his perpetual nihilism, Svidrigailov announces he is "going to America," before commiting suicide.

Contributors

HAROLD BLOOM is Sterling Professor of the Humanities at Yale University and Henry W. and Albert A. Berg Professor of English at the New York University Graduate School. He is the author of over 20 books, including *Shelley's Mythmaking* (1959), *The Visionary Company* (1961), *Blake's Apocalypse* (1963), *Yeats* (1970), *A Map of Misreading* (1975), *Kabbalah and Criticism* (1975), *Agon: Toward a Theory of Revisionism* (1982), *The American Religion* (1992), *The Western Canon* (1994), and *Omens of Millennium: The Gnosis of Angels, Dreams, and Resurrection* (1996). *The Anxiety of Influence* (1973) sets forth Professor Bloom's provocative theory of the literary relationships between the great writers and their predecessors. His most recent books include *Shakespeare: The Invention of the Human* (1998), a 1998 National Book Award finalist, *How to Read and Why* (2000), *Genius: A Mosaic of One Hundred Exemplary Creative Minds* (2002), and *Hamlet: Poem Unlimited* (2003). In 1999, Professor Bloom received the prestigious American Academy of Arts and Letters Gold Medal for Criticism, and in 2002 he received the Catalonia International Prize.

EDWARD WASIOLEK is Professor Emeritus of Slavic Languages & Literatures at the University of Chicago.

ROBERT LOUIS JACKSON is the B.E. Bensinger Professor of Slavic Languages and Literatures at Yale University.

MALCOLM V. JONES is Emeritus Professor in Residence at the Department of Russian and Slavonic Studies at The University of

Nottingham. He has written many articles on Russian authors, and published two books on Dostoevsky.

ROGER B. ANDERSON is the author of *Dostoevsky: Myths of Duality* and co-editor of *Russian Narrative & Visual Art: Varieties of Seeing.*

RAYMOND J. WILSON III is Professor of English at Loras College in Dubuque, Iowa.

FRANK FRIEDEBERG SEELEY has published articles on Dostoevsky and Gogol.

GERALD FIDERER has published articles on Henry James, Dostoevsky, George Orwell, and D.H. Lawrence.

R.E. RICHARDSON teaches Russian literature at Boston University.

GILES MITCHELL teaches at the University of North Texas. In addition to publishing scholarly articles, he is a poet whose collections include *Love Among the Mad* and *Some Green Laurel.*

LAURA A. CURTIS is the author of *The Elusive Daniel Defoe* (1984).

RICHARD PEACE is Professor Emeritus at the University of Bristol. He is the author of several books on Russian authors.

ALBA AMOIA is the author of books on Jean Anouilh, Edmond Rostand, Thomas Mann Fiorenz, and Albert Camus.

NINA PELIKAN STRAUS is a Professor of literature and member of the creative writing faculty in the School of Humanities, as well as a member of the interdisciplinary women's studies faculty, at Purchase College.

Bibliography

Alm, Brian M. "The Four Horsemen and the Lamb: Structure and Balance in *Crime and Punishment*." *McNeese Review* 21 (1974–75): 72–79.

Anderson, Roger B. *Dostoevsky: Myths of Duality*. Gainseville, FL: University of Florida Press, 1986.

———. "*Crime and Punishment*: Psycho-Myth and the Making of a Hero." *California Slavic Studies* 11 (1977): 523–38.

Bakhtin, Mikhail. *Problems of Dostoevsky's Poetics*. Minneapolis: University of Minnesota Press, 1984.

Berry, Thomas E. "Dostoevsky and Spiritualism." *Dostoevsky Studies* 2 (1981): 43–49.

———. *Plots and Characters in Major Russian Fiction*. Vol 2. Hamden, CN: Archon Books, 1978.

Breger, Louis. *Dostoevsky: The Author as Psychoanalyst*. New York: New York University Press, 1989.

Brody, Ervin C. "Meaning and Symbolism in the Names of Dostoevsky's *Crime and Punishment* and *The Idiot*." *Names* 27, no 2 (June 1979): 117–40.

Burnett, Leon, ed. *F. M. Dostoevsky (1821–1881): A Centenary Collection*. Colchester, UK: University of Essex, 1981.

Cassedy, Steven. "The Formal Problem of the Epilogue in *Crime and Punishment*: The Logic of Tragic and Christian Structures." *Dostoevsky Studies* 3 (1982): 171–90.

Catteau, Jaques. *Dostoyevsky and the Process of Literary Creation*. Trans. Audrey Littlewood. Cambridge: Cambridge University Press, 1989.

Chapple, Richard L. *A Dostoevsky Dictionary*. Ann Arbor: Arids, 1983.

Conradi, Peter J. *Fyodor Dostoevsky*. New York: St. Martin's Press, 1988.

Cox, Gary. *Crime and Punishment: A Mind to Murder*. Boston: Twayne, 1990.

Danow, David K. *The Dialogic Sign: Essays on the Major Novels of Dostoevsky*. New York: Peter Lang, 1991.

Dostoevsky, Anna. *Dostoevsky: Reminiscences*. Translated and edited by B. Stillman. New York: Liveright, 1975.

Frank, Joseph. *Dostoevsky: The Seeds of Revolt 1821–1849*. Princeton: Princeton University Press, 1976.

———. *Dostoevsky: The Years of Ordeal 1850–1859*. Princeton: Princeton University Press, 1983.

———. *Dostoevsky: The Stir of Liberation 1860–1865*. Princeton: Princeton University Press, 1986.

———. *Dostoevsky: The Miraculous Years 1865–1871*. Princeton: Princeton University Press, 1995.

Gide, A.P.G. *Dostoevsky*. Westport, CT: Greenwood, 1981.

Goldstein, David I. *Dostoevsky and the Jews*. Austin: University of Texas Press, 1981.

Hanan, David. "*Crime and Punishment*: The Idea of the Crime." *Critical Review*, no. 12 (1969): 15–28.

Hingley, Ronald. *Dostoyevsky: His Life and Work*. New York: Scribner's, 1978.

Holk, Andre van. "Moral Themes in Dostoevsky's *Crime and Punishment*." *Essays in Poetics* 14 (1989): 28–75.

Jackson, Robert Louis. *The Art of Dostoevsky: Deliriums and Nocturnes*. Princeton: Princeton University Press, 1981.

———. *Dialogues with Dostoevsky: The Overwhelming Questions*. Stanford: Stanford University Press, 1993.

———. *Dostoevsky: New Perspectives*. Englewood Cliffs, NJ: Prentice-Hall, 1984.

Johnson, Leslie A. *The Experience of Time in* Crime and Punishment. Columbus, OH: Slavica, 1985.

Johnson, Tamara, ed. *Readings on Fyodor Dostoyevsky*. San Diego: Greenhaven Press, 1988.

Jones, Malcolm V. *Dostoevsky: The Novel of Discord*. New York: Barnes & Noble, 1976.

———and Garth M. Terry, eds. *New Essays on Dostoevsky*. Cambridge: Cambridge University Press, 1983.

———. *Dostoevsky After Bakhtin: Readings in Dostoevsky's Fantastic Realism*. Cambridge: Cambridge University Press, 1990.

Jones, John. *Dostoevsky*. Oxford: Clarendon Press, 1983.

Kjetisaa, Geer. *Fyodor Dostoyevsky: A Writer's Life*. Trans. Siri Hustvedt and David McDuff. New York: Viking, 1987.

Koprince, Ralph G. "The Question of Raskol'nikov's Suicide." *Canadian American Slavic Studies* 16, no 1. (1982): 73–81.

Kraeger, Linda, and Joe Barnhart. *Dostoevsky on Evil and Atonement*. Lewiston, NY: Edwin Mellen Press, 1992.

Krag, Erik. *Dostoevsky: The Literary Artist*. New York: Humanities Press, 1976.

Leatherbarrow, William J. *Fedor Dostoevsky. Boston: Twayne*, 1981.

———. "Raskolnikov and the 'Enigma of His Personality.'" *Forum for Modern Language Studies* 9 (1973): 153–65.

Lynch, Michael F. "Dostoevsky and Richard Wright" Choices of Individual Freedom and Dignity." *Chiba Review* 12 (1990): 25–40.

Maze, J.R. "Dostoyevsky: Epilepsy, Mysticism, and Homosexuality." *American Imago* 38 (1981): 155–83.

Miller, Robin Feur, ed. *Critical Essays on Dostoevsky*. Boston: G.K. Hall, 1986.

Morson, Gary Saul. "How to Read *Crime and Punishment*." *Commentary* 93, no. 6 (June 1992): 49–53.

Murav, Harriet. *Holy Foolishness: Dostoevsky's Novels and The Poetics of Cultural Critique*. Stanford: Stanford University Press, 1992.

Panichas, George A. *The Burden of Vision: Dostoevsky's Spiritual Art*. Chicago: Gateway, 1985.

Nuttall, A.D. Crime and Punishment*: Murder as Philosophic Experiment*. Sussex University Press, 1978.

Rice, James. "Raskol'nikov and Tsar Gorox." *Slavic and East European Journal* 25, no. 3 (Fall 1981): 38–53.

———. *Dostoevsky and the Healing Art*. Ann Arbor: Ardis, 1985.

Rising, Catherine. "Raskolnikov and Razumov: From a Passive to Active Subjectivity in Under Western Eyes." *Conradiana: A Journal of Joseph Conrad Studies* 33, no. 1 (Spring 2001): 24–39.

Struas, Nina Pelikan. *Dostoevsky and the Women Question*. New York: St. Martin's Press, 1994.

Terras, Victor. *F.M. Dostoevsky: Life, Work, and Criticism*. Fredericton, Canada: York Press, 1984.

Wellek, Rene, ed. *Dostoevsky: A Collection of Critical Essays*. Englewood Cliffs, NJ: Prentice-Hall, 1964.

Zdanys, Jonas. "Raskolnikov and Frankenstein: The Deadly Search for a Rational Paradise." *Citara* 1 (1976): 57–67.

Acknowledgments

"Fyodor Dostoevsky: *Crime and Punishment*" by Harold Bloom. From *How to Read and Why*: 166–173. © 2000 by Harold Bloom. Reprinted by permission of the author.

"Crime and Punishment," by Edward Wasiolek. From *Dostoevsky: The Major Fiction*: 67–84. © 1964 by The Massachusetts Institute of Technology. Reprinted by permission of The Massachusetts Institute of Technology Press.

"Philosophical Pro and Contra in Part One of *Crime and Punishment*" by Robert Louis Jackson. From *Twentieth Century Interpretations of Crime and Punishment*, ed. Robert Louis Jackson: 26–40. © 1974 by Prentice-Hall, Inc. Reprinted by permission.

"Raskol'nikov's Humanitarianism" by Malcolm V. Jones. From *Canadian-American Slavic Studies* 8, no. 3 (Fall 1974): 370–380. © 1974 by Charles Schlacks, Jr. and Arizona State University. Reprinted by permission.

"Raskol'nikov and the Myth Experience," by Roger B. Anderson. From *Slavic and East European Journal* 20, no. 1 (Spring 1976): 1–17. © 1976 by the American Association of Teachers of Slavic and East European Languages. Reprinted by permission.

"Raskolnikov's Dream in *Crime and Punishment*," by Raymond J. Wilson III. From *Literature and Psychology* 26, no. 4 (1976): 159–166. © 1976 by Morton Kaplan. Reprinted by permission.

"The Two Faces of Svidrigailov," by Frank Friedeberg Seeley. From *Canadian-American Slavic Studies* 12, no. 3 (Fall 1978): 413–17. © 1978 by Charles Schlacks, Jr. and Arizona State University. Reprinted by permission.

"Raskolnikov's Confession," by Gerald Fiderer. From *Literature and Psychology* 30, no. 2 (1980): 62–71. © 1980 by Morton Kaplan. Reprinted by permission

"Svidrigailov and the 'Performing Self'," by R.E. Richardson. From *Slavic Review* 46, no. 3/4 (Autumn–Winter 1987): 540–52. © 1987 by The American Association for the Advancement of Slavic Studies. Reprinted by permission.

"Pathological Narcissism and Violence in Dostoevskii's Svidrigalov," by Giles Mitchell. From *Canadian-American Slavic Studies* 24, no. 1 (Spring 1990): 1–18. © 1990 by Charles Schlacks, Jr. Reprinted by permission.

"Raskolnikov's Sexuality" by Laura A. Curtis. From *Literature and Psychology* (1991): 88–106. © 1991 by Morton Kaplan. Reprinted by permission.

"Motive and Symbol: *Crime and Punishment*," by Richard Peace. From *Dostoyevsky: An Examination of the Major Novels*: 34–58. © 1992 by Gerald Duckworth and Company Ltd. Reprinted by permission.

"*Crime and Punishment*," by Alba Amoia. From *Feodor Dostoevsky*: 51–70. © 1993 by The Continuum Publishing Group. Reprinted with the permission of the publisher.

Straus, Nina Pelikan. "Why Did I Say 'Women!'?": Raskolnikov Reimagined." From *Diacritics* 23, no. 1 (Spring 1993): 53–65. © 1993 by The Johns Hopkins University Press. Reprinted with permission of the Johns Hopkins University Press.

Index